Athletic Journal's
Encyclopedia of Football

ATHLETIC JOURNAL's
ENCYCLOPEDIA OF FOOTBALL

Edited by Tom Ecker and Bill Calloway

Parker Publishing Company, Inc.

West Nyack, New York

Library of Congress Cataloging in Publication Data
Main entry under title:

Athletic journal's encyclopedia of football.

    1. Football coaching--Addresses, essays, lectures.
I. Ecker, Tom. II. Calloway, Bill
III. Athletic journal. IV. Title: Encyclopedia of
football.
GV954.4.A73   796.33'2077   77-25127
ISBN 0-13-050047-X

Printed in the United States of America

What This Encyclopedia
Offers You

In 1921, two coaches, Major John L. Griffith and George "Potsy" Clark, noted that while other phases of education had publications for the dissemination of knowledge, athletics was not so blessed. Also, at that time, the number of football texts was extremely limited.

To fill this void, *Athletic Journal* was begun. The first issue had but twelve pages, and in that first issue the publishers stated: "There should be at this time a medium through which coaches may exchange ideas and students of athletics may receive discussions pertaining to the leading athletic sports."

The original concept, it will be noted, called for an exchange of ideas, and no attempt has ever been made to categorically state that there is but one right way to perform a fundamental or to execute or stop a given play.

From that original issue of twelve pages, *Athletic Journal* has grown over the years by leaps and bounds to its present status as one of the most respected publications in the coaching field. This encyclopedia brings together in one volume those football articles that we believe will be most beneficial to you, the football coach.

Working with the total cooperation and immeasurable assistance of Jack Griffith and his able staff at *Athletic Journal,* we culled through more than 2,000 football articles consisting in the neighborhood of three million words, as well as countless photographs and diagrams.

You will quickly notice that many of the game's outstanding names are included: George Allen, Bear Bryant, Frank Broyles, Paul Dietzel, to cite just a few, while other top names are not present. Limited to space, we had an extremely difficult job limiting the articles to just those that now appear, but the final criterion for selecting the articles was how well each particular article would help you to produce winning teams.

These 49 articles represent the top thinking in the game today. Read "The Houston Veer" and "Counters Off the Houston Veer" by Billy Willingham and Barry Sides, two long-time assistants at the University of Houston. Perhaps you prefer the Wishbone or the "I." If you do, there are articles analyzing various aspects of these two offenses. See in Chapter 3 what Coach Raymond had to say about the famous Delaware Wing-T Options.

One of the most exciting chapters in this invaluable encyclopedia is Chapter 14—The Offensive Backfield. Here in this one chapter alone is the combined expertise of Ara Parseghian, Pepper Rodgers, Frank Broyles and George Allen.

As a student of the game of football, you will find this timeless resource guide another valuable contribution to football coaching from *Athletic Journal*.

Tom Ecker
Bill Calloway

Table of Contents

Part I
OFFENSE

1 / The Veer

THE HOUSTON VEER

by Billy Willingham and Barry Sides

Billy Willingham
University of Houston

Barry Sides
University of Houston

There are several veer options, but our favorites are the inside veer and the outside veer.

The features of the inside veer (or 13 veer) that make it different from other options are: 1) pursuit is walled off by the play-side tackle, guard, and center; 2) two receivers are releasing downfield as pass receivers and/or blockers ahead of the pitch if the option gets that far; and 3) the quarterback may hand off to the fullback, keep the ball, or pitch to the running back.

Diagram 1-1 shows the offensive set that is used to run this play.

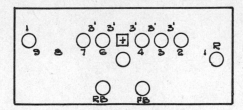

Diagram 1-1

The tight end and the inside linemen from tackle to tackle take a 3-foot split

The fullback and the running back line up foot-to-foot with the offensive guards, with their feet 4½ yards from the ball.

The quarterback seats the ball, drives off his opposite foot, and meshes with the fullback. No mention is made of his angle leaving the center. As he leaves the center, he picks up the first man outside the offensive tackle and keys him; if the defensive tackle remains stationary or goes up the field, then the quarterback gives the ball to the fullback.

If the defensive tackle closes down, the quarterback removes the ball from the fullback's stomach and runs a normal option on the end. As is true in the case of any other play, the quarterback must run the play a thousand times before he acquires the necessary feel and confidence. The decision as to whether or not the fullback gets the ball rests with the quarterback.

As shown in Diagram 1-2, the fullback lines up foot-to-foot with the guard at a depth of 4½ yards. On the snap of the ball, the fullback slashes at the seam between the guard and tackle. As he feels the ball in his stomach, he places a soft squeeze on it. Again, the decision as to whether or not the fullback will get the ball is made by the quarterback, not the fullback.

The running back lines up foot-to-foot with the guard at 4½ yards. On the snap of the ball, he pushes off his outside foot and maintains a pitch position with the quarterback. The flanker or running back lines up wide enough so that a back from the inside cannot cover him on any deep cut. He runs a 40-yard dash.

The tight end blocks the secondary man who is responsible for the force. By splitting the flanker so that he cannot be covered by a back from the inside, the tight end will be blocking on the safety or the monster. His technique is to release across the face of the end, applying outside pressure on the end, and then get position on the safety (Diagram 1-3). When he is facing an eight-man front, the tight end may be in a normal or a flexed position. In either case, his assignment is the same (Diagrams 1-4 and 1-5).

The right tackle's basic assignment is to block the linebacker on or to the inside. Against an even defense he will either get on the linebacker quick (Diagram 1-6) or he will block what we call a combination with the guard (Diagram 1-7).

Two other situations which the tackle must be aware of are his opposing linebacker stunting into the guard-center gap, or the down lineman being so strong the guard cannot handle him. In the first case, we use a gap block call (Diagrams 1-8 and 1-9). Gap switches the assignment of the guard and the tackle, that is, the guard blocks the linebacker and the tackle blocks the lineman.

In the second case, the tackle double-teams with the guard (Diagrams 1-10 and 1-11). The only other thing which can occur is that there is no linebacker, in which case the tackle double-teams with the guard (Diagram 1-12). When the tackle faces the seven-man front, odd, he should stretch the defense another foot. If the defensive tackle appears to declare inside, the right tackle should call under to the guard. Then the guard

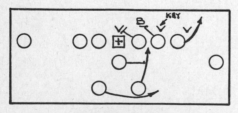

Diagram 1-2

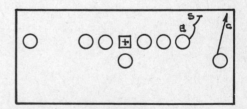

Diagram 1-3

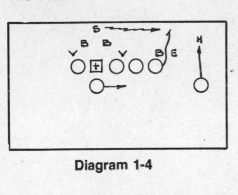

Diagram 1-4

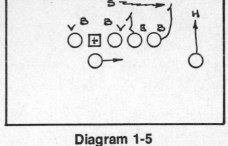

Diagram 1-5

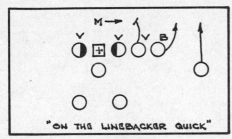

Diagram 1-6

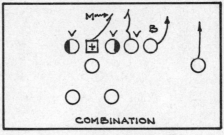

Diagram 1-7

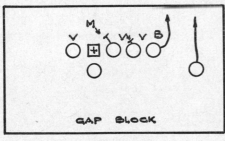

Diagram 1-8

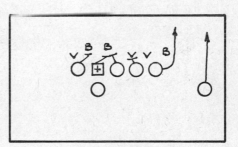

Diagram 1-9

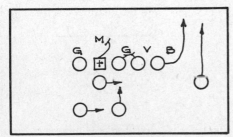

Diagram 1-10

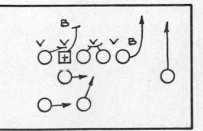

Diagram 1-11

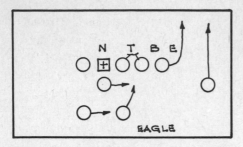

Diagram 1-12

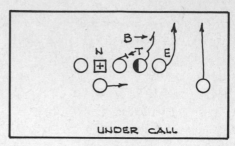

Diagram 1-13

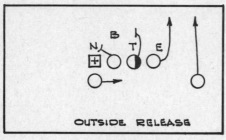

Diagram 1-14

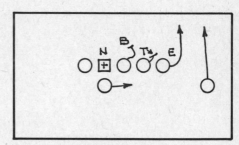

Diagram 1-15

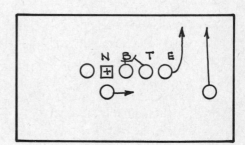

Diagram 1-16

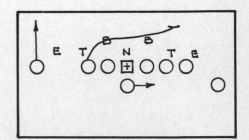

Diagram 1-17

Diagram 1-18

Diagram 1-19

should fire out on the slant tackle, and our right tackle will bounce the slant tackle and pick up the linebacker (Diagram 1-13). We allow the tackle to release outside the defensive tackle in case the defensive tackle alignment prevents the inside release and the right tackle does not want to call under (Diagram 1-14). If, as the tackle releases outside, the defensive tackle goes with him, then he locks on to the defensive tackle (Diagram 1-15). This is an under call on, but the defensive tackle stunts out.

The right guard's assignment (Diagram 1-16) is to block any down lineman from head-on the center to the near shoulder of the tackle.

Diagram 1-17 shows the right guard coming off the nose man on a 5-2 to the linebacker if the linebacker moves up close to the line of scrimmage.

Diagram 1-18 shows the center blocking the zero man through the play-side gap.

As shown in Diagram 1-19, the left guard blocks the base. The left tackle releases inside the No. 2 man and blocks the first man outside the tight end and keys him. If he stays on the line or goes up the field, he hands off. If the key closes down, the quarterback withdraws the ball and options on the safety.

In the outside veer, the fullback takes a normal alignment and, on the snap of the ball, slashes at the seam between the end and the tackle (Diagram 1-20). As the fullback feels the ball in his stomach, he applies a soft squeeze. Again, the decision as to whether the fullback gets the ball rests with the quarterback.

The running back has the same alignment, movements, and responsibilities he had on the 13 veer.

The flanker or R man runs a streak.

The tight end has the responsibility for the linebacker on or inside. His technique is the same as the tackle uses on 13 veer.

He can: 1. get on the linebacker quick (Diagram 1-21); 2. double-team with the tackle (Diagram 1-22); and 3. use a combination (Diagram 1-23).

On an eight-man front, the tight end must realize that only one man can be turned loose. Therefore, he must block the man over him (Diagram 1-24).

The right tackle blocks the same as he did in 13 veer.

The right guard, center, and left guard block the base. The left tackle's and left end's assignments are the same as on 13 veer.

The main pass that is used off the veer series is an option pass or run. This play has the following features: 1. A quick pass to the tight end up the seam between the middle coverage and the wide outside coverage of the secondary versus our basic set. (Diagram 1-25). 2. This quick pass helps our offensive team have some control over how that area is defended. 3. If the tight end is covered, the quarterback will run a normal option on the end. 4. If the ball is pitched to the running back, again the play is run or a pass is thrown.

The tight end's release from the line of scrimmage is the same as it was on 13 veer except now he is a receiver instead of a blocker. According to his alignment, he should be sure that he cannot be covered by a linebacker from the inside. The quarterback will attempt to get the ball to the tight end after he clears the fullback. If the tight end is

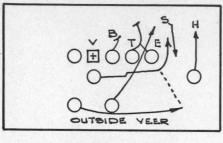

Diagram 1-20

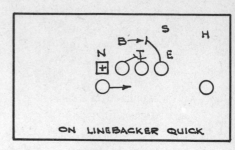

Diagram 1-21

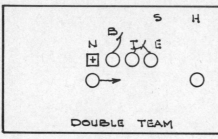

Diagram 1-22

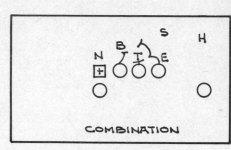

Diagram 1-23

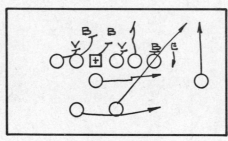

Diagram 1-24

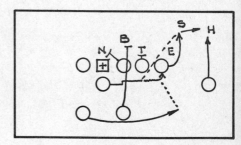

Diagram 1-25

covered, and the quarterback comes down with the ball, he turns immediately to the outside and becomes the flat receiver for the running back on a pass-run option on the defender in the flat.

The quarterback seats the ball, pushes off his left foot, meshes with the fullback, clears, and checks the tight end. If he is open, the ball is delivered to the tight end. If the tight end is covered, the quarterback comes down with the ball and runs an option on the end man on the line.

The fullback slashes at the seam between the center and the guard, makes a good fake, and attempts to screen the linebacker. If there is a defensive lineman in the guard-tackle gap, the fullback should make sure he hits with enough force to drive the defensive man off the line of scrimmage.

The running back pushes off his left foot and maintains a pitch position as the quarterback moves down the line of scrimmage. If the quarterback pitches the ball, the running back checks the flanker or R man first to see if he is open. If the R man is covered, he should run a pass-run option on the defender in the flat with the tight end.

The flanker or R man runs a streak. The right tackle blocks the man on him or the first man outside on the line of scrimmage. This must be an aggressive block. The right guard blocks a lineman in the area from head-on the center to the inside shoulder of the tackle. The center, left guard, and left tackle block the man on or in the right gap. These blocks must also be aggressive.

The inside veer or 13 veer, the outside veer or 12 veer, and the quick pass option are the focal points of our offense. The balance of the offense is designed to be used after these plays have been fully defensed.

COUNTERS OFF THE HOUSTON VEER

by Billy Willingham and Barry Sides

Billy Willingham
University of Houston

Barry Sides
University of Houston

We feel the counter series complements the veer or the triple option phase of our game. It provides the regular option in which only one force man is optioned and gives us a called counter play with the wide option threat. Space will not allow a discussion of all that is involved in this offense; therefore, we shall only describe the previously mentioned plays which are a large part of our total offense.

Counter assignments are as follows: Left Tackle—Blocks the base man, No. 2, or pulls versus a wide 5 technique. Left Guard—Blocks the base man, No. 1. Center—Blocks the base man, 0. Right Guard—Blocks the base man No. 1. Right Tackle—Blocks the base man, No. 2. Left End—Runs a streak. Tight End—Forces an inside release and blocks the safety. Flanker—Runs a streak. Running Back—Pushes off his left foot and takes a 12-inch jab step with his right foot, keeping his shoulder parallel with the line of scrimmage. Then he slashes at the left leg of the center and cuts off his block. Fullback—He can either fill over the outside shoulder of the guard or step up and run wide, faking the counter option (Diagram 1-26). Quarterback—Seats the ball and pushes off his left foot. He takes a short jab step with his right foot, a short jab with his left foot, and places the ball in the running back's pocket. Then he continues the counter option route. No mention is made of depth. Two changes in blocking can be made. We use a fold block on both even and odd defenses (Diagrams 1-27 and 1-28).

The counter option will be shown to the split end side. This play is used when we get a man coverage or a rotated situation. Left End—Runs a streak. Left Tackle—Tries to misdirect the man over him (Diagram 1-29); if he cannot do that, he tries to hook the base man, No. 2 (Diagram 1-30); and if he cannot, he will pull and lead, passing up the base man to let the quarterback option him (Diagram 1-31).

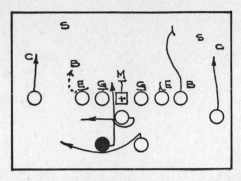

Diagram 1-26

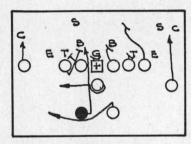

Diagram 1-27

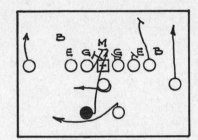

Diagram 1-28

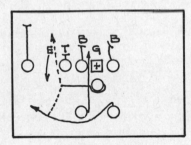

Diagram 1-29

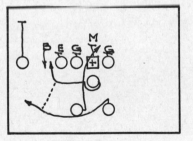

Diagram 1-30

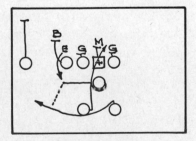

Diagram 1-31

The misdirection block mentioned previously is used when a defensive man is playing the offensive man's head as a key to determine his blocking objective. The offensive player should fire out with his head on the side of the man away from the hole. He is expected to fight in the direction we want him to go. The offensive man should hit the defensive player's inside leg with his shoulder, and just as he hits his leg, he should swing his legs and body around and whip the defensive man's legs out from under him. Usually it will end in a reverse body block. This type of block should not be used if the defensive man is playing fairly loose because the offensive player will miss him. It is an excellent block for defensive players who are playing hard nose and delivering a good hard blow on the offensive man.

Left Guard—Blocks the base man, No. 1. He can also use a misdirection block. Center—Blocks the base man, 0. Right Guard—Blocks the base man, No. 1. Right Tackle—Blocks the base man, No. 2. Tight End—Forces an inside release and blocks the safety. The counter option is also run to the strong side with the same assignments. The difference is that the tight end now blocks the force of the secondary (Diagram 1-32).

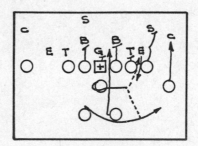

Diagram 1-32

The counter option pass comes off this series. It is similar to the pass run off the veer. This pass is in our offense in order to keep the defensive player ready to cover the tight end, who is driving up the field in the seam between the defensive safety and the defensive man who is covering the flanker. Hopefully, covering the pitch and the tight end will cause the defense some problems.

Tight End—Runs the seam route by releasing outside the defensive end. He should look for the ball quickly. If he is covered right after the quarterback clears the fullback and is unable to throw to him, then the tight end should break for the sideline and be ready for the pass-run option by the running back on the defender who is covering the flat (Diagram 1-33).

All Linemen—Block the man on or in the right gap. This must be an aggressive block.

Flanker—Runs a streak.

Fullback—Pushes off his right foot and takes a slide step to the inside with his left

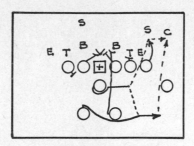

Diagram 1-33

foot, keeping his shoulder parallel to the line of scrimmage. Then he slashes at the right leg of the center, meshing with the quarterback, and makes a strong fake.

Running Back—Takes a jab step toward the line of scrimmage with his left foot and then maintains a pitch position as the quarterback goes down the line of scrimmage. If the quarterback has to pitch to him, the running back should look deep for a flanker if he is covered, and then execute a pass-run option on the defender in the flat with the tight end.

Quarterback—Seats the ball, takes a short jab step with his left foot, a short step with his right foot, then pushes off his right foot and pivots. He should mesh with the fullback and allow him to make a strong fake; if he is covered, the quarterback should come down with the ball and run a normal option on the end man on the line.

Another phase of our offense is the draw, which is used in conjunction with our dropback passing game. It has the effect we need in order to slow down penetration that can hurt our options. In our opinion, this play is a must in order to run the Houston type of offense. The assignments and coaching points are as follows:

Tight End—Releases outside, looks for a quick pass, and blocks the middle third.

Right tackle, Right Guard, Left Guard, and Left Tackle—Set quick to the inside in a good football position. They should make the defense think they are blocking for a dropback pass. As soon as they reach this position, they should attack their assigned defensive man and take him any way they can. Their assignments will be the same as dropback pass protection, guards on the No. 1 men and tackles on the No. 2 men versus a seven-man front (Diagram 1-34). When meeting an eight-man front, block the first defensive man to the outside. The center and the remaining back should block the two inside defensive men (Diagrams 1-35 and 1-36).

Center—The technique of the center is to set quick and take the zero man any way he can; if the zero man does not take a side, the center should work his body to one side so the back can cut off his block.

Split End—Runs a streak and blocks the man who is covering the deep.

Flanker—Streaks and blocks the man who is covering the deep.

Fullback—Takes a slide step inside as if he were running the counter. Use a slight hesitation. Receive the ball from the quarterback and run for daylight.

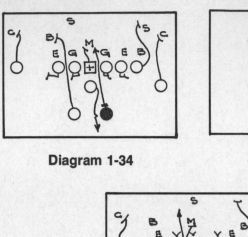

Diagram 1-34   **Diagram 1-35**

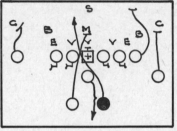

Diagram 1-36

Running Back—Blocks the No. 2 man; if it is an eight-man front, block the inside linebacker.

Quarterback—Look at the tight end as if to hit him on a quick pass, then retreat from the line of scrimmage and place the ball in the pocket made by the fullback.

The last series we will discuss is our passes off the fullback slant. The fullback slant is a convenient slant off the weak side (Diagram 1-37).

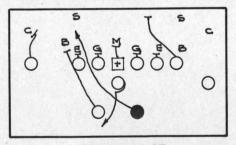

Diagram 1-37

These passes are used as the basis for attacking the weak side with two-man cut combinations. They are used to place pressure on a defense that overplays our strong side. The assignments on our fullback slant passes are as follows: Tight End—Blocks the end man in the rush (may be called out on individual cuts). Right Tackle, Right Guard,

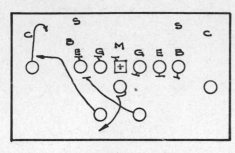

Diagram 1-38

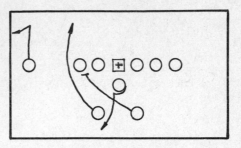

Diagram 1-39

Center, Left Guard, and Left Tackle—Block the man on or in the left gap. Split End—Run a 12- to 15-yard curl. Flanker—Runs a streak. Fullback—Pushes off his right foot at the inside leg of the tackle. Make a hard fake and block the end man in the rush. Running Back—Slashes the No. 3 man, fakes a block, and slides into the flat. Quarterback—Seats the ball, pushes off his right foot, and pivots on his left foot. Mesh with the fullback. After the fake is made, set up 5 to 7 yards deep behind the left tackle. Look for the split end first (Diagram 1-38).

Combination cuts can be run with the split end and the running back. As an example, when we call an outside cut by the split end, the running back runs up the seam (Diagram 1-39).

The offense we have described is a series that we feel complements our basic veer or triple option.

COACHING THE VEER BACKFIELD

by Joe Collins

Joe Collins
Central State University, Ohio

The veer offense, the triple option from split backs, has changed the roles of present-day quarterbacks. Reading the defense by the quarterback in a triple option offense is one of the most challenging and exciting offensive wrinkles in football. A quarterback can defeat a defense both physically and mentally as well as control the tempo of the game.

Physically, a quarterback must have several qualities; however, great speed is not one of them. A quarterback who has great speed will enhance an offensive attack, but it is not one of the prime requisites. Therefore, I believe the tools needed in order to become a great veer quarterback can be taught and improved. Every quarterback cannot have great speed, but each one can improve himself through drills on the physical requirements by doing them daily. Quarterbacks should have six qualities as follows: 1. A mental grasp of defensive football. 2. Poise. 3. Quick hands. 4. Quick feet. 5. Quick eyes. 6. A burning desire to become a leader and a winner.

Coaches can give their quarterbacks a mental grasp of defensive football. Poise and a burning desire to become a leader and a winner depend on the athlete's pride. Through daily drills and the willingness to work, a quarterback can develop quick hands, quick feet, and quick eyes.

As will be seen, the quarterback plays a far greater role in the veer offense than in any other offense seen thus far. That is why he must be coached with patience and understanding and given encouragement at every opportunity.

A quarterback's steps, arm movement, and eye action must be 100 percent mechanical. Thirty minutes a day during and before each practice are devoted to this area. When the ball is snapped, the quarterback focuses his attention on the defensive tackle (assuming option blocking versus a 5-2 defense). The quarterback's first step should be 18 to 25 inches at heel depth. Then he extends the ball over his lead foot. He must keep his arms extended as the ball is placed in the fullback's pocket, while the fullback is sprinting to meet the ball at the aim point.

The quarterback's second step is the most important. It is an adjustment step which prepares him to go on to the outside option key. The speed of the fullback determines the speed of the adjustment step. After the ball is placed in the fullback's pocket, the quarterback must begin his second step. He must not rush this step because it will bring him too close to the fullback, binding him and not allowing him to work with extended arms. As the fullback and quarterback mesh, the quarterback begins to take his second step, gaining ground into the line of scrimmage and shifting his weight as he rides the fullback into the line of scrimmage. It is during this ride that the decision to give or keep is made by the quarterback. The end of the adjustment step should leave the quarterback in a sprinter's stance with his adjustment foot forward and his knees flexed.

If the decision not to give has been made, then the quarterback must immediately pull the ball from the fullback and shift his attention to the second option key, the defensive end. The speed of explosion after the fullback ride is important in attacking a defensive end. The longer it takes the quarterback to option its second key, the more time the defense has to get their backside into the pursuit.

After his second step, the quarterback should be in a position in which his shoulders are parallel with the sideline, his adjustment foot is forward, and his weight is shifted and centered through his inside hip to the ball of his adjustment foot. Now he is prepared to step to and attack the defensive end.

The quarterback must position the ball in his hands in preparation for the pitch—if there is one. His hands should be positioned on the ball in exactly the same manner as they would be for a pass. The quarterback's arms should be in a comfortable position at his waist, with the ball directly in front of his belt buckle.

The play of the defensive end determines whether the ball is pitched or kept. If the play of the defensive end dictates that the quarterback pitch, then he starts a lifting motion with his arm. He lifts his right arm when he options to the left. The elbow of his pitch arm should come up just before he starts to rotate the wrist and thumb of his pitch arm down. This motion is a rotation of the hand and forearm similar to passing the ball. A soft but firm, end-over-end pitch is developed that is easy to handle but is not floating to the back.

The quarterback, if time and the defensive end permit, after the decision to pitch is made, should focus his attention on the back who is in the pitch position. The focusing on the pitch back and the lifting motion of the elbow and wrist should be coordinated. However, this is not always the case, and frequently the quarterback must execute a blind pitch. For this reason we spend a great deal of time practicing on the quarterback pitching the ball to the backs.

If the play of the defensive end tells the quarterback not to pitch, then the quarterback must turn directly up the field at a 90° angle.

The dive back's main responsibility is to hit the aim point and mesh with the quarterback at exactly the same spot, 100 percent of the time, and this can never be overemphasized. The steps of the quarterback, the timing, and general success of the play depend upon this factor. Fumbles can be the result if the dive back runs to a different spot on every play.

The dive back must approach the mesh with a wide pocket. As he feels the quarterback place the ball into the pocket, he should roll his arms gently over the ball. If the quarterback decides to give, then the dive back squeezes the ball. However, the dive back does not take the ball from the quarterback; the quarterback gives it to him. The dive back must learn to feel when the quarterback is giving him the ball (mesh drill) as opposed to faking to him.

If the dive back does not receive the ball, he must continue to fake through the line of scrimmage. Backs have a tendency to stop after the fake or when the defensive tackle puts a hand on them. If the dive back stops at the line of scrimmage, then the quarterback will be forced around him, causing the quarterback to delay in attacking the defensive end and destroying the timing of the play.

When the dive back does not receive the ball and is not tackled at the line of scrimmage, he must block the linebacker or continue downfield and pick up the safety.

The back who is running the pitch route must align himself in and maintain the pitch relationship. Since backs have a tendency to float in toward the quarterback, proper pitch relationship and distance from the quarterback must be emphasized. This must be done in the first two steps, and then the pitch back must focus all his attention on the quarterback. The pitch back's main responsibility is to catch the football. Only after catching the football should he look up to key the block on the contain man. The techniques used in catching the football are practiced daily. When the pitch back sees the quarterback beginning to pitch, he should place his outside or back arm at the bottom of his jersey numbers, with the palm of the hand facing the line of scrimmage and the fingers outstretched. When he is catching the ball, this hand has a backboard effect. His front or inside arm should be below waist level, with the elbow slightly in back of his body and the palm of this hand facing upward. The pitch back must watch the ball into his hands.

If the quarterback gives to the dive back, the pitch back is responsible for carrying out his fake before turning up the field. This will help prevent the defense from falling back inside.

However, if the quarterback keeps the ball and turns up the field, the pitch back must hustle up the field with the quarterback to get back into the pitch relationship. A pitch downfield will be made occasionally, and it often results in a scoring play.

Meshing of the quarterback and fullback is the most difficult phase in the option offense. It must be executed perfectly and be mechanical in order to prevent fumbles, negative yardage, any slowing down or hesitation on the part of the quarterback or the fullback, and poor pitch relationship.

At first, the quarterback will have a tendency to overstep or understep, causing either a collision with the fullback (overstepping) or missing the hand-off (understepping). Thus, it should be emphasized to the dive back that he must always hit the same aim point. Then the quarterback can get the feel of where the back will be all the time and can adjust his first step accordingly.

Our mesh drill (Diagram 1-40) is practiced in what is referred to as the mesh box. This box can be painted or lined on any field, or tape can be used when practicing in a gymnasium.

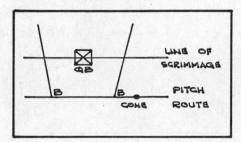

Diagram 1-40

The dive route is drawn from the heel depth of the backs, depending on how deep the backs are set, through the aim point and 3 yards past the line of scrimmage. This is done to emphasize to the backs that they must continue faking although they may not have the football. The dive back must hit the same aim point continually. This cannot be overemphasized. Now the quarterback will have the feel of the dive back. Thus, the quarterback can work with extended arms, because he knows how far his first step must be to reach the dive back's pocket. A cone, which prevents the back from floating to the quarterback, is also placed on the pitch route to insure proper pitch relationship.

This one play will figure to be 30 to 40 percent of the total running offense, so that much practice time should be devoted to this area daily.

The running pitch is executed by the quarterback and the pitch back running down the line in the pitch relationship. This drill (Diagram 1-41) will give the quarterback the feel of running and pitching the ball. It is worked on before practice while running from sideline to sideline.

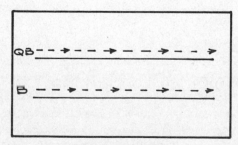

Diagram 1-41

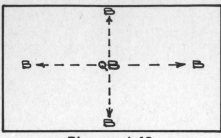

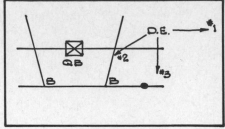

Diagram 1-42   **Diagram 1-43**

The circle drill (Diagram 1-42) is executed with the quarterback in the middle of four backs and pitching quickly to each one in succession. The quarterback and the backs should maintain the pitch relationship.

The purpose of this drill is to devote more time and work to the technique of pitching the ball, that is, rotating the elbow up with the wrist and thumb turned down. The quarterback can actually pitch the ball more than he can in any other drill. In all pitch drills, the quarterback, if he is right-handed, should pitch the ball twice as many times with his left hand than with his right and vice versa.

The end drill (Diagram 1-43) is the routine that is used to perfect the second phase of the option, that of attacking the defensive end. To achieve maximum proficiency from both an offensive and defensive standpoint, this drill should always be live, using the starting defensive ends. It will give the quarterback a more accurate read while helping to sharpen the technique of the defensive ends against the option. This drill is practiced from the mesh box, with the defensive end taking his normal alignment.

The three reads the quarterback will see from the ends are the cat and mouse or float read, the crashing end, and the end taking the pitch.

Since the cat and mouse read is the look the quarterback sees most frequently, time should be spent practicing against this read. The end has the quarterback in this read but is trying to position himself to help on the pitch. The crashing end read is seen when the defensive end comes immediately for the quarterback at the snap of the ball. This is the primary reason why the quarterback, after deciding on the dive whether to give or keep, must immediately focus his attention on the defensive end. This read often results in a blind pitch by the quarterback. The quarterback must pitch as soon as he sees the defensive end crashing. If the quarterback who is practicing this drill is inexperienced at running the option, then this phase should be used sparingly until he has gained confidence in himself and the option.

The third read of the end drill is that of having the defensive end take the pitch. This read tells the quarterback to turn up the field immediately with the football.

As can be seen, the veer offense requires patience, hard work, and a great deal of time and practice. It can be run on any down and in all situations. Therefore, the coach can limit the work on his passing attack or simplify the attack. The veer running attack coupled with play-action passes, plus a simplified passing attack, can complement each other while presenting a great many problems to a defense.

2 / The "I"

THE SLOT I

by Dan Devine and Bob Frala

Dan Devine
University of Notre Dame

Bob Frala
Formerly, University of Missouri

There are many reasons why the I formation is good and has caught on, but we are going to give the reasons we adopted it and how it has been used.

We had been using a form of multiple offense with an unbalanced line, balanced line, T, and various flanker and backfield sets. Many formations and many plays were used. Of course, any formation has its advantages and disadvantages. However, we felt, particularly with the unbalanced line in our system, that it was extremely difficult to know how it was going to be defensed, whether they were going to stay on the ball or shift over a man. This is confusing, not only to the defense regarding what the offense is going to do, but it is equally confusing to an offense not to know how the defense is going to set. The main reason we changed from multiple offense to the I formation is the soundest one of all, it suited the personnel better than any other.

These are the reasons we like the I formation. First, and perhaps most important of all, better execution of plays is achieved because fewer plays are run, and with the flip-flop of personnel, less learning is involved. We like the quarterback-tailback featured in our offense which is the backbone of the I. Probably the greatest advantage of the I is that it permits a team to feature one great running back in the tailback slot. Also, more than one great runner is not necessary in the offense. We also like the fact that the halfback does not have to block in this offense as he did previously in conventional offenses. Normally, the halfback type of player is not big and sturdy enough to do that type of work, and we are able to utilize the big powerful player (the fullback) for most of the blocking.

Using the balanced line is superior to the unbalanced line, in our opinion, because, as mentioned previously, the offense is more likely to know how the defense is going to play. In addition, it is easier to flip-flop, substitute, and have the depth in a balanced line than it is in an unbalanced line.

35

Our basic formation (the slot I) places the slotback and split end on the same side and the tight end on the opposite side. Thus, passing strength is provided on one side, the slot side, and running strength on the tight end side. Therefore, in a commonly used defense such as the monster, the monster man cannot support on the running strength side and then be able to drop off to cover the passing strength side. He must select a side, and whichever side he chooses, we feel the slot I will make him ineffective. The slot I is the ideal formation to use to attack the ever-popular 5-2 monster defense.

At this point, mention should be made of the tailback. One of the reasons the tailbacks have been doing so well in picking up yardage is, not only are they fine athletes and have opportunities to carry a greater number of times than backs running from other formations, but their position is the greatest place from which a back could possibly carry the football. The tailback is in the middle of the formation and can hit every hole. In addition, his depth enables him to see the hole open better, and he can hit square to the line of scrimmage, which enables him to cut to daylight more easily. Not detracting from the great backs, we feel that running from the tailback position makes it easier to gain yards, and tailbacks would not have done as well had they been running from the conventional halfback position.

With the slot I, great specialization can be achieved from the other personnel. As an example, the slot-side guard does more pulling than the tight end side guard. Naturally, the split end is completely different from the tight end. We have found it much easier to position our personnel in the slot I.

Every player on the line is flip-flopped. This is a basic carry-over from the use of the unbalanced line. By flip-flopping our line we can better utilize the ability of the players. The best pulling guard does most of the pulling. In addition, the time spent learning the plays is cut in half. The only thing that changes on a flip-flop is the play becomes a left-handed technique versus a right-handed technique. Most coaches teach a player to block with either the left or right shoulder; therefore, there is no technique problem.

Probably the greatest advantage of the slot I is that it permits the use of the best blockers against both sides of the defense. Normally, our three best blockers are placed on the tight end side, and that is where most of the running yardage will be gained. If the team is setting in a formation with the tight-side men to the right, they block the defensive left side. If the formation is switched with the tight-side men to the left, they would be working against the weaker defensive linemen. Now all our strength has been pitted against the opponent's weakness.

The weakness in flip-flopping the personnel is that it is not quite as easy to have the depth with the flip-flop of the personnel as would be the case with a completely mirrored attack on a balanced line that is not flip-flopped. For instance, the next best tackle cannot cover the opposite side without learning new assignments because the assignments are different. In fact, due to the lack of depth caused by flip-flopping, we are working a little more toward the mirror attack. As is true in any offense, a team cannot have everything.

Diagrams 2-1 and 2-2 show the basic formation of the slot I. The numbering system is perfect for flip-flopping the personnel as the numbers are also flip-flopped. The small

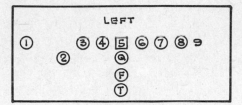

Diagram 2-1

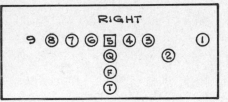

Diagram 2-2

numbers are on the side of the small split end and the big numbers are on the side of the
big tight end. As an example, if the team is in a right formation, the one hole is to the right
and wide to the split end. A 51 play would be exactly the same if the line flip-flopped,
went to a left formation, then called 51, and ran wide left. Our offensive linemen are
referred to by the number of the hole they are in. As an example, the tight-side tackle is
called the 7 man because it is also the 7 hole. They are not actually referred to as the left
tackle or the strong-side tackle.

The plays are called by two digit numbers, the last digit referring to the hole or area
that is run to and gives the linemen their blocking rules. Sometimes word calls are added
to vary blocking schemes. The first digit refers to the backfield or play series, not
specifically to the ball-carrier. We do not have a 2 back or a 3 back, but we do have a 20
series, a 30 series, a 40 series, a 50 series, etc.

To make it easy to remember, anything in the 20's or 30's (20 and 30 both begin
with T) states that the quarterback goes to the tailback first, whether he gives or fakes to
him. The 40's and 50's (40 and 50 start with F) state that the quarterback goes to the
fullback first, either giving or faking. The 20 through 50 series are running plays. The 90
series is used for dropback passes. The 80's are special passes, and the 70 series is used
for sprint-out passing. Play action passes usually assume the same number as the running
play that is being used, but *pass* is added to the call.

In our opinion, the slot formation is superior to the basic pro look of the weak-side
end being split with a wide flanker (Diagram 2-3). We have a four back offense rather
than a three back offense in that the slotback is available as a ball-carrier, and he can do
anything the tight end does in the pro formation such as blocking and receiving. When
the weak-side end is split off in the pro, basically all that is done is to weaken that side
for running plays. Using the split end on the slot side spreads the defense and forces the
important spread between the safety and the strong halfback. On both formations the

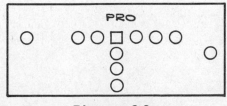

Diagram 2-3

defense is forced to cover the weak-side end, man-for-man, unless they are in a 4-deep, and then the weak safety could double.

Our quarterbacks read the situation and always throw strong-side. Thus the slot gives basically the same advantages in passing, and the double tight end running threat is gained plus the extra running back in the attack. The slot left and right are our two basic formations, and the team runs most frequently from them. However, we do not feel a team can operate out of just two formations. How many others are used depends on the personnel and the defenses with which the team is confronted. Some of our supplementary formations follow.

On obvious passing situations the tight end is split to better enable him to get out. Many times the second-string split end is substituted for him to provide a better receiver for the play (Diagram 2-4).

As shown in Diagram 2-5, the backs are also split, which enables them to get in the pass patterns a little better. When this is done, the team usually shifts from the I.

On occasion our slotback is stepped up and the split end is back (Diagram 2-6).

The balance of the plays are diagramed from the right formation. They are mirrored from the left formation but the personnel flip-flops and the assignments stay exactly the same. As an example, the 6 man does the same thing on a 37, whether it be from the left or right formation.

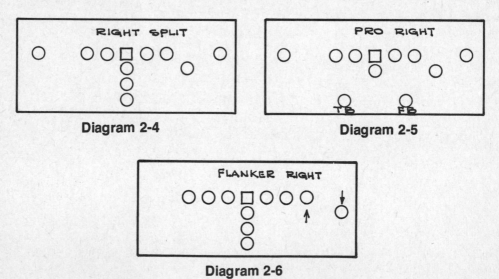

Diagram 2-4   **Diagram 2-5**

Diagram 2-6

Diagram 2-7 shows possibly our most basic bread-and-butter play. It is particularly effective versus a 5-2 in that a double-team is achieved on the tough nose guard, who frequently loops a great deal. All other players have an angle block, with the linebacker being isolated for the fullback to block. The tailback merely cuts off the fullback's block. Our quarterback reverse pivots on the 20 and 30 series, which allows the fullback to clear without the quarterback seeing him.

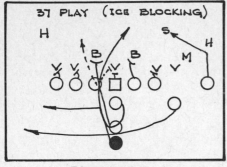

Diagram 2-7

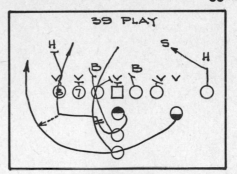

Diagram 2-8

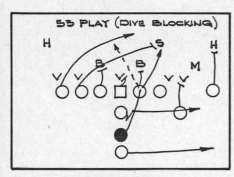

Diagram 2-9

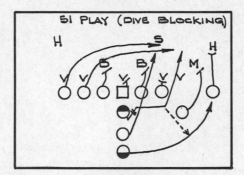

Diagram 2-10

Diagram 2-8 shows the 39 play which is the companion to the 37 play. It is a great option play which has been very kind to us. Notice the blocking is almost the same as it was for the 37 play, even to the point of the 7 man using an influence block. The 8 man goes first at the end to make it appear the same, and he can also prevent a hard, quick crash by the end. It is important that the quarterback make a great fake, because a delay is necessary to permit the slotback to get in position. On the options the quarterbacks are instructed to think keep unless they are forced to pitch due to the end closing. Naturally, we would prefer the pitch, but we find the quarterbacks execute better this way. The option is simplified for them. Our quarterbacks use a soft, one-handed pitch with the nearest hand. On this play the defense is always optioned. It is our best outside play versus a monster defense, hitting at the weakest spot of this defense.

Nothing more than the basic fullback dive which has been around a long time is shown in Diagram 2-9. It has worked well in that the nose guard will stunt a higher percentage of the time away from the monster. The play features basic, man-for-man blocking which all coaches use.

The quarterback is told to front out on all 40 and 50 series because the fullback is closer and hits quickly. Having both the front out and the reverse pivot destroys the linebacker's keying the movement of the quarterback.

The points of execution for the quarterback are the same as they were for the 39 play (Diagram 2-8) except that it is a quicker and shorter ride to the fullback (Diagram 2-10).

On both options the responsibility is placed on the halfback to be in the proper pitch position, which is about 4 yards back and 2 yards in advance of the quarterback. We want to option the end on this play. It it is a balanced defense (no monster), the slotback blocks on the line of scrimmage, as would the tackle on a 6-2 defense.

This is a very quick-hitting option. The same type of option is also run to the tight end side and is called 59. The tight end blocks according to the slotback's rule.

A fine play-action pass comes off 51, which is called 51 pass in which the split end runs a corner route and the slotback goes in the flat with the tailback blocking the end.

Another bread-and-butter play which every I team runs is shown in Diagram 2-11. It is one that works well with the back breaking to daylight. Some of our best gains have come off this play when the tailback broke clear back, behind the nose guard. It is an excellent play to use to counter the fast pursuit seen today. We want the quarterback to get the ball to the tailback quickly and as deep as possible so that he can run to daylight.

A very fine pass similar to the basic sprint-out is shown in Diagram 2-12, but the 22 is being faked. Incidentally, we changed the name to 12 pass because we want to automatic both it and 22 play by reading the monster. It works best when there is no monster, but it is excellent to counter a monster man who is playing in tight support on the off-tackle hole. It is a quick fake by the quarterback because we want him to be ready to throw quickly.

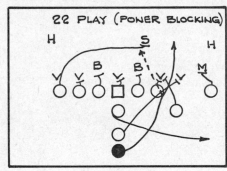

Diagram 2-11

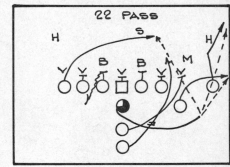

Diagram 2-12

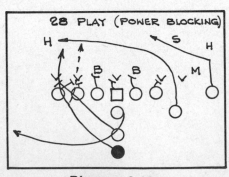

Diagram 2-13

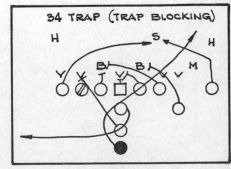

Diagram 2-14

We have also used this play as a true sprint-out with the tailback also lead blocking, but favor using the play action because so many monster defenses are encountered and it is necessary to fake in order to freeze the monster man. It is an option run-throw by the quarterback. To hit the crossing end is effective but it is difficult to get the quarterback to do it.

Diagram 2-13 shows a play which is exactly the same as 22 but is actually a better play for our team because we have our three best blockers on that side. Also, the short side of the defense is being attacked. The effectiveness is helped by the 22 pass threat, which offsets the slotback not being as good a blocker as the tight end.

One of the truly fine plays that we developed is shown in Diagram 2-14. It provides a great counter to flow, which is one of the weaker points of the I. Defenses are attacked predicated on the linebacker's going with the flow. The tailback must establish direction to the left before he cuts back. It is somewhat delayed in order to allow the defense to react. Needless to say, our tackles like this play and have made some fantastic blocks.

Speaking of counter action, we also counter back with the slotback. This formation is versatile and almost everything can be run from it.

Diagram 2-15 shows a play which will provide two different blocking schemes at each point of attack without additional learning being required of the players. By merely flip-flopping the personnel as we do, the defensive right tackle can be trapped either with the guard or the tackle, depending on whether the call is right 34 or left 56, using the blocking scheme that is most effective. This is also an excellent play for the fullback and is a long-time standard in football.

Our 90 series consists of dropback passes. Diagram 2-16 shows a play where favorite dropback patterns can be used, which include checking backs out into the pattern. It is perfect in that our protection is designed where the backs block the linebackers in case of a red-dog. Also, we do not have to have our tailback blocking the big defensive end all the time. It is called big man on big man, which is merely having the guards and tackles block the big defensive linemen, and the backs take the smaller linebackers. We feel the idea has considerable merit and have been very pleased with the results.

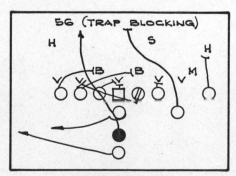

Diagram 2-15

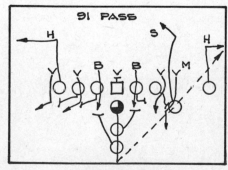

Diagram 2-16

We have three basic blocking rule systems: 1. power blocking; 2. ice blocking; and 3. trap blocking.

1. Power Blocking Rule—front side is inside, on, linebacker. a. Inside means any man between the linemen and the next inside man. b. On means any man directly on the lineman's nose. c. Linebacker means the nearest linebacker to the lineman as the blocker.

Backside Rule—from center to tackle is on, backside gap, linebacker.

2. Ice Rule. a. On the front side—the end and tackle block the first man outside on the line of scrimmage. Front-side guard—block on the center, inside, on, linebacker. b. Center block—on, or the backside gap. c. Backside guard and tackle—block according to the power rule, on the back side, on, backside gap, linebacker.

3. Trap Blocking—56 Play—Eight man—first man inside the linebacker. Seven man—far removed or the middle linebacker. Six man—on center, inside, man on, influence block the first outside man. Five man—on or backside. Four man—pull the front-side block first. Man on 4 or past 4. Three man—inside, on, release. One man—release to the safety.

34 Play—mirror the previously mentioned rules except switch the back-side tackle and the guard's assignment.

On any power play that is designed as such, we merely say power block this play, which means to block on the front side, inside, on, linebacker. This is the simplest of all blocking rules. These rules are used against a stunting defensive team.

Our isolation blocking is limited because there are only two plays in which the team uses the ice block.

The trap blocking is standard for any trap that is put in the offense.

Coaches will find they can incorporate their own bread-and-butter plays and philosophy into this offense very easily. Naturally, they will want to include more fullback or slotback plays if they have a good runner in these spots. If the quarterback is a good sprint-out man, he could be featured. We always let our personnel dictate the type of plays that are used. In our opinion, the slot I is an offensive theory and formation that has tremendous advantages.

THE WIDE I

by John Pont, Jake Van Schoych and Bob Baker

John Pont
Northwestern University

Jake Van Schoych
Northwestern University

Bob Baker
Michigan State University

The wide I should be used when the available material is compatible with it and with those maneuvers which are run from this alignment. Primary consideration should be given to the abilities of the players, and the approach of *what can be done* must be used before proceeding to *what must be done* to be successful offensively. The entire operation is flip-flopped, using the term IPRO for a right-handed set (Diagram 2-17) and ICOM for a left-handed set (Diagram 2-18). Since we have a long side (four men) and a short side, the linemen are designated long tackle, short tackle, etc. Again, this is done to be compatible with the material, because seldom do two tackles have identical speed, so the quicker of the two is placed to the short side (he has no tight end to help him block) and the other tackle goes to the long side with the tight end. This, we feel, simplifies material selection and has a tendency to force the defense to align themselves in a standard method. Our deep backs use a three-point stance and align four yards and six yards deep from the ball. The wide men set at a ten-yard minimum.

The wide I alignment forces the defense to stretch, and by stretching (to cover the two side receivers), gives us more room to operate in. The fact that we have more area

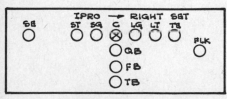

Diagram 2-17

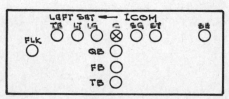

Diagram 2-18

43

results in more long-gainers. By its initial alignment, the stacked backfield places two men in a relatively good position to block down the defensive container, and if two blockers cannot take one defender, then we have problems that are difficult to solve. Also, the stacked backfield offers excellent position to execute the power off-tackle, which is a sound and fundamental play necessary to the entire offensive structure. This alignment also lends itself to the running quarterback, which affords the offense methods of attacking the corners of a defense with the utmost speed and optional features. These methods are certainly effective if a coach has a quarterback with a high degree of all-around athletic ability.

We shall describe some maneuvers from the formation IPRO. Notice Nos. 1, 2, and 3 are blocked in reference to the guards, tackles, and tight end. Further notice we have two basic plays with actions resulting from these plays. Power is a basic play with its companion being power pass to the on-side rollaway to the backside. Slant is also a basic play with the belly coming off in the basic action.

Our power play is shown in Diagram 2-19. Split End—He should take the man in his deep third. Short Tackle—Should keep the No. 2 man to his outside. Short Guard—Should keep the No. 1 man to his outside. Center—If the defense is odd, take 0; if it is even, take the safety man. Long Guard—Take No. 1. Long Tackle—Take No. 2. Tight End—He should double-team with the tackle on No. 2 against an odd defense; on an even defense he takes No. 4; and on a gap defense he blocks No. 3. Flanker—He should take the man in his deep third. Quarterback—He should pressure lift with his hands on the center's tail. Ride the center forward for the ball. Bring the ball into the stomach with both hands. Reverse pivot at a 135° angle and move quickly to the exchange spot 3 yards deep. Look the ball into the pocket and use both hands to give it to the tailback. Then bring the hands back to the hip as if to hide the ball. Sprint to the outside, faking the power pass play. Fullback—He should lead step-block the first man outside his offensive tackle's block, No. 3. Use a shoulder block. He should keep his head up and eyes open, approach his man on a straight line, and dig him out. Only if the man gives himself up and commits to the inside will the fullback use a cut-off block and bury him. On a gap call, block No. 4. Tailback—He should take a lead step in the direction of play. Drive straight in and square up to the line of scrimmage. Keep the head up, eyes open, and aim for the tackle area. Do not reach for the ball. The tailback should make a pocket for it by holding the elbow up and let the quarterback give the ball to him. The primary hole is on the

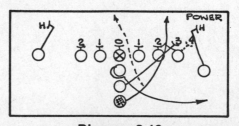

Diagram 2-19

outside shoulder of the tackle. If this hole is closed, he should cut back sharply to the inside and take the first route that shows daylight. Accelerate through the hole looking for the blockers downfield.

Diagram 2-20 shows the power pass play. Split End—He should run a streak cut. Short Tackle—He should execute set step protection. Short Guard—He should use step protection. Center—If the defense is odd, he should take 0, and then turn the backside even. Long Guard—He should take No. 1. Long Tackle—He takes No. 2. Tight End—He should double-team with the tackle on No. 2 versus an odd defense; against an even defense he takes No. 3. Flanker—He should execute his cut at 9 yards. Quarterback—Pressure lift with the hands on the center's tail. Ride the center forward for the ball. Bring the ball into the stomach with both hands. Reverse pivot at a 135° angle and move quickly to the exchange spot 3 yards deep. Look the ball into the pocket and make a good ride on the tailback. Hide the ball on the hip and sprint to the outside. Look for a receiver and hit him if he is open; if the receiver is covered, run. On all power pass plays, the sequence will be: first choice, pass; second choice, run. Fullback—He should lead step-block the first man outside his offensive tackle's block. Against an odd defense he should take No. 3; against an even defense take No. 4. He should keep his head up, eyes open, run straight at his man, and dig him out. If a flood pass is called, he should slip out into the flat and look for the ball over his outside shoulder. Tailback—This player should take a lead step in the direction of play. He should drive straight in and square up to the line of scrimmage. His head should be up, eyes open, and he should aim for the tackle area. He should make a pocket for the ball, but on this play he does not take it. The primary hole is on the outside shoulder of the tackle. If this hole is closed, butt back sharply to the inside and take the first daylight route. He should accelerate through the hole and run as if he had the ball. On this play, the tailback should be tackled.

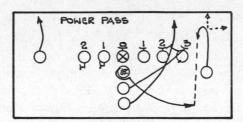

Diagram 2-20

Our rollaway play is shown in Diagram 2-21. Split End—He should run inside and deep. Short Tackle—Take No. 2 in. Short Guard—Take No. 1 in. Center—If the defense is odd, take 0; if it is even, reach on-side. Long Guard—Pull and take the first color to show inside. Long Tackle—Take No. 2 out. Tight End—Bump No. 3, and then take a 95° angle course, reading for the inside linebacker. Flanker—Run a streak pattern. Quarterback—Pressure lift with the hands on the center's tail. Ride the center forward for the ball. Reverse pivot at a 135° angle. He should fake the ball to the running back as

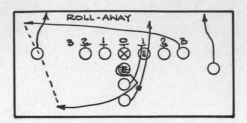

Diagram 2-21

he did on the power play. The action should be fluid. Make a good ride. The quarterback should key the defensive end, and also the block being thrown on him by his guard. If the end is coming, pull up and throw from inside the pocket. If the end is holding or retreating, then the guard will stay on him. Therefore, the quarterback should sprint outside for a pass-run option. He should call "go" to alert the guard if he runs. Fullback—Lead step drive for the front side guard area. Fill block for the guard who is pulling. He should make sure he gets into the line of scrimmage. Be under control with the legs and body. Use a shoulder block. Tailback—On this play, the tailback does not get the ball, and he should run a tighter course. Aim for the outside leg of the offensive guard.

The slant play is shown in Diagram 2-22. Split End—He should take the man in his deep third. Short Tackle—Take No. 2 out. Short Guard—Take No. 1 out. Center—If the defense is odd, take 0; if it is even, block back. Long Guard—He should take No. 1 any way he can, and long. Long Tackle—Take No. 2 out, and stick right and long. Tight End—Take No. 3 out. Flanker—He should take the man in his deep third. Quarterback—Pressure lift with the hands on the center's tail. Ride the center forward for the ball. Bring the ball into the stomach with both hands. Open pivot at a 60° angle, step deep, and reach to meet the fullback. Look the ball into the pocket and use both hands to give to the fullback. Get the ball to the fullback early so he can secure it and concentrate on running. Let the hands and shoulders rotate toward the line for a short ride. As he rides, the quarterback should step down the line, not into the line. As the blocking back passes, the quarterback should fly to the outside and key Nos. 3 and 4. Fullback—He should take a lead step in the direction the play is called. Get width on this first step. He should keep his eyes open, head up, and aim for the inside leg of the tackle.

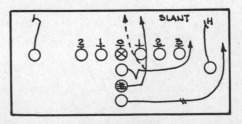

Diagram 2-22

His shoulders should be square to the line so he can cut. Make a pocket with the inside elbow up. He should not reach for the ball, but let the quarterback give it to him. Use go blocking, option, and run for daylight. He should accelerate through the hole, looking for his blockers downfield. Tailback—He should take a cross-over step in the direction the play is called. Fly to the outside, stay 4 yards outside and in front of the quarterback, and fake a belly play. He should make a move as he would in receiving a pitch from the quarterback, secure a make-believe ball, and run. He should make sure he turns the corner.

Diagram 2-23 shows the belly play. Split End—He should take the man in his deep third. Short Tackle—Take No. 2 out. Short Guard—Take No. 1 out. Center—If the defense is odd, take 0; if it is even, block back. Long Guard—Take No. 1 in. Long Tackle—Take No. 2 in. Tight End—Take No. 3 in. Flanker—He should take the man in his deep third. Quarterback—Pressure lift with the hands on the center's tail. Ride the center forward for the ball. He should bring the ball into his stomach with both hands. Open pivot at a 60° angle and step deep to meet the fullback. Look the ball into the pocket, make a good ride on the blocking back (the key to the play is ride), and use quick, jerky action. Let the hands and shoulders rotate toward the line. As he rides, the quarterback should step down the line, not into it. As the fullback passes him, he should fly to the outside key guard for inside or outside go. When he clears the line, the quarterback should sprint toward the outside contain man and make the pitch off him. If he is forced to turn up inside or lose his pitch man, he should be a runner, cut back to the inside, and use the blockers downfield. If he has a clear field outside, he should take it and go. Fullback—Take a lead step in the direction the play is called. Get width on this first step. The fullback should keep his eyes open, head up, and aim for the inside leg of the tackle. His shoulders should be square to the line so he can cut. He should form a pocket for the ball, but he does not take it. The fullback should be tackled on this play; if he is not, he should block the linebacker. Tailback—He should take a cross-over step from the I formation, a drop step from regular formation, and go in the direction the play is called. Fly to the outside, and stay 4 yards outside and in front of the quarterback. Be ready for the quarterback to turn up the field. Look for a pitch, catch the ball, put it away, and then run. If the quarterback does not pitch, get a block.

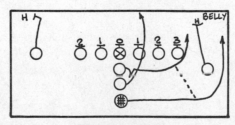

Diagram 2-23

THE FLEXIBLE I

by Ray Graves and Fred Pancoast

Ray Graves
Formerly, University of Florida

Fred Pancoast
Vanderbilt University

Through the years, football coaches have designed a variety of offensive systems, and each in its own way has had a place in advancing the game of football. In our opinion, the use of the I formations in recent years has had the greatest impact on offensive football up to the present time. Variations of the principles of the I have been widely and successfully used by many coaches, and the effect makes it appear as though the formation will have a hold for many years to come.

After some years of experimenting, we found a system which utilizes great flexibility and diversity of formation alignments by the movement of only one player. This system has proved effective because it emphasizes a high degree of efficiency from a limited number of plays used from a variety of formations.

Arriving at an adequate yet simple formation call system requires a great deal of attention. There are many ways to accomplish this. First, it must be established that ten of the eleven offensive players will assume a fairly standard alignment, with only the tight end and the split end moving to one side or the other, directed by a right or left formation call. Many coaches would prefer to utilize a flip-flop principle of moving guards and tackles to the strong or weak side with this call. We have tried both and found that linemen over a long period will do a more effective job when they stay to a constant side.

The two backs who remain constant are the fullback (up back) and the tailback (deep back). As in most formations, the up back should possess good inside running ability and be the better of the two blockers. The deep back should be both a strong inside runner and an effective outside runner, plus be strong and durable, because he will be called upon to carry the ball more than twice as often as the other backs.

The up back should align himself directly behind the quarterback and 3½ yards from the ball. He should assume a three-point square stance, which will allow him to move quickly in any direction.

The deep back should align himself directly behind, and one yard deeper than, the up back. He is placed in an upright, two-point stance with his hands on his knees. This position allows him a full view of the defense and his quarterback who, on occasion, will send him in motion by a flip of his heel. Diagrams 2-24 and 2-25 show the right and left formations.

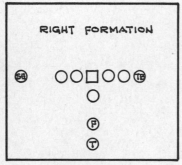

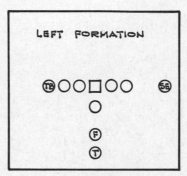

Diagram 2-24 **Diagram 2-25**

Flexibility of formation is gained through varying the alignments of the eleventh player, who is called the rover. In order to play this position adequately, a player must possess a variety of abilities. He must be a strong inside blocker, an excellent pass receiver, and be a threat as a ball-carrier. If a player of this caliber is not available, the degree of efficiency of this system will be hampered.

In developing a call system to use in directing the rover to a desired alignment, we found the use of a number with which to assign his positions to be the most effective. A number preceding a play call sends him to a position to the direction call of the formation. As an example, suppose the play called is 24 Lead. Then the desired alignment of the rover is achieved to the strong side by preceding the alignment number with the play call. Let us say we would like him split wide as a flanker. The call would, therefore, be (3) 24 Lead. The (3) directs this alignment. Diagram 2-26 shows strong side alignment variations.

Alignments of the rover to the weak side of the formation are numbered in the same manner, with the call of *over* added to assign him to corresponding positions to that side. The weak side offers an added position due to the position of the split end to that side. This alignment, which places the rover at a position from 5 to 7 yards from the split end, is assigned the number 4. We refer to this alignment of the split end and the rover as twins. Many effective pass route combinations can be gained from this alignment.

With the fourth position added to the weak side, it must be pointed out that the 3 position will station the rover in a position equidistant between the weak tackle and the split end, as shown in Diagram 2-27.

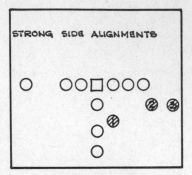

Diagram 2-26

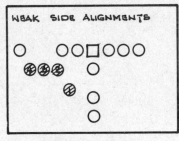

Diagram 2-27

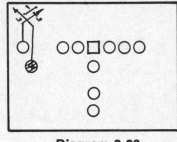

Diagram 2-28

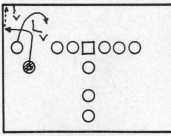

Diagram 2-29

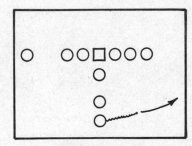

Diagram 2-30

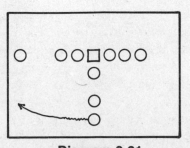

Diagram 2-31

An example play called to the weak side would be I Right Over (3) 24 Lead. This is the same play that is used to illustrate strong side alignments, and will be explained in detail.

Although the 3 and 4 alignments may seem similar, there is a difference between the two, especially in regard to pass coverage. For example, when the defense is employing a basic man coverage on the two, split end, and rover, the 4 or twins alignment is more effective. This alignment places the defenders who are covering the two in positions very close to each other and makes them vulnerable to mistakes. They even run into each other when they are covering crossing patterns, as shown in Diagram 2-28.

The 3 alignment is preferred when encountering the basic zone coverages. This is true because of the added stretch that is placed on the defense when the rover is placed in a slot position between the split end and the weak tackle. This principle is more effective when the alignment is placed to the wide side of the field. A pattern, as shown in Diagram 2-29, would be effective in this case.

Adding to the effectiveness and flexibility of this system is a simple method of placing motion into the call system. Although we are sure there are others, we use three variations of motion, each in its own way, thus placing an added strain on the defense.

The deep back or tailback is in a position to move before the snap to either the weak or the strong side of the formation. When directed to the strong side, the call of *fly* is used, as shown in Diagram 2-30.

A call of *race* is used to send him to the weak side, as shown in Diagram 2-31. In all cases, the extension of motion is set by the desired play and is directed by the quarterback in his signal call system.

A third variation is utilized by placing the rover in motion and is directed by the word *cross*. Naturally, this should not be done from a 3 or 5 alignment. However, the rover can be used from a 1 or 2 position to either a strong or weak alignment. His movement will always take him across the backfield to the opposite side of his alignment and in front of the fullback. As shown in Diagram 2-32, he is leaving from a strong side 2 alignment, and in Diagram 2-33 from a weak side 1 alignment.

One of the simplest, yet probably the most effective, plays which can be used from this formation system is the split T option. Although the techniques are different from the basic split T, the principles are the same.

In the execution of this play, the quarterback's responsibility plays a major role. The alignment of the formation must isolate the defensive end to either the strong or the weak side in order for the play to be effective. This can be done from any of the previously discussed alignments. However, we would prefer to run the play to the side of one or two split men in order to obtain a crack-back blocker on the inside fill. Therefore, we will illustrate the play run from two formation variations.

Run first to a strong side 3 alignment, as shown in Series A, the play is called as follows: I Right 318. The 3 directs the alignment of the rover and the 18 is the play. Our split T series is 10, with even numbered holes to the right and odd numbered holes to the left.

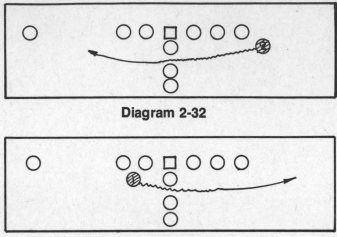

Diagram 2-32

Diagram 2-33

Play is initiated by the quarterback taking a lateral and then a cross-over step down the line and sprinting towards the defensive end who, we hope, has been isolated by the strong end's and the tackle's blocks on anything to the inside. When reaching a point just short of his arm's reach, the quarterback should slow himself by taking short, choppy steps. Then he will either pitch the ball to the tailback or keep himself to the inside. This decision is made on the position of the defensive end.

In order to gain the proper pitch relationship with the quarterback, the tailback must start by taking a short, quick counter step away from the play call. This step serves two purposes: 1) to allow the fullback clearance in front of him, and 2) to place him in a position 3 yards deeper and 2 yards wider than the quarterback when and if the pitch is made.

The two key blocks are normally made by the split man and the fullback. On the snap, the split man takes a bucket step to the inside. He should continue to the inside, looking for a block on the first fill man, who will be either the strong safety or the linebacker. The block should be of the high screen type, emphasizing that he maintain contact as long as possible.

The initial angle taken by the fullback is most important. He must aim at a point 1½ yards deeper than the defensive end and continue on this line until just before reaching him. Then he goes either inside or outside the defensive end, and after passing him, gains an inside-out position on the widest man to show outside. The type of block is the same as that used by the split man on the inside fill. If the ball is pitched to the tailback, an alley should be created by their two blocks, as shown in Diagram 2-34.

Another aspect is added to the play when it is run to a weak side 4 alignment, as shown in Diagram 2-35. Now the play is called I Right Over 419, and it is run to the left. The principles of the play are the same, except that an extra blocker is gained by the split end. He should drive the man who is covering him as deep as possible with a high screen type block.

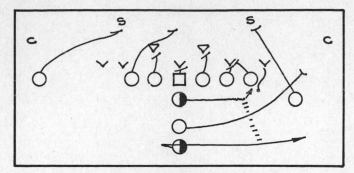

Diagram 2-34

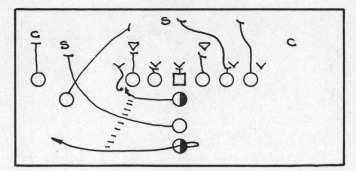

Diagram 2-35

The take-off from 18-19 is an off-tackle play called 14-15. This play, as shown in Diagram 2-36, starts out appearing the same as 18 or 19. The quarterback starts down the line, employing the same action that is used in running the option. On his fourth step, he comes to a stop, steps back as far as possible toward the tailback, and makes a hand-off to him. The tailback starts at the same angle as he would on 18 and 19, but after his third step, he plants his outside foot and starts to the inside toward the hand-off point.

The blocks of the strong ends and tackles are the same as they were for 18-19, hoping for a seal-off to the inside. Now the fullback will aim for a point one yard deeper than the defensive end, hoping that he will come up the field a little way to play the option. He is assigned to kick the end out with an inside-out shoulder block, hoping to create an alley for the tailback.

The same play to the weak side from a strong side 3 formation would be called I Right 315. Many times when this play is used to the weak side, a blocking change-off is used between the tackle and the guard. This is especially true against an off-set defense, as is shown in Diagram 2-37.

The 20 Series is basically a power series, with the threat of the power play by the tailback always present. The power play, 24 Lead, was used to illustrate formation calls earlier in this chapter. As shown in Diagram 2-38, the play attempts to isolate a linebacker by blocking the tight end outside and the strong tackle on-inside. Naturally,

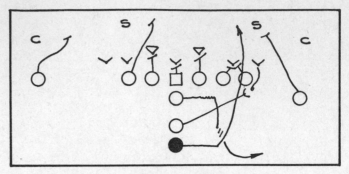

Diagram 2-36

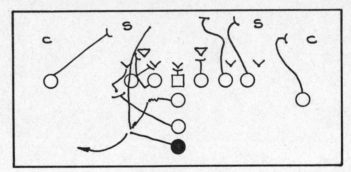

Diagram 2-37

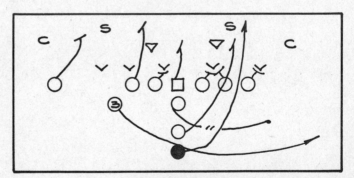

Diagram 2-38

the play is more successful against a stack or off-set defense, which is usually run to stop the option. Now the quarterback executes a deep, two-step reverse pivot, attempting to make the hand-off as deep as possible to the tailback. The hand-off should be made with both hands, and the quarterback should be riding slightly with the ball before pulling his hands out. After the hand-off, the quarterback makes a fake pass on the corner, and if the rover has been placed into the trail position, he fakes the option. The tailback starts with an over-and-up step with his near foot to allow the fullback to clear and direct his angle of attack toward the line in as perpendicular a manner as possible. This position allows him freedom to bend back to the inside in case a hole has not been created. The fullback is responsible for the linebacker over or nearest the strong tackle, and he heads directly for him on the snap. His block should be a nose-to-numbers block, attempting to collapse the linebacker or turn him to one side or the other. In most cases, the tailback should run off his block. This play can be run to the strong side with the rover in any position.

A take-off play of 24-25 Lead would be our 28-29 Easy. This is a wide option type play with easy blocking, referring to the tight end's block on the cornerback to his side. This play requires the rover to be placed in a position from which he can gain a pitch relationship with the quarterback, which means that he must be in a 1 or 2 position to either the strong or the weak side. The quarterback begins play with the same reverse pivot used in the 24-25 play. Now he will give the tailback a short ride, take the ball from the tailback, note quickly the position of the defensive end, and use the same principles on 18-19, which means he will keep inside himself or else pitch the ball wide to the rover. The tailback drives straight for the outside leg of the tackle, with no over-up step. When the ball is placed into his stomach by the quarterback, the tailback will start a gradual bend back to the inside with a low, hard-driving fake into the line after the ball has been taken out.

The fullback has the same blocking responsibility as he would on 24-25 Lead. If the linebacker has taken a fake of the tailback, he will continue on for the strong safety. Employ the on-side tackle block rule on-outside, using reach technique when the man is on the outside. The tight end must drive his outside shoulder into the man on the outside, keeping his head close to the inside. After holding the block for two full counts, he releases inside and blocks the cornerback to the outside with high screen technique. The rover leaves on the snap count, except when he is in a strong 2 position, in which case, he must be placed into two-step cross motion. Then he should pick up the option relationship with the quarterback. When receiving the pitch from the quarterback, the rover should run inside or outside on the tight end's block. Diagram 2-39 shows the play run from a strong side 2 alignment, and Diagram 2-40 shows the play run from a weak side 2 alignment.

When the play is run to the weak side, the split end takes up an easy assignment and the quarterback must locate the defensive end well behind the tailback with a fake. The right end is not protected by the tight end's slow block on the defensive end; therefore, the quarterback must pitch the ball immediately after taking it from the tailback, if the end is on fire.

There is a tendency for the defense to key either the fullback or the tailback from the I formation, so it is important that counter type plays be placed into the scheme of attack due to the similarity in quarterback action when incorporating this into our 20 Series. The word *counter* added to a play call tells the fullback always to drive on the weak side guard and the tailback over the strong side tackle. The quarterback executes the same reverse pivot used in 24-25 Lead. The off-tackle trap call, 26-27 counter trap shown in Diagram

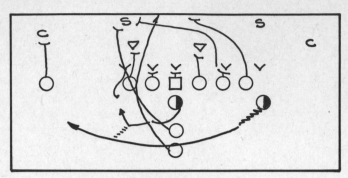

Diagram 2-39

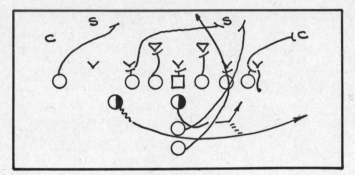

Diagram 2-40

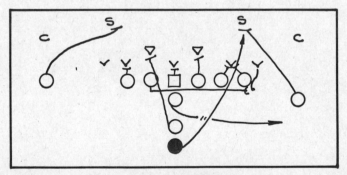

Diagram 2-41

2-41, is a tailback play to the strong side. As the quarterback takes his first step in a reverse pivot, the fullback will pass close enough for an adequate fake but without an actual fake to him. The quarterback continues in one motion into the second step and the hand-off point to the tailback. After the hand-off, the fake is the same one that is used on 24-25 Lead. The tailback takes over and up-steps to gain the proper angle. After receiving the hand-off, he looks for a hole to open inside and for the pulling guard's block on the defensive end. The fullback drives hard for the inside leg of the defensive

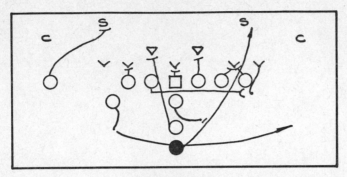

Diagram 2-42

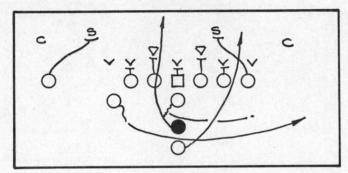

Diagram 2-43

guard, faking as if he were receiving the ball when he passes the quarterback. The tight end and the strong tackle block the inside, and the strong guard pulls and kicks out on the defensive end.

Diagram 2-42 shows how the rover, when he is placed in a weak side 1 or 2 position, can help block on the defensive end with a wide fake of the 28 play.

The fullback play to the weak side is 20-21 counter, as shown in Diagram 2-43. All backfield ball-handling is the same as it was in the 26-27 counter trap, except the ball is given to the fullback on the first step and the fake is made to the tailback on the second step. All blocking in the line is zone or rule, and the fullback has the option of running for daylight anywhere from the weak tackle to the strong guard.

Many times this play is successful when cross motion is added by the rover from a weak side 2 position. His movement across the backfield before the snap will frequently move a linebacker from the point of attack, which often will allow the play to go for a long gainer (Diagram 2-44).

In every offense there is a need for a special or trick play. This play, if used at the proper time under ideal circumstances, can yield long yardage, or, of course, it might result in a big loss. It is therefore advisable that a play of this type be used sparingly and under conditions where a loss would not be disastrous.

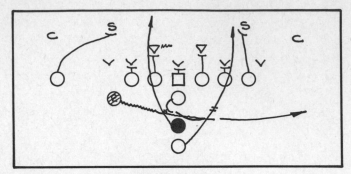

Diagram 2-44

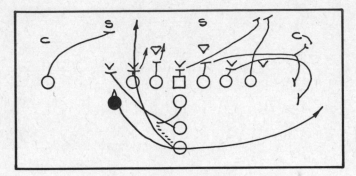

Diagram 2-45

The play that has been the best to us in this category is shown in Diagram 2-45.

It is especially effective when the defense rotates toward the rover, who is lined up to the weak side in a 2 position. If the chase from the strong side with action away ever becomes lax, then the chances for a big play are practically insured.

Play begins as though a routine off-tackle play is starting to the weak side. The techniques for the quarterback, tailback, and fullback are the same as they are in any 20 Series play, except the fullback will kick out on the first man to show outside the weak tackle's block in order to secure a pitch to the rover. A short jab step toward the line with the outside foot is made by the rover before he gains a trail position behind, and two yards deeper than, the tailback's alignment before the snap. He should be directly behind the center and ready to receive the pitch from the quarterback, who has given a good extended ride fake to the tailback. Weak side linemen use normal blocking rules, and then release to the play area. The tight end releases as though he were going into a deep pass route or a block on the safety man. This will tend to drag the cornerback deep and toward the middle. The strong tackle blocks on-outside for two counts, and then releases to the outside. After clearing the line, he fans back up the field toward the defensive end, who will start into recovery after seeing the ball pitched. At this point, the tackle is ready to pick him up with a peel-back block. The strong guard uses the same rule blocking, then releases down the line and looks back over his outside shoulder for a second peel-back block. If there is none, he continues to the outside, looking for an inside-out block on the corner who, at this point, will be starting to recover. The center blocks the on-near gap (toward the play) for two counts. Then he starts down the line toward the play and watches for the strong guard. If he has executed a peel-back block, he will continue out for a block on the corner; if not, he should turn directly up the field and look for the safety. The ball-carrier should be ready to give enough ground to clear the strong tackle's block on the chase man, and then follow the guard's or the center's block downfield.

The primary strength of the I formation is running; therefore, it is logically sound to say that the most effective way to throw would be from play action or after faking one of the running plays which have been explained.

The pattern that is shown in Diagram 2-46 seems at first glance a very simple one, but as simple as it may seem, it has been our most productive.

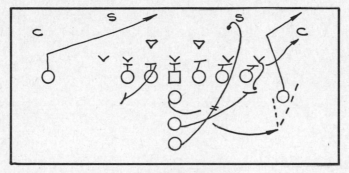

Diagram 2-46

Because the run play 24-25 to the strong side is probably the strongest, it naturally serves as the best faking action in use.

The pattern or play is called 28 or 29 pass. The 20 Series, of course, directs the backfield action and the number 8 or 9 directs the route of the wide receiver and the route complementary to it, in this case the tight end's. As was the case in the run plays, pass routes are numbered even to the right and odd to the left. The entire play called from the most favorable formation would, therefore, be I Right 328 Pass.

The quarterback executes a two-step reverse pivot making a two-handed ride fake to the tailback, and then continues to the corner with the option of throwing to the rover, tight end, or, if containment has broken down, he has the run option.

The tailback fakes 24 or 25 Lead and if he is able to clear the line, hooks up in the strong linebacker zone. The fullback drives hard, directly for the defensive end, and executes a hook block on him. It is important that the fullback does not try and lead the defensive end up the field, because normally he will read this angle as pass and contain up the field. The rover or flanker back starts directly inside as though he were cracking back on the safety. In doing so, he should watch the movement of the cornerback or halfback to his side. When the rover has continued inside far enough to lose the cornerback's attention, he breaks back to the outside. If the rover has fooled the corner, he continues deep in behind him; if not, he flattens his angle and runs toward the sideline in front of the cornerback.

The tight end executes a turn-out block for one count and then releases into the quick flat, developing a foot race between himself and the linebacker or the strong safety. If double coverage has occurred on the flanker, he adjusts his route by hooking up halfway between the flanker and his original position.

The split end runs a shallow drag route through the post to hold off the safety. By a simple change of the second digit in the play call, different routes can be run, as shown in Diagram 2-47. The same or a different route can be run from a different formation call, as shown in Diagram 2-48.

A pattern that is directed away from the backfield action is commonly referred to as a bootleg pass. This type of pass can be effective if the defensive secondary rotates too quickly toward the initial direction of play. The play shown in Diagram 2-49 is an effective one because it gives the quarterback the possibility of three choices of receivers.

The play is called I Right 338 Bootleg. In this case, the backfield action is directed

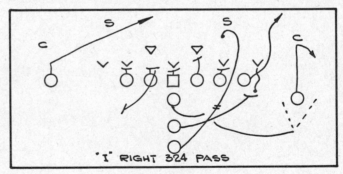

Diagram 2-47

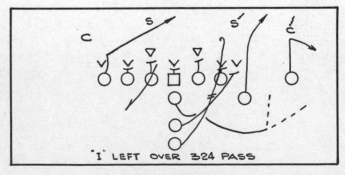

Diagram 2-48

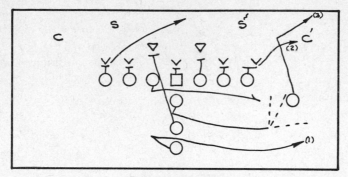

Diagram 2-49

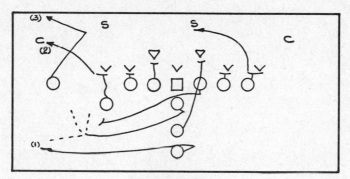

Diagram 2-50

by a fake to the fullback and, in our system, is labeled as the 30 Series; as is the case in the 28 or 29 pass, the second digit directs the route of the two outside receivers.

The quarterback opens with a deep, one-step pivot to meet the fullback, gives him a short ride fake, and then reverses to the opposite side of the formation. In doing so, he should pay particular attention to maintaining proper spacing with the pulling guard because the defensive end will usually chase deep up the field, requiring him to pull up to throw. His choice of receivers in the order of preference are: 1) tailback, 2) tight end, and 3) flanker. Many times the quarterback can continue wide with the ball, drawing coverage from the cornerback to contain on him. The flanker executes the route described for play 28 or 29. The route of the tight end is also the same, except he must deepen it to 8 to 10 yards to create better spacing between himself and the two other receivers.

The tailback takes a false step toward the initial direction of the play and then changes direction toward the tight end side. He should give ground, continually gaining position to receive a pass behind the line and over his inside shoulder.

In this case, the split end should bring down the split to 5 yards and false block for two counts on the man who is covering him before going into the shallow drag route. Thus, the quick backside chase on the quarterback is limited.

Another version of this play is achieved by merely changing the formation call, as shown in Diagram 2-50. The play is called to the weak side of the formation and from a 2 alignment of the rover. Now the play is called I Right Over 239 Bootleg.

There are other run and pass plays which are used in our system. We have, however, attempted to give some information on the structure of our system and those plays that have been the most productive for us. We do hope that in some way we have stimulated the thinking of football coaches, and what we have offered may be of some value to them in their future planning.

3 / The Wing T

THE DELAWARE WING T

by Ted Kempski

Ted Kempski
University of Delaware

The Delaware wing T is more than a formation. It is a philosophy of attack based on the anticipation of certain adjustments forced upon the defense due to the position of the wingback. It is a four-back running system that forces the secondary to play at least three deep, due to the presence of three deep receiving threats. Thus it is readily apparent that although the Delaware wing T is a ground-oriented attack, it is equally dependent on an interrelated passing game.

Although the wing T has undergone drastic changes during the past two and one-half decades to stay abreast of the increased defensive sophistication, the basic principles designed and developed by Dave Nelson and Tubby Raymond remain intact.

1. The wing T is designed for consistency, strength, and is ball control oriented.

2. The formations are characterized by a wingback, so there is the threat of at least three deep receivers.

3. The quarterback threatens the flank either with action toward or away from it on every play, providing either an additional threat to the attack flank or misdirection threatening the flank away from flow.

4. All three backs are close enough to the formation so that they may be used as blockers, as ball-carriers, or for deception.

5. The offense is designed in complete backfield series, each of which presents multiple threats to the defense on each play.

6. It has a balance of passing that is predominantly play action in nature.

7. The spread of receivers is accomplished by ends, and is made to accommodate the running game, not as a mechanism to enhance the passing game.

The numbering system employed is a three-digit system. The first digit identifies the formation; the second, the series or backfield action; and the third, the point of attack. The formation may be modified with a prefix and the blocking adjusted with a suffix. Holes are numbered from 1 to 9, going from right to left. Thus 1 through 4 are synonymous with right and 6 through 9 are synonymous with left.

Formations

Since the wing T is actually a multiple formation attack, there are numerous formations. In spite of this multiplicity, however, there are six basic formations which are primary. When the first digit is 1, the wingback is placed to the right, and when it is 9, the wingback is left. The six basic formations are shown in Diagram 3-1.

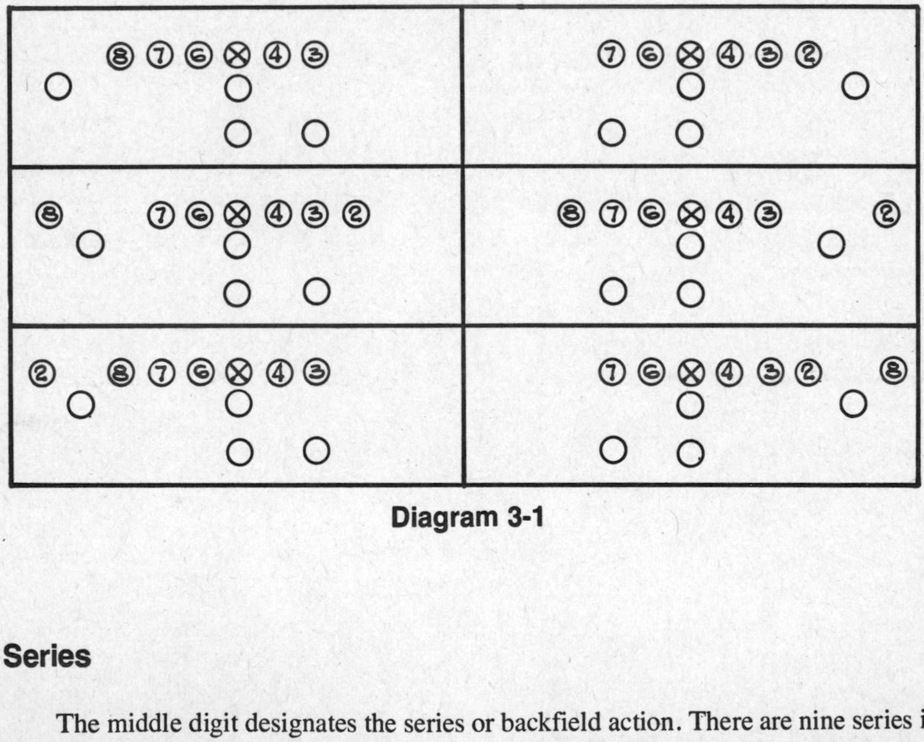

Diagram 3-1

Series

The middle digit designates the series or backfield action. There are nine series in all—five which are primarily running series and four which are primarily passing series. Diagram 3-2 shows the nine series.

The 20, 30, 40, 80, and 90 series are running series and the teen, 50, 60, and 70 series are passing series. The 20, 30, and 80 series comprise about 80 percent of the Delaware wing T. The other series are used merely to complement the basic attack. The 80's and 40's make up the belly series, with the 80's representing about 90 percent of the total.

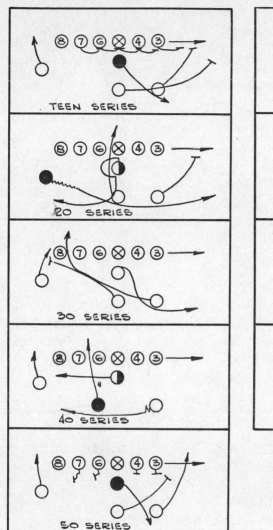

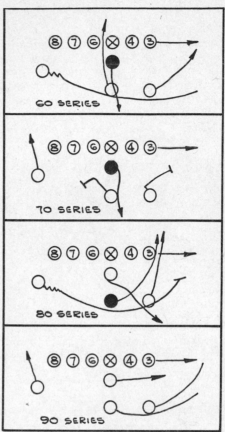

Diagram 3-2

Point of Attack

The third and last digit is the point of attack or hole to be hit. There are nine points of attack, numbered from right to left. With the exception of the two flank areas, the holes are numbered over the seven offensive linemen. These linemen are referred to by these numbers. The last digit, not only indicates the area of attack, but also assigns the man who is the original lead-on, wall-off backer and indicates the direction of flow of the backfield. With the third digit 1 through 4, the direction of flow is to the right; 6 through 9 is to the left (Diagram 3-3).

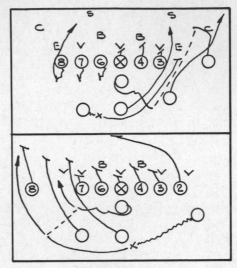

Diagram 3-3

The belly series is the heart of the wing T because it provides great balance to the attack, virtually eliminating any tendencies. In the belly series the fullback is used similar to the tailback in the I formation attack.

The belly series is broken down into six categories: 1) Power belly. 2) Veer belly. 3) Quick belly. 4) Counter game. 5) Passing game. 6) Option game.

1. Power Belly

The power belly is the heart of the fullback game. It can best be described as a group of plays that has the fullback running a circular path for the inside leg of the tackle. Generally, the attack side halfback leads through the hole, one yard in front of the fullback. The quarterback pivots to 45°, riding the ball to the fullback at a depth of 2½ yards, enabling the fullback to hit the hole directly or wind back over center (run to daylight). The off-side halfback leaves in early motion and blocks the outside man on the line of scrimmage 1 yard in front of the quarterback, who fakes a belly keep pass.

Diagram 3-4 shows five different blocking schemes used with the power belly: 1) Normal isolation. 2) On. 3) X-Block. 4) Gut. 5) Wham.

In using the various blocking schemes, it must be realized that there are four different alignments at which the play can be directed. This is important because some blocking schemes are restricted by formation. For example, normal blocking must be run to a diveback, since the halfback's block through the hole is primary (Diagram 3-5). The four alignments are: A) Diveback and tight end (4-man side). B) Tight end and wingback (3-man side). C) Diveback and spread end (3-man side). D) Spread end and wingback (2-man side).

A. *Diveback and tight end*. This is the most powerful, and thus the most consistent,

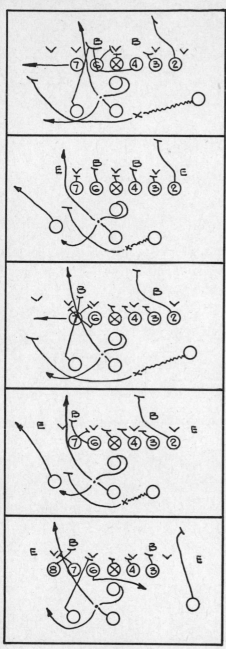

Diagram 3-4

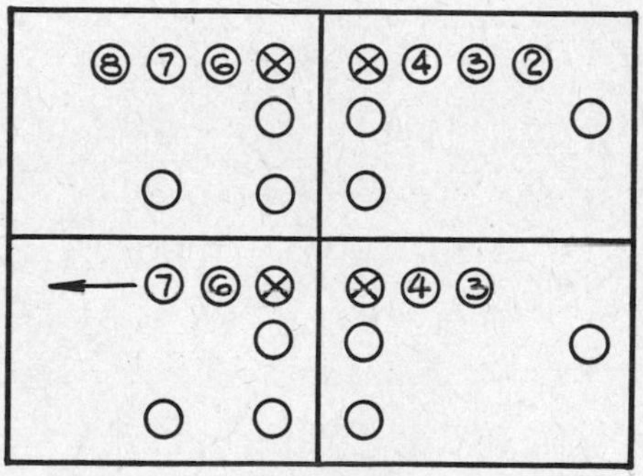

Diagram 3-5

area. All five types of blocking may be used, since all four of the primary blockers are present. Due to the powerful setup, the defense generally focuses a great deal of attention on this area. As a result, there is a very slight chance for a long gainer.

B. *Tight end and wingback*. This area of attack is effective because of the outside influence of the wingback on the defensive player who is responsible for sealing the hole. Since there is no diveback, normal and wham blocking cannot be used.

C. *Diveback and spread end*. This has always been a successful area of attack because the defense usually places its emphasis on the wingback. Both power blocking and finesse blocking may be used at this area. Since there is no tight end, wham blocking cannot be used.

D. *Spread end and wingback*. This area, which has only two of the four primary blockers, uses finesse blocking entirely. Gut blocking is the most popular by far, but *on* has been used with some success. Eighty-three gut and eighty-seven gut are excellent draw type plays.

2. Veer Belly

The veer belly is quicker and wider than the power belly, and works in conjunction with the option. This series is particularly effective against a seven-man front, since it places tremendous pressure on the end, who must seal and contain (Diagram 3-6).

The fullback runs a straight path for the inside leg of No. 2 (tight end) and turns upfield upon receiving the ball. The quarterback pivots as flat and as fast as possible, rides the ball to the fullback 1 yard behind the tail of the tackle, and springs past the face of the defensive end, faking the option. The onside halfback influences by faking an outside block on the end, releasing to the secondary. The off-side halfback leaves in early motion and runs an option path, looking for the pitch.

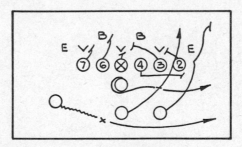

Diagram 3-6

As shown in Diagram 3-7, there are three different blocking schemes used with the veer belly: A) Down. B) Gut. C) Normal (lead post).

Down blocking is the most sound in that all gaps are checked and there is a block in at the hole as well as a block out. If the defensive end is concerned about the outside, gut is an excellent adjustment because the guard can then turn up on the linebacker. Normal blocking is used when the defensive tackle is not reacting inside and the power of the lead post is required.

3. Quick Belly

The quick belly is used as a change-up and as a method of combining some of the

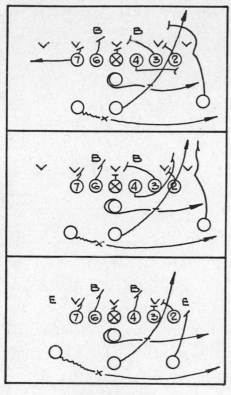

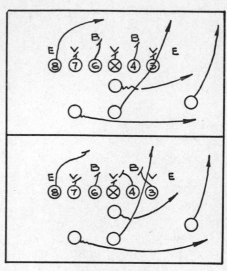

Diagram 3-8

Diagram 3-7

wishbone attack with the wing T. Although the potential for this series is great, it has not been employed to any extent.

The fullback dives for the outside leg of the guard as the quarterback fronts out to 45° to execute a ride with the fullback. Then the quarterback sprints past the defensive end and takes an option. The onside halfback runs an arc and blocks the secondary support, setting up the option. The off-side halfback leaves in early motion and runs an option path, looking for the pitch.

The quick belly (Diagram 3-8) utilizes two blocking schemes: A. On. B. Triple.

4. Counter Game

Diagram 3-9 shows the four counters that are employed in the belly series: 1) 184 CT (tackle trap). 2) 187 Quarterback at 3. 3) SL 181 Sally. 4) SPR 181 Reverse at 9.

The Tackle Trap (184 CT) is the best play in the belly series, and is possibly the best play in the entire Delaware wing T. It has been used in every situation from long yardage through normal to goal line. It is successful due to its deception and the fact that the primary blocks are maintained over a four-man base in addition to the trap.

Also, an excellent play is 187 QB at 3, which is a quarterback counter. It has been a great change of pace in that it forces the linebackers to be entirely honest.

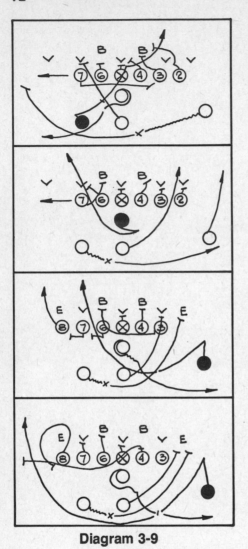

Diagram 3-9

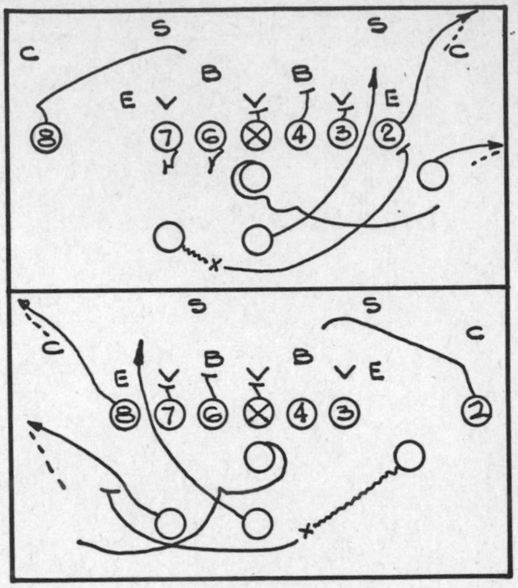

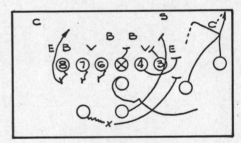

Diagram 3-10

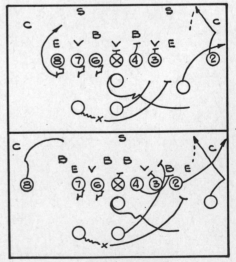

Diagram 3-11

Diagram 3-12

The Sally is an excellent draw type play which has produced some long gainers. It is used as a change-up and, as a result, is secondary.

The reverse is used to take advantage of a poorly disciplined team. It is good because it enables the offense to get speed outside with misdirection.

5. Passing Game

The belly passing game is broken down into two categories based on formation: 1) To a tight end. 2) To a spread end.

This passing game to a tight end is used to augment the running game by developing conflicts of seal or contain for the end, and support or cover for the corner (Diagram 3-10).

The spread and belly passing attack is an excellent means to use to throw individual patterns. This particular group of patterns works so effectively due to the fake to the fullback. The fullback's fake makes it difficult to get any underneath coverage. It is necessary for the inside linebackers to check the fullback first, and the outside line-backers have the problem of covering or supporting (Diagram 3-11).

If the defense employs a man-for-man secondary, deep inside cuts are very good. The two best are shown in Diagram 3-12.

The belly screen to the tight end is also very good against a team that pursues aggressively (Diagram 3-13).

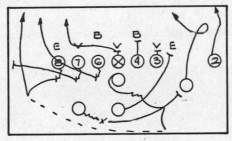

Diagram 3-13

6. Option Game

As previously mentioned, the option game is directly related to the veer belly. Two methods of blocking are employed: 1) On blocking. 2) Down blocking.

On blocking is used when the secondary is playing man-for-man or keying the wingback-tight end combination. It is also effective to the weak side versus a hard, strong rotation (Diagram 3-14).

Down blocking is used to complement 182 Down, and is an excellent way to run an option, using the guard as a lead blocker (Diagram 3-15).

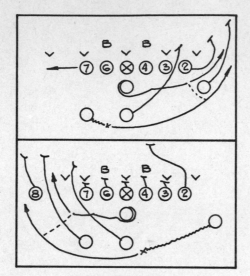

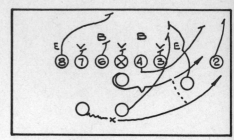

Diagram 3-15

Diagram 3-14

WING T OPTIONS

by Harold R. Raymond

Harold Raymond
University of Delaware

The fundamental of an effective football offense is consistency. If a team is going to drive the football or control it, the offense must be consistent. This, of course, not only means executing football plays which have the greatest chance of success, but also avoiding bad plays which force the team into long yardage situations or turn the ball over to the opponent. The football play with the greatest chance of success is generally conceded to be the one which is executed with respect to the defense. It is a play that is called at the line of scrimmage or one which during its execution has optional routes or points of attack such as the triple option. Neither the audible nor the typical option appealed to us. Calling audibles is subject to error, and option plays are risky in that they expose an offensive back to a defensive man who is not blocked.

We tried to incorporate the advantages of the audible and optional plays into the system. In place of audibles, rule assignments were developed which are applicable to almost every defensive stunt or spacing. But perhaps even more important, through the use of shifting formations we have limited, and to a degree, controlled, the number and complexity of the defenses that have been observed.

In our offense there are two aspects of optional football plays. Virtually all of the plays are designed to give the ball-carrier an optional route if the primary opening does not materialize. There will be a wall-off block one notch short of every planned opening so the ball-carrier will have blocking if he elects to wind back. It is necessary for the ball-carrier to establish a perpendicular path to the line of scrimmage just before he crosses that line. Turning up the field with the ball at the line of scrimmage makes it possible for the ball-carrier to take full advantage of the blocking he receives.

The quarterback fakes keeping the ball after handing off, either with the flow of the play or away from it. This action sets up the option play in the offense that we feel is analogous to the typical option play. When the quarterback keeps the ball at the flank, he executes the option of keeping the ball or passing it forward. When considering the urgency of consistency, it makes sense to throw the ball forward rather than to risk the consequences of tossing it backward.

Before explaining these principles with two plays of the wing T, let us describe our shifting techniques. The team shifts from one wing T formation to its mirror formation, or uses a three back I as a pre-shift formation. Five backs are also incorporated into a three back I formation, with the tight end lining up behind the quarterback. This pre-shift formation employs the right and left halfbacks as split ends at a width of 4 yards. The tight end takes his position behind the quarterback, followed by the fullback. The deep back is a flip-flop halfback because he can play either right or left halfback (Diagram 3-16). The tight end shifts to the side designated by the formation call, while one halfback becomes the split end and the other becomes a dive back. The deep back assumes the position of the wingback. Since the split end assignments are the same as those of the wingback, the positions become interchangeable and provide many formation possibilities, including an unbalanced line.

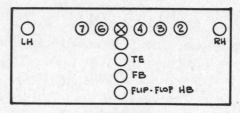

Diagram 3-16

The Sweep

Let us assume the team has shifted into an unbalanced wing T formation to the right (Diagram 3-17). The right halfback, having shifted to the spread end position to the right, now finds himself between 4 and 6 yards outside of the original position of the tight end. The exact width depends upon the alignment inside him. If a man from the defensive front plays head-on him, he will go all the way to 6 yards or stop when he finds he can soften the flank by having a defender drop off in the walk-away position or force him to crash across the line of scrimmage.

The spread end's assignment is to block the first man he can legally block on the line of scrimmage or wall off on the next free man.

The wingback shifts to a position 2 yards outside the tight end's original position and 2 yards off the ball. His assignment is to block the first free man to the inside. We feel it is important to recognize that being 2 yards off the ball makes it difficult for a man to penetrate inside him and destroy the sweep.

The tight end will adjust his split to as wide as 6 feet from the tackle if someone plays head-on him. His assignment is to block a man in the gap, and then wall off.

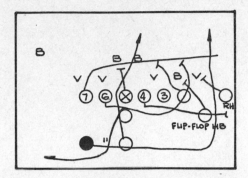

Diagram 3-17

The tackle's assignment is to block his gap, and then the nearest linebacker.

All three men involved in establishing the flank have angles on their opponents and the advantage of having optional assignments if no one is immediately to their inside.

The right guard pulls, gets 2 yards of depth, and reads the block of the flank. He will block out on the first man outside the split end's block.

The center blocks a man on him or away from the attacking flank.

The backside guard pulls and turns in to wall off at first daylight. This block is primary if the halfback elects to wind back.

The weak-side tackle blocks flat at the cut-off, and will block out on delayed support of the flank.

The fullback briefly gives the midline to the quarterback. Then the quarterback reverse pivots, bringing the ball to his body, and moves to the hand-off spot on the midline at a depth of 4 yards. The fullback veers back up the middle, off the center's block.

The left halfback receives the hand-off and immediately begins reading the wall-off blocks at the flank, running parallel with the line of scrimmage. Once he establishes the most effective wall-off area, that is, either the spread end or the wingback, he will turn up the field off his right guard, who blocks out, forming a running lane directly up the field.

The ball-carrier's flat speed to the sideline sets up the right guard's block out, and the depth of the guard brings the ball-carrier and this primary block close together. When the ball-carrier reads the opening, he will cut directly up the field, crossing the line of scrimmage at a perpendicular angle, hopefully with the left guard just in front of him.

The quarterback fakes at a depth of 5 yards away from the point of attack, and now it can be seen that the defensive front is being threatened at three points of attack—the quarterback at one flank, the fullback up the middle, and the sweep at the other flank.

The Quarterback Bootleg

One of our most effective plays has been the quarterback bootleg away from the sweep action, which has just been described with the quarterback keeping the ball. It is considered our option play. Diagram 3-18 shows it from a slot formation. The tight end

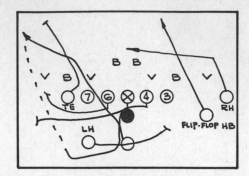

Diagram 3-18

releases inside the man on him and runs a flag pattern. If the defensive halfback is well disciplined to the corner, the end may run the alternate route of an out cut at least 15 yards deep. The left tackle blocks a man in his gap or a man on him. The attack side guard pulls flat and hooks the first man at the flank who has reacted to the tight end's inside release. This guard is not being asked to do the impossible, but is allowed to block the first man he thinks he can block in.

The fullback fills quickly for the guard while the center blocks the first man on him or to his right. The backside guard pulls flat, allowing the fullback to release, and then gets 3 yards depth and blocks the first man outside of the left guard's block. The quarterback, after faking to the fullback and the sweeping left halfback, now finds himself threatening the flank close to the off-side guard, who is ready to block out for him. After making his block, the fullback slips into the weak-side flat. The wingback runs a post pattern while the spread end runs a crossing pattern. Many options are available to the quarterback on this play. He has a legitimate running play with blocks both in and out at the flank. He is able to dump the ball to the fullback if the flank is not established, or he may pass to any open receiver.

The wing T has been an effective offense for us. We feel at least some of our success can be attributed to the offensive principles described here, which tend to keep the number of mistakes down and eliminate the bad football play, which destroys a drive.

SWEEP SERIES

by John M. Yovicsin

John Yovicsin
Formerly, Harvard University

Basically, ours have been T teams. In putting things together for this series, we borrowed from the single wing advocates and also from the T teams that were running a power type attack.

The reasons behind our thinking were that we wanted to better utilize the backfield talent, particularly several strong runners with average speed and a good blocking quarterback. Then, too, three of our halfbacks were former single wing tailbacks.

As we go into the plays, we are sure the similarity to the single wing type of attack will be noticed. Our line-up is standard, although the backs are probably placed a little deeper than they are on many teams (Diagram 3-19).

The play in the series that is used more often than any other is the end run (Diagram 3-20). We feel this play must be run well and shown often enough to make the opponents outside conscious when they are setting up their defenses for our team. As a result, it is our thinking that the team has a better opportunity to run the inside attack successfully. Statistics show that this play has been run less each year since it was put in, and there is a definite increase in the number of inside plays that are run from this series.

The plays against the 5-4 defense will be diagramed and discussed since, at least in our league, more of this defense than any other is seen.

The block on the defensive end is a key block. The right end steps with his near foot, driving into the end with a high shoulder block into the numbers. Then he releases to pick up the first man to the inside, who is usually the linebacker. The right tackle blocks the defensive tackle. It is important to stop any penetration by the defensive linemen, since we try to clear our guards. The right guard pulls and leads at a minimum depth of two yards. If the end has penetrated, the right guard will drive into him, double-teaming with the right halfback. If the guard can clear, he turns the corner and blocks the safety man.

79

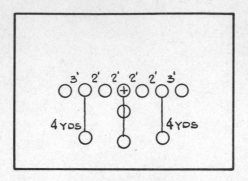

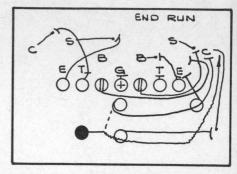

| **Diagram 3-19** | **Diagram 3-20** |

The center blocks the man over him. The left guard pulls and leads at a depth of three yards, looking to the inside to pick up any pluggers. If he clears, he turns the corner and peels to the inside, picking up the first pursuit man. The left tackle, after filling to check the plugger, releases downfield and blocks back. The left end blocks downfield on the safety man. The right halfback drives directly for the defensive end, and using a body block, hooks the end. The fullback gaining only one yard will block out on the cornerman, using either the shoulder or body block. The quarterback pivots and with two hands pitches a soft dead ball to the left halfback, and then leads at over a depth of three yards. He will look to the inside for penetration, turn up the field, checking the block on the safety man, and then block the first man to show. The left halfback lead steps, gaining a little depth, and runs laterally, turning up the field behind the quarterback, making his cut according to the blocks in front of him.

The option end run or pass (Diagram 3-21) is closely associated with the end run and is run similar to the end run. These two plays support one another very well. The play is an important part of the sweep series and is run as often as the defensive reaction permits. If the defensive cornerman is coming up fast and playing the end run hard, then the option play will be run and probably the pass will be either to the end or the halfback. Of course, this is not always true, because some of our most successful runs have been made when the option play was called and the halfback decided to run. The players like this play, and considerable time is spent working on it.

The right end will drive at the defensive end with a shoulder block, just as he does on the end run. Then he will release, sprinting downfield, and run an angle-out pattern, generally breaking at ten yards. This maneuver and pattern will be varied depending upon the release that is met. The right tackle has the same assignment he does on the end run. He will block on the defensive tackle. The right guard will pull and lead at the same depth he uses on the end run. If he meets the end in his path or finds him inside, he will block him. If the end has penetrated, the right guard will continue and block the cornerman. The center will block the man over him. All of the blocks are aggressive and executed in the same manner as the block on the end run. The left guard pulls and leads at the same depth he uses on the end run. He looks to the inside to pick up any plugger. If he

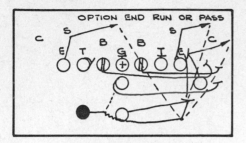

Diagram 3-21

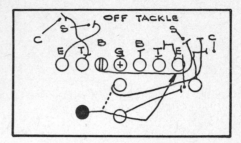

Diagram 3-22

clears, he will check the block on the end or turn downfield on the run call by the left halfback and peel to the inside, blocking the first man to show. The left tackle sets up and blocks the tackle with a passive type block. The left end releases as he would on the end run to block the safety man, and runs an angle-in pattern. The right halfback drives at the defensive end, positioning himself for the hook block, makes a good fake, and then slides out to the flat at approximately a depth of five yards. The fullback leads at the same depth he uses on the end run, looking to pick up the defensive end. If the guard has blocked the end, the fullback will check this block and help if he is needed or block on the cornerman. With deep penetration by the end, the fullback will block him, because by now the guard will have cleared behind the end. The quarterback will pitch the ball and lead just as he did on the end run. He will look to the inside for pluggers and check the block on the end. If he clears, he will pick up the first man, who may be the cornerman if the fullback and right guard are blocking on the end or lead up the field on the run call by the left halfback. The left halfback will take the ball in the same manner he does on the end run. He will immediately hold it in his hands, preparing to pass. The reaction on the cornerman will determine what he will do. If the cornerman comes up playing the end run, we feel he should have a good chance to hit the right halfback in the flat. With the cornerman playing pass, we would normally prefer to have our back run. However, the backs are encouraged to run any time they feel they have a good chance to make five yards, regardless of the reaction of the cornerman.

The off-tackle play (Diagram 3-22) is run similar to the end run. If the defensive end is found reacting to the flow or to the pressure of our halfback, our players feel they should be able to run inside him. They hope the end run will be effective enough to force his type of defensive reaction. If they do not get it, they still have the option of running the play to the outside.

The right end will step to the defensive end and shoulder block as he did on the end run, and then block back on the tackle. The right tackle blocks the defensive tackle with help from the end. The right guard blocks on the linebacker. The center will block the man on him. The left guard pulls and leads, and checks the block on the end. If he sees daylight to the inside, then the left guard will lead through the hole, blocking the first man to show. If the defensive end closes the hole, then the right guard will drive into him, double-teaming the end with the fullback. The left tackle fill releases downfield and blocks back. The left end releases and blocks on the safety man. The right halfback drives directly for the defensive end as he did on the end run, fakes a hook block on the end, and then blocks out on the cornerman. The fullback blocks out on the defensive end. The quarterback pitches the ball and leads as he did on the end run, and then blocks the safety man. The left halfback takes a short lead step plus two steps and cuts back into the off-tackle hole. If he sees daylight, he hits into the hole, following the left guard. If the end has closed the hole, he will veer outside and pick up the quarterback as he did on the end run. We feel by making this play an option off-tackle or end run, additional pressure has been placed on the defense. It has helped the team in attacking at this hole.

The trap play (Diagram 3-23), as our off-tackle play, begins similar to the end run. If the defensive tackle has been giving our players some problems on the other two plays, then the quarterback will come back with this play.

The right end drives at the tackle, placing outside pressure on him, and then blocks on the linebacker. The right tackle doubles on the linebacker with the end. The right guard and center double-team the man over center. The center sets the man up and then releases to handle any plugger. Again, the left tackle fill releases downfield and blocks back. The left end releases and blocks on the safety man. The right halfback drives at the end as he did on the off-tackle play, fakes a hook block, and then releases downfield on the safety man. The fullback blocks out on the end. The quarterback pivots left and pitches the ball directly and firmly to the left halfback. He does not lead the left halfback on the pitch as he did on the other plays. After the pitch, he runs the same path he used on the end run and off-tackle plays. The left halfback takes a lead step and receives the ball. Then he cuts into the trap hole, running close to the double-team and cutting off the block on the linebacker.

If our players find that the man over center and the linebackers are going with the flow and pursuing fast, they like to come back with the buck play (Diagram 3-24).

The ends will release downfield and block on the safety men. The tackles will block on the defensive tackles. The guards will hit out and block on the linebackers. The center will handle the man over him and block him in either direction, because the back will cut off his block. The right halfback drop-steps with his inside leg and drives directly at the center, cutting off his block. The quarterback will pivot left, faking the pitch to the left halfback, and hand the ball to the right halfback. He will gain a little depth in executing this pivot, making room for the halfback to cut to either side of the center's block. The fullback will lead as he does on the end run. The left halfback will fake taking the pitch from the quarterback and running the end run.

We do not use the reverse play (Diagram 3-25) too often, but it has proved to be a good change of pace. Fast pursuit is an important part of all defensive play today, and we hope that with this play we will keep the forces at home just a little longer.

The left end releases downfield as he would on a play away from him, and then peels back, blocking the first man to show. The left tackle blocks on the tackle, stopping

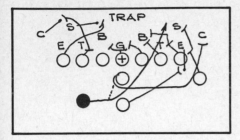

Diagram 3-23

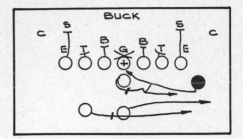

Diagram 3-24

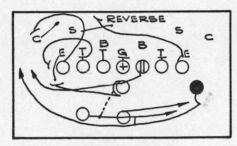

Diagram 3-25

any fast penetration, and then releases and peels to the outside, blocking back at the line of scrimmage. The left guard blocks on the linebacker. The center blocks the man over him. The right guard pulls and leads at a depth of three yards, checking the block on the end by the quarterback. The right tackle blocks the defensive tackle. The right end shoulder blocks on the defensive end and releases downfield on the safety man. The quarterback pitches to the left halfback as he did on the end run and then leads to the left, blocking on the defensive right end. The fullback blocks on the left end as he does on the trap play. The left halfback takes the ball from the quarterback and runs just as he does on the end run. He will give the ball to the right halfback with his right hand, placing it into his near hip, and then carry out his end run fake. This exchange is made approximately behind the right tackle. The right halfback drop-steps with his inside leg and sprints back and to his left, gaining a depth of five yards, and levels off. Running at a depth of five yards, he takes a hand-off from the left halfback and follows the right guard.

We hope we have presented some ideas which may be of assistance in developing a successful wing T offense.

INTEGRATING THE PRO I
WITH THE WING T

by Mike Lude and Paul Lanham

Mike Lude
Colorado State University

Paul Lanham
Washington Redskins

The wing T offense has been an effective method of moving the football since its inception at the University of Maine in 1950, and it has continued to develop at the University of Delaware through the efforts of Dave Nelson and his staff, of which we were privileged to be a part for many years.

We have been cognizant of the trends in intercollegiate football. One of these is the use of a flanking back and a split end. In other words, there is an increasing use of the pro-style offense.

A great deal of thought, study, hard work, discussion, and experimentation on these three important methods of offensive football was done. After considerable deliberation, we decided that we did not want to scrap our basic wing T attack. The problem then was to add a variation to the basic offense, an innovation whereby our personnel could be used to maximum efficiency, and not lose the effectiveness and consistency which had been established with our wing T. To do so, it was decided to integrate a few of the basic wing T plays with a pro I alignment. We have been pleased with the apparent results thus far.

In this article, we will take four basic wing T plays and show how integration was accomplished. The four plays were equally divided between run and pass. The two running plays were 134 counter and 147 wham, providing us with a power play and a counter play. The two passes were 161 quick (a drop-back pass) and 101 sprint-out. Actually, using our mirrored offense, there would be eight plays. The corresponding play on the opposite side of the offensive front could be understood easily by holding the illustrations and diagrams up to a mirror and observing them. The mirrored plays of those presented, using our numbering system, are as follows:

Running Game: 134 Counter—Mirrored 936 counter. 147 Wham—Mirrored 943 wham.

Passing Game: 161 Quick—Mirrored 969 quick. 101 Sprint-Out—Mirrored 909 sprint-out.

Numbering System

The communication necessary for efficient team operation can be transmitted effectively by means of a three-digit number plus a few descriptive words (Diagram 3-26). The first digit indicates the formation; the second, the backfield series and techniques; and the third digit indicates the point of attack.

The basic spacing and point of attack are shown in Diagram 3-27.

Tight 134 Counter—Diagram 3-28. Assignments: Number 2—on, over, outside. Number 3—widen, across to a linebacker (this is the first backer-up on No. 4 or to the off-side). Number 4—lead, principle. Number 5—post, lead. Number 6—area, post, away. Number 7—inside out. Number 8—block the middle one-third. Right

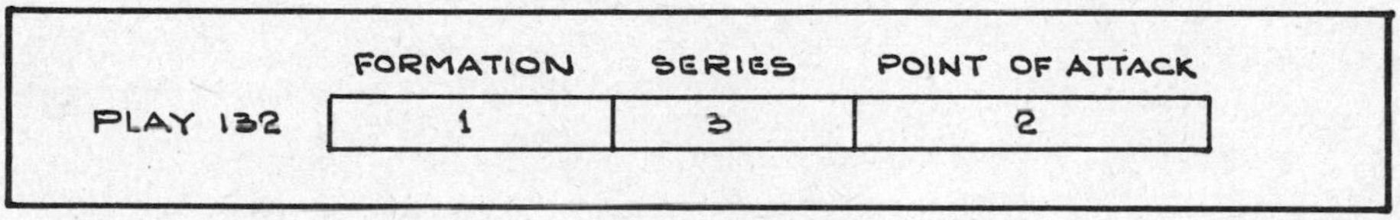

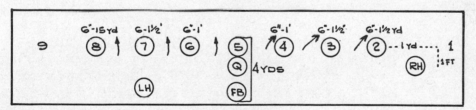

Diagram 3-26

Diagram 3-27

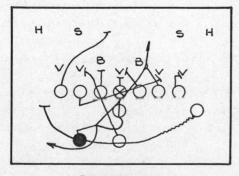

Diagram 3-28

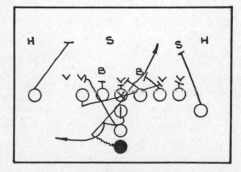

Diagram 3-29

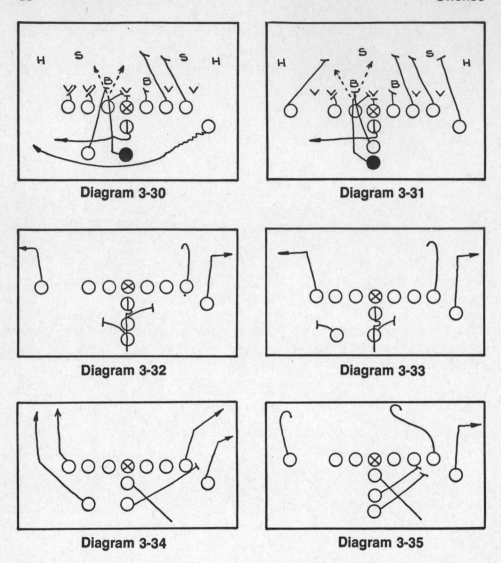

Diagram 3-30   Diagram 3-31

Diagram 3-32   Diagram 3-33

Diagram 3-34   Diagram 3-35

halfback—fly, fake the sweep at 9, and block the first man outside the tight lineman. Left halfback—carry at 4 and rock the weight on the left foot. Receive the ball, drive for a lead, and post. Fullback—check block, and use the outside leg of No. 6 as a landmark. Quarterback—reverse pivot, hand inside to the left halfback, and bootleg at 9.

Pro I 134 Counter—Diagram 3-29. Play Assignments: All internal line assignments remain the same. Number 8—split about 8 yards and block the middle one-third. Right halfback—split about 8 yards and block the middle one-third. Left halfback—take 3 steps for early motion, pivot, receive the ball, drive for the lead, and post. Fullback—check block and use the outside leg of No. 6 as a landmark. Quarterback—reverse pivot, hand inside to the left halfback, and bootleg at 9.

Tight 147—Diagram 3-30. Play Assignments: Number 2—block the middle one-third. Number 3—on, inside release to cut off. Number 4—on, linebacker, away gap, and cut off. Number 5—on, linebacker (over or away), and away gap. Number 6—on, away gap, and lead. Number 7—on (easy way), outside gap, and linebacker. Number 8—on, outside gap, and linebacker. Right halfback—fly, fake the outside belly at 9 and keep a 2 x 5 yd. relationship with the quarterback. Left halfback—clean up the hole, and landmark the 6 or 7 seam. Fullback—step up and out, landmark the 6 or 7 seam, and read the block of the left halfback. Quarterback—reverse pivot, give to the fullback, and fake a keep at 9.

Pro I 147—Diagram 3-31. Play Assignments: All internal line assignments remain the same. Number 8—split about 8 yards and block the middle one-third. Right halfback—split about 8 yards and block the middle one-third. Left halfback—carry at 7—step up and out, landmark the 6 or 7 seam, and read the block of the fullback. Fullback—clean up the hole and landmark the 6 or 7 seam. Quarterback—reverse pivot, give to the left halfback, and fake a keep at 9.

Pro I 161 Q—Diagram 3-32. Play Assignments: All internal line assignments remain the same. Number 8—split about 8 yards and run an out pattern at 12 yards. Right halfback—split about 8 yards and run an out pattern at 12 yards. Left halfback—step up and get inside position. Block the first man who rushes outside No. 7. If no one comes, help inside. Fullback—step up and get inside position. Block the first man who rushes outside No. 3. If no one comes, help inside. Quarterback—sprint back three steps and set to throw.

Tight 161 Q—Diagram 3-33. Play Assignments: Number 2—hook at 12 yards. Number 3—take the second man outside No. 5. Number 4—take the first man outside No. 5. Number 5—on, over, and backside. Number 6—second man, on, outside No. 5. Number 7—third man, on, outside No. 5. Number 8—out pattern at 12 yards. Right halfback—out pattern at 12 yards. Left halfback—set up and get inside position, block the first man who rushes outside No. 7. If no one comes, help inside. Fullback—step up and get inside position. Block the first man who rushes outside No. 3. If no one comes, help inside. Quarterback—sprint back three steps and set to throw.

Tight 101 Sprint-Out—Diagram 3-34. Play Assignments: Number 2—corner pattern. Number 3—block the third man, on, over, outside No. 5. Number 4—block the second man, on, over, outside No. 5. Number 5—block his man, on, over, first man on the attack side. Number 6—he should step down to his inside, cup protection. Number 7—he should close down to his inside, cup protection. Number 8—break route. Right halfback—run out the pattern at the contain man. Fullback—block the fourth man on, over, outside No. 5. Left halfback—divide route. Quarterback—receive the ball, step out at a 45° angle, sprint five steps, and pull up.

Pro I 101 Sprint-Out—Diagram 3-35. Play Assignments: Number 2—run an 8 pattern and then hook at 15 yards. All internal line assignments remain the same. Number 8—split about 8 yards, run a curl at 12 yards. Right halfback—split about 8 yards and then run an out pattern at a depth of 12 yards. The left halfback is the personal escort for the quarterback. Fullback—block the fourth man on, over, outside No. 5. Landmark 1 yard outside No. 2. Quarterback—receive the ball, step at a 45° angle, sprint five steps, and pull up.

There are many more plays which can and have been incorporated into this total concept. However, our objective was to show how four basic plays were selected, and then the details which are important to their success were covered. Our space is limited, but we want coaches to realize how easily these two effective formations can be put together into one style of offensive football.

It is our hope that this material will prove to be of value to those coaches who have used the wing T and are looking for ways of keeping up with trends in modern offensive football. We also are hopeful that there will be a few adventurers who will have courage enough to use their imagination and thereby be amazed at the seemingly unlimited avenues this basic idea will open.

In our opinion, many of the outstanding coaches are men who pride themselves as teachers. The better a coach teaches, the more objective he can be in analyzing critically his system as well as his techniques. The result will be that he will more nearly realize his aims and objectives.

4 / The Wishbone

THE WISHBONE OFFENSE

by Rudy Feldman

Rudy Feldman
San Diego Chargers

The wishbone offense is a running offense. The alignment of the backs provides for a strong running attack. As a consequence, the passing attack suffers. The quarterback in the wishbone offense must have a great deal of athletic ability. He must be able to run, must have the perception to execute the triple option, and he must be able to pass. Of course, the quarterback should also possess the many other qualities necessary to direct any offense successfully.

It is important for a team that is running the wishbone attack to limit their offense and strive for perfect execution of a few basic offensive plays. The wishbone offense provides a mirrored attack so that the same plays can be run to the left or the right. It also provides a goal line to goal line attack. Here again the exception occurs when a score is needed in a hurry. It is not an effective offense if a team is behind by several touchdowns, or if it is necessary to score with very little time remaining. The feature we like best about the wishbone offense is that it forces the opponent to play a balanced defense. Whether we play against a seven- or eight-man front defense, we know that the defensive team must assign responsibilities for the quarterback who may keep the ball, and for the pitch to the trailing back. In addition, someone must be assigned to defend the potential receiver who is sprinting down the field. The formation is designed for the purpose of executing the triple option either to a tight end or a split end (Diagram 4-1).

The fullback has his feet 4 yards from the ball. He is in a four-point stance. The halfbacks are aligned behind the guards at a depth of 5 yards. They are in a three-point stance.

Triple Option Blocking Assignments. The blocking assignments for the triple option are simple and remain constant regardless of the defense. The on-side end stalks the outside one-third. He sprints in an effort to get outside and beyond the defensive

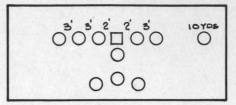

Diagram 4-1

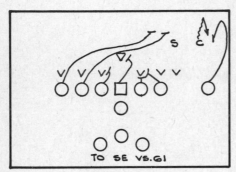

Diagram 4-2

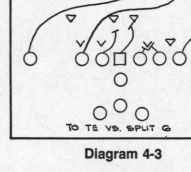

Diagram 4-3

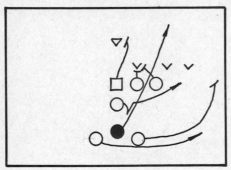

Diagram 4-4

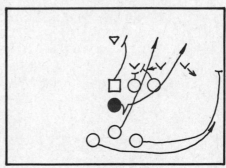

Diagram 4-5

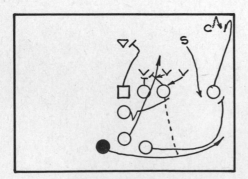

Diagram 4-6

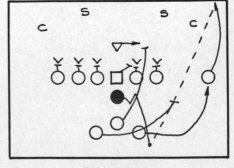

Diagram 4-7

man who is defending the outside one-third. When he recognizes that the defensive man stops to react to the run, the end maintains a position between the defensive man and the trailing back.

The on-side tackle will lead to the inside. He blocks the first defensive player to the inside, either a lineman or a back. The on-side guard will block the first lineman inside the on-side tackle. The center will block a man over, the on-side gap or the nearest linebacker. The off-side guard will seal the first man on the off-side. The off-side tackle and end will sprint across the field. Diagrams 4-2 and 4-3 depict this against a 6-1 and a split 6 defense.

Backfield Execution of the Triple Option. As the name implies, it is necessary to execute two distinct options. The first is between the fullback and quarterback. The second is between the quarterback and the trailing back. Because of this concept, we do not block the two end men on the line of scrimmage. The inside option is executed against the second man in, and the outside option against the end man on the line. We call the first defensive man outside our tackle the key. The quarterback will open step with his on-side foot and stab the ball back to the fullback. He will ride the fullback one step. We call this the decision step because at the end of this ride, he must decide whether to leave the ball with the fullback or keep it himself. His instruction is to leave the ball with the fullback unless the key takes the fullback. If the key does not take the fullback, the quarterback leaves the ball and continues a lateral fake (Diagram 4-4). If the key takes the fullback, the quarterback should pull the ball, continue down the line, and execute the outside option. The quarterback's instruction is to run inside the defensive end (Diagram 4-5). When the end takes the quarterback, the quarterback should pitch the ball with his on-side hand to the trailing back (Diagram 4-6).

The fullback will step with his on-side foot and run a course over the outside hip of the on-side guard. He must see the ball and take a soft squeeze on the ball. He will run the course described, and he should run hard enough to break arm tackles when the ball is left with him. When the quarterback pulls the ball, he must continue on the course and become a faking back. This phase of the play requires a great deal of time to work out properly.

The on-side halfback sprints to the sideline. His assignment is to execute a hook block on the defender who is responsible for the pitch. The off-side halfback will also sprint to the sideline. He must be ready for the pitch. When the ball is pitched, he must catch it and utilize the block on the on-side halfback. When the quarterback keeps the ball, the off-side halfback should turn up the field and maintain a pitch position.

Triple Option Pass. Obviously, if the defense does not respect the on-side end going down the field, the triple option pass must be part of the offense. On a pass the offensive linemen cannot go downfield; therefore, our instruction is to block the nearest defensive lineman aggressively. The backfield assignments change, but we emphasize that they should appear as much like the triple option as possible. The quarterback will open step with his on-side foot and stab the ball back to the fullback. He will ride the fullback one step and then drive off his front foot, setting up at a depth of about 5 yards to throw deep to our split end. The fullback will step with his on-side foot, close over the ball, run the same course he used on the triple option, and block the nearest on-side linebacker. The on-side halfback will run his triple option course. The off-side halfback will come across as he did on the triple option, but his assignment will be to block the defensive end. The split end will sprint up the field, outside and beyond the defensive man, and be responsible for the outside one-third (Diagram 4-7).

HALFBACK BLOCKING ON THE TRIPLE OPTION

by Robert Ford and Raymond Murphy

Robert Ford
New York State University

Raymond Murphy
University of Pittsburgh

The block of the lead halfback in the wishbone is an extremely important factor in making the triple option attack go. Here we would like to present the two aspects of his block, the arc scheme and the load scheme, both from a philosophical and a technical viewpoint.

The halfbacks align, straddling the inside leg of the guard at a depth 5 yards from the ball. They can align in a two- or three-point stance, although we have gone entirely to the two-point stance. This alignment assists them in reading the perimeter, and negligible speed is lost when they must hit straight ahead.

In the past, wishbone teams have had the lead back take a step with his outside foot directly toward the sideline and parallel with the line of scrimmage. Then he took his second and third steps along the same line, and on his third step, he had to recognize who was responsible for the pitch. Then he went at that defender's outside leg (Diagram 4-8).

The defense could give the offense some problems by crashing the pitch key on the quarterback in an attempt to force the pitch quickly and possibly to rattle the quarterback mentally and physically (Diagrams 4-9 and 4-10). They could also develop problems for the offense by running the pitch key out and filling with a defensive back. Since this would give the quarterback a keep read, he would turn up the field only to be confronted by the defensive back in a 1-on-1 (Diagrams 4-11 and 4-12).

The offense could combat both of these defensive efforts by running a load blocking scheme. Against the crashing pitch key, the halfback goes directly at the pitch key area and blocks the man who shows (Diagrams 4-13 and 4-14).

This move by the halfback enables the quarterback to step around the pitch key, come to the outside, and option the next man, which places tremendous pressure on the defense. Versus a pitch key that runs out and is followed by a fill from the secondary, the

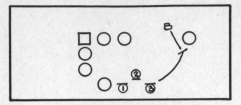

Diagram 4-8

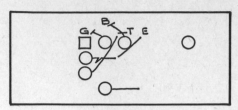

Diagram 4-9

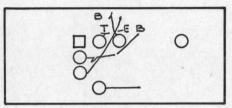

Diagram 4-10

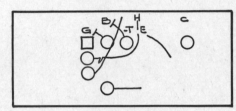

Diagram 4-11

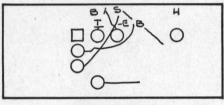

Diagram 4-12

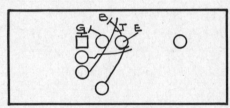

Diagram 4-13

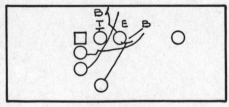

Diagram 4-14

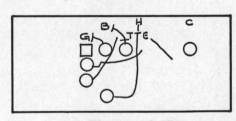

Diagram 4-15

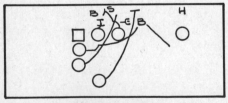

Diagram 4-16

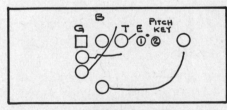

Diagram 4-17

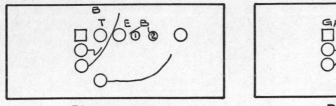

Diagram 4-18

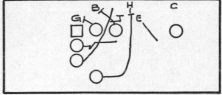

Diagram 4-19

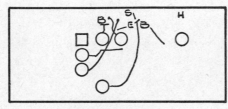

Diagram 4-20

load blocking scheme combats this nicely. The quarterback is permitted to turn up the field behind a lead blocker (Diagrams 4-15 and 4-16).

The problem with the blocking scheme mentioned previously is that it turns into a guessing game. If the offense has an arc blocking scheme on and the defense runs a secondary fill, the offense has a bad play. Thus, teams are running load more frequently. While a safer blocking scheme is presented, the offense is prevented from fully exploiting the corner and breaking the long one.

It is possible for the offense to combat this situation, especially if the halfbacks are in a two-point stance. The halfback must be able to recognize the pitch key. As the halfback takes his first step with his outside foot toward the sideline and parallel to the line of scrimmage, he looks at the pitch key. He continues to look at him on his second and third steps. On his third step, he must make a decision based on what the pitch key did. If he stayed at home or closed down, the halfback will continue on his arc scheme and take the man coming out of the secondary who is responsible for the pitch (Diagrams 4-17 and 4-18).

If the pitch key runs out or up the field, or moves to take the pitch, the halfback plants and comes up into the alley. To be sound, the defense is going to fill with someone out of the secondary. By continuing the halfback on the arc scheme, he would be wasted, because the quarterback's key to run or pitch indicated run, and he is going to keep the ball (Diagrams 4-19 and 4-20).

The lead blocker uses a cut block for both the arc and the load schemes. Although the execution of the block is similar, the blocker's task is more difficult for the arc scheme, since the defender is more conscious of protecting his outside leg, which is the target point of the cut blocker.

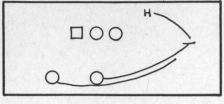

Diagram 4-21

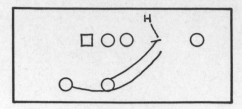

Diagram 4-22

The lead blocker must pin the defender to the inside; therefore, when he is running the arc scheme, as soon as he recognizes the secondary defender who is responsible for the pitch, he takes an aggressive angle at the defender and attacks his outside leg. The aggressive angle serves a twofold purpose. First, it shortens the corner, giving the ball-carrier additional running room; second, it provides the blocker with a better blocking angle. The blocker's aggressive angle alters the ball-carrier's course, since he is taught to position himself on the outside hip of the lead blocker. Therefore, the ball-carrier's altered course forces the defender to attack more aggressively, setting up the easier block for the lead blocker (Diagrams 4-21 and 4-22).

As the lead blocker attacks the outside leg of the defender, he maintains his feet until he is about to step on the defender's toes. At this point, the blocker fires his head, arms, and shoulders past the defender, and sinks his inside hip into the defender's outside hip. The block is completed by using an inside roll, throwing the outside arm and leg up into the defender and rolling through him to help tie up the defender. The key coaching point to insure pinning the defender to the inside is to emphasize a body position on contact that has the head facing up the field and the shoulders parallel to the goal line. The only difference when using the load scheme is that the aggressive angle is already established by a route which aims immediately for the outside leg of the pitch key.

The cut block is the only block that is taught to our backs, and is used for both sprint and action passes. This particular block enables the back to handle defenders much bigger than himself without absorbing any physical punishment. At times it is possible to throw an excellent cut block and completely miss contact with the defender. However, if the blocker has his head and shoulders facing up the field and the ball-carrier is on the outside hip of the blocker, the defender will be pinned inside and the ball carrier will be past the defender.

We have found that the heavy, bell-bottom, pop-up dummy is best for practicing the cut block. During our daily fundamental period, each halfback takes 12 cut blocks on the pop-up bags—6 using the arc scheme and 6 the load scheme. These blocks are divided 3 each between left and right. The one additional drill used is to incorporate the cut block with reaction to defensive movement. In this drill various perimeter reactions for deferring the pitch are initiated, and the lead back must take the proper reaction and cut block. Although line defenders make the reaction, the lead back blocks pop-up dummies that are placed according to where the blocker would contact the defender for each

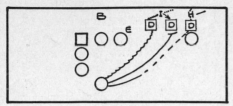

Diagram 4-23

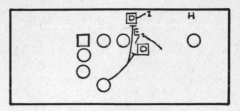

Diagram 4-24

particular reaction (Diagrams 4-23 and 4-24). The only time the lead back blocks line defenders is in a scrimmage situation.

The combination of the cut block and reading the perimeter defense has enabled us to attack the perimeter successfully using the wishbone offense, despite having very small halfbacks.

PASSING FROM THE WISHBONE

by Tom Beck

Tom Beck
Elmhurst College, Illinois

With the evolution of the fast-striking and deceptive triple option, the wishbone formation proved its adaptability to the coach who is run-oriented. Although we like the wishbone and triple option, we believe in a balanced offense. In our opinion, the wishbone can provide the versatility that is necessary for an effective run/pass offense. Our offensive thinking is to have a balanced attack both left and right, inside and outside, and between run and pass.

Due to the general thought that the wishbone is not a passing formation, it is important for the players to recognize that passes can be made effectively from the wishbone. Our players must believe they can run or pass from any spot on the field and at any time. We do not want them to feel that the only alternative left to them is the pass.

Some coaches may believe that a sound passing attack cannot be developed from the wishbone for the following reasons: 1. Too much time is needed for practicing and executing the triple option. 2. The backs, due to their depth and position, are not able to get into pass patterns effectively, thus enabling the defense to concentrate on two primary receivers.

Although considerable time must be spent on drilling for the effectiveness of the triple option, there is still time to develop a balanced passing attack if simplicity is maintained.

The second point can easily be remedied by using motion. Our wishbone is dressed up by employing motion on approximately half of the running and passing plays. Motion will provide four additional formation looks and should cause some major adjustments in the secondary. Motion with the right halfback to the tight end side (Diagram 4-25) gives us a balanced Pro formation. Motion with the left halfback to the split end side (Diagram 4-26) gives us two wide receivers to one side with a balanced backfield. Motion right

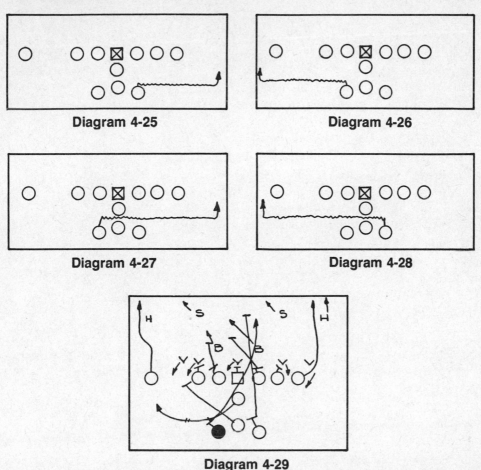

Diagram 4-25   Diagram 4-26

Diagram 4-27   Diagram 4-28

Diagram 4-29

with the left halfback gives us a Pro formation with a strong backfield (Diagram 4-27), and motion left with the right halfback gives us a strong backfield look with two wide receivers left (Diagram 4-28). Our tight end and split end are flip-flopped.

Our passing attack consists of the following five basic blocking schemes, plus the draw play: 1) Option. 2) Sprint. 3) Cup. 4) Screen. 5) Bootleg trap.

The halfback draw is run off sprint action (Diagram 4-29). This play is basic to our pass offense.

Against a 5-2 defense, the following rules apply:

Ends—Fake the defensive back deep and outside. When he reacts to the play, attempt to screen him to the outside.

Tackles—Set up in pass protection and steer the defensive tackle to the outside.

Guards—Set up and show pass, hold for one count, and then attack the linebackers.

Center—Take the nose man in the direction he wants to go.

Quarterback—Open up to the left and bring the ball back to the left halfback. He should continue with the fake by bringing an imaginary ball to his chest and taking his sprint route.

Left Halfback—Take one step laterally and then set up to block. The quarterback will bring the ball to him. Read the center's block, follow the lead blocker, and get yardage north or south.

Fullback—Take a sprint blocking route and block the defensive end outside of our tackle. Attack him aggressively.

Right Halfback—Take a normal sprint route that is two steps behind the center to seal backside leakage, hold for one quick count, and then lead the ball-carrier through daylight. Hopefully the block should be on the defender who is assigned to the middle one-third of the field.

We believe our draw play is effective because it starts with misdirection and includes a personal protector, the backside halfback, leading through the hole. Because it is set up from our sprint attack, a threat must be established with the sprint-out passing attack.

Two of our most successful pass plays have been the bootleg (Diagram 4-30) and the pass of the trap play.

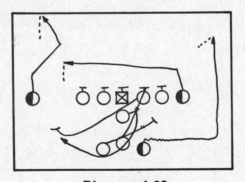

Diagram 4-30

Split End—Execute a good inside fake before going flag. Beat the halfback deep.

Tight End—He should clear the line of scrimmage and look for the ball as he passes the last linebacker. He should avoid linebackers who are trying to check him. His depth will vary. He should get depth gradually, and usually he will be between 8 and 15 yards deep.

Line—Block aggressively.

Right Guard—Pull and block the contain man. Be under control. His block is the key block.

Quarterback—Fake to the fullback, fake a hand-off to the halfback, hide the ball, and look over the shoulder, reading the guard's block. React inside or outside.

Fullback—Receive the fake and fill for the guard. His route should be slightly tighter than it would be on a normal option.

Left Halfback—Receive the fake and block outside of the tackle.

Right Halfback—Motion and run a throwback pattern. The ball may be thrown to him.

Motion is used on the bootleg to get predetermined rotation in the secondary and to influence defensive thinking to the right. Due to the fast pursuit of the defense when our option is run, this play has been successful. The faking of the option right initiates misdirection.

Our trap pass comes off one of the basic plays (Diagram 4-31). Its success must rely upon a good fake by the quarterback and halfback. Our players have not been dropped for a loss on this play, and on many occasions have had 4 or 5 seconds of protection before releasing the ball. It has been a long-gaining pass play.

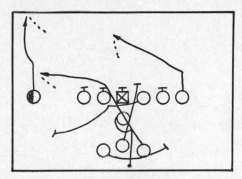

Diagram 4-31

Split End—Deep pattern, start lazy. ,

Tight End—Post

Line—Block aggressively.

Right Guard—Pull and form a cup.

Quarterback—Reverse pivot, fake a trap play, and retreat straight back. Look for the primary receiver first, and then the secondary receivers.

Left Halfback—Fake a trap, pull up, and form a cup.

Fullback—Fill for the right guard.

Right Halfback—Fake a trap, avoid being tackled, and proceed to the flat. Do not get out too fast.

We also like to run the pass shown in Diagram 4-32, especially against a team that uses an eight-man front to stop our option, thus leaving themselves in a three-deep.

If the defensive halfback widens with the extended motion and then covers the one-third zone, we want our tight end to run in the seam between the outside and the

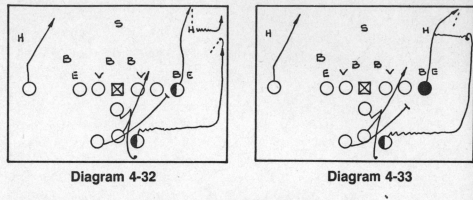

Diagram 4-32   **Diagram 4-33**

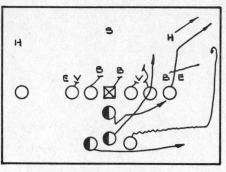

Diagram 4-34

middle one-third (Diagram 4-32). We know the linebacker must then cover the extended motion, which is a very difficult task.

If the defensive halfback covers the motion halfback all the way (man coverage), our tight end sprints for the flag, getting a big cushion between himself and the safety (Diagram 4-33).

If the defense covers motion with the outside linebacker (Diagram 4-34), we believe they seriously hamper themselves in defending against our option to that side. The three pass plays show a pass without motion, in the direction of motion, and away from motion.

In addition, individual and combination patterns from sprint, cup, and option projections, along with our screens, are run. Simplicity is maintained in our terminology and approach yet enough variety is emphasized to meet all game situations.

5 / Goal Line Offense

THE GOAL LINE ATTACK

by Charles McClendon

Charles McClendon
Louisiana State University

Before going into our goal line offense, we would like to tell why our style of attack was adopted.

When we started the I formation, the team moved the ball from the 20-yard line to the 20-yard line with more big plays than ever before, but scoring inside the 10-yard line was something else. Trying to score with a two-man backfield was a problem; therefore, we changed to different goal line plays, which were not a true part of our offense and resulted in more fumbles and missed assignments than ever before. We finished the season kicking 14 field goals. This proved only that we had a good field goal kicker and a very poor goal line offense.

After this trying season, we set our sights on spring practice with emphasis on a strong goal line attack. This led to a three-man backfield formation which we called the strong I. The formation is set up with the quarterback, tailback, fullback, and the splitback, who doubles as a flanker in the I formation, and the halfback to the side of the formation in the strong I.

From experience, we felt the formation and plays had to be part of our basic attack, one that we would use along with the I, on any down, and any place on the field. Therefore, it would be in our practice plan every day. We felt this would help eliminate mistakes on the goal line.

In this attack, there are two inside running plays to the strength side and two outside running plays, one to strength and one to the split end. These running plays, plus two pass patterns, are the basis of the strong formation attack.

The base play is definitely the off-tackle play to the strength. This, we feel, is a play that the opponents have to stop. From this play, other plays are selected according to the play of the defense.

The Off-Tackle Play (toward formation)

Splitback—Blocks the end man on the line.

Fullback—Leads through the point of attack for the linebacker.

Tailback—As the ball-carrier, he takes a slight open step to keep his shoulders parallel to the line. His point of aim is the outside hip of the offensive tackle. He should always be ready to dive or hit the soft area.

Quarterback—He reverses, gets the ball deep to the tailback, and uses a good outside running fake to set up the next play.

The Double Wham (toward formation)

Splitback—Leads through the point of aim, the inside hip of the offensive tackle, and has the responsibility of blocking any outside linebacker.

Fullback—Leads through the point of aim, the outside hip of the offensive guard, and has the responsibility of blocking any inside linebacker. We like the fullback and splitback to be shoulder to shoulder.

Tailback—As the ball-carrier, he takes a slight open step to keep his shoulders parallel to the line. His point of aim is the outside hip of the offensive guard. He should always be ready to dive or hit the soft area.

Quarterback—Reverses and gets the ball deep to the tailback. He should execute a good outside fake.

The Quarterback Keep (toward formation)

Splitback—Blocks the end man on the line. He starts at the inside leg of the end but attacks his outside thigh.

Fullback—He starts as if he were going off-tackle approximately two steps and then veers outside, behind the splitback, to block the widest outside man. The steps by the fullback are important.

Tailback—Fakes an off-tackle play. If possible, he should dive. The tailback's fake is definitely one of the keys to the play.

Quarterback—As the ball-carrier, he reverses and has a good ride fake to the tailback. He hides the ball and follows on the hip of the fullback.

The Counter Option (away from formation)

Splitback—Does not counter, but takes off and gets himself in a proper pitch position outside the defensive end. He should be approximately 5 yards deep.

Fullback—Takes a slight counter step, and then goes down hill to a point of aim, which is the defensive end's outside leg. If the defensive end is in this area, the fullback blocks him; if not, he continues up the field and seals. If there is any doubt, the fullback should block the end.

Tailback—Takes a slight counter step and leads to the wide outside man. Normally the defensive back covers the split end.

Quarterback—Takes a counter step, a slight open step, and then a crossover step away from the play. He pushes off and starts back down the line to option the end man. He keeps or pitches according to the end play.

The Keep Pass

Splitback—He sprints to the play side. After clearing the fake area, he starts downhill as an extra protector.

Fullback—Blocks the end man to the play side.

Tailback—Executes a good fake at the point of aim, which is the gap between the tackle and guard. Then he blocks the linebacker or any player who is free in this area.

Quarterback—Reverses, executes a good ride fake to the tailback, and then comes out to run or pass. This pass is run with individual pass patterns called.

In conclusion, we learned it is necessary to have a planned attack for short yardage and the goal line. We also believe it is necessary to strengthen the formation at this time, because the opponents are going to strengthen their defense.

THE GOAL LINE PASSING ATTACK

by John McGregor

John McGregor
Fleming High School
Roanoke, Virginia

In our opinion, goal line offense is the most important phase of any offense. The number of times a team scores is the only statistic that can measure offensive success effectively. In order to be successful at the goal line, the offensive players must be able to run right at the defense consistently, but there will always be a time when a 3-5 or 4-4 situation is confronted which calls for a pass. To achieve the goal of scoring every time they are inside the 10-yard line, the offense must have a passing game to complement its running game.

Since there is not much room to operate when establishing a goal line passing game, the offense must take advantage of the way goal line defenses are forced to play. The goal line defense is virtually forced to commit first to the run. By using play action passes, the Mike linebacker can be controlled and then a zone can be flooded where the Mike cannot help.

The problems presented when the Mike linebacker is held by play action and a zone is flooded are shown in Diagram 5-1. The quarterback should read the strong safety. If he goes with the fullback to the corner, the tight end should come open. If he reads the tight end's release and takes him, then the quarterback must make a decision on the corner-back's reaction to the crossing routes by the fullback and the split receiver. The quarterback can read with greater efficiency if he is able to recognize immediately whether it is man or zone coverage, and thereby gain the advantage of being able to anticipate what will transpire.

Diagram 5-2 shows our play pass 14, which places the goal line defense at a great disadvantage. The coaching points involved in executing this pass are as follows: The split receiver runs a corner comeback route that forces the cornerback to cover him all the

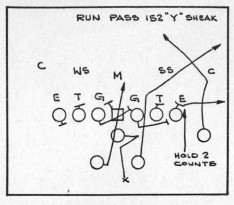

Diagram 5-1

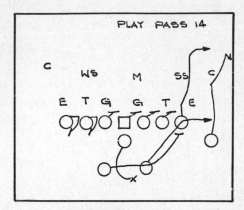

Diagram 5-2

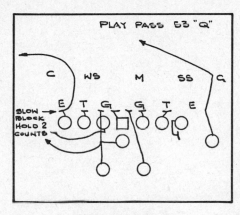

Diagram 5-3

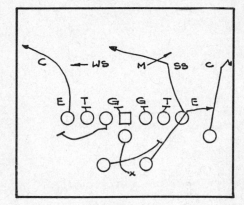

Diagram 5-4

way into the corner of the end zone. At this point, the objective is to remove one man completely from the pass coverage. The tight end takes an inside release and runs an outside curl. He must run away from the middle linebacker. If he does not beat the middle linebacker, we do not have a play. The fullback runs right at the defensive end and just dips by him. His route is straight down the line of scrimmage. The strong safety must make a decision as to whether to cover the tight end or the fullback. The quarterback reads the strong safety.

Another play action pass that exerts great pressure on the goal line defense is shown in Diagram 5-3. This pass places pressure on the weak cornerback. If he supports run, the quarterback dumps the ball to the tight end, who held his block two counts before going into the flat. If the cornerback stays off and covers the flat, the quarterback runs. The fake of the dive play must be good enough to hold the weak safety.

If the weak safety keys the guard and there is a threat to the successful completion of the play shown in Diagram 5-3, we then run the action shown in Diagram 5-4. The two most important points to emphasize on the pass shown in Diagram 5-3 are that the end

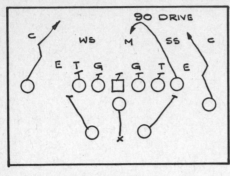

Diagram 5-5   **Diagram 5-6**

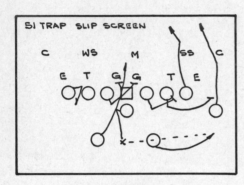
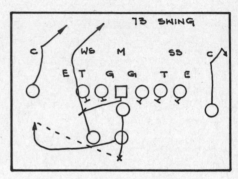

Diagram 5-7   **Diagram 5-8**

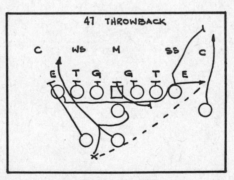

Diagram 5-9

should slow block for two counts, thus giving the weak cornerback a run key, and the quarterback must threaten him with the run.

Diagrams 5-5, 5-6, 5-7, 5-8, and 5-9 show plays that can be run with the quarterback taking a three-step drop. They are quick routes and must be run correctly in order to defeat goal line pass coverage. These plays are designed to attack the cornerback's playing man coverage with an inside pad.

The most demoralizing thing that can be done to a football team is to defeat its players where they feel they are strongest, and that is exactly what is done with the 90 drive play (Diagram 5-5). The key to making this a successful play is in the correct running of the route. The receiver should drive off at a 45° angle for two steps, then take one step straight up, which should force the cornerback to give up his inside pad. After taking the inside pad away, break back at the 45° angle. We have been successful in defeating teams at their strength with this route.

The 90 drive play is complemented by running the 90 drive-out (Diagram 5-6). The receiver should get into the defender as if he were trying to force his way inside. Use the defender to push off and change directions to go out.

Some special plays that seem to have merit are shown in Diagrams 5-7, 5-8, and 5-9. We have found that it is wise to have at least one of these ready for each game, because we never want to demoralize our own team by not having a weapon that can get them into the end zone when the big play situation arises.

We believe our players can score with the pass. Our goal line passing attack is an integral part of the goal line attack, and we do not wait until our backs are to the wall before a pass is thrown. In order to be successful passing on the goal line, the coach must believe in what he is doing, and he must sell his players on his system.

6 / The Passing Game

PASSING FUNDAMENTALS

by Lee Corso

Lee Corso
Indiana University

When writing about the passing game from an offensive set, certain basic principles and theories must be discussed.

The basic principles that must be considered in all passing games are as follows: 1. Protection. 2. Individual routes. 3. Unit patterns. 4. Tips for receivers.

Without protection, the team will not have a passing game. The quarterback will spend more time on the seat of his pants, and the prone position is not the best position from which to throw the ball. It is difficult to make the ball spiral when the quarterback is on his back.

There are many types of line protection. Two of the most commonly used are the cup or area protection and the number or out block system. We will not go into detail on the lineman's techniques, but will present the principles of each of the types of protection.

In the cup protection, each lineman has a predetermined area to protect. Linemen are not interested in specific players, but have zones they are instructed to protect. A lineman should step forward a few feet, make contact, and drop back to protect his area. The linemen should all retreat a few feet and form a cup or pocket. The quarterback is instructed to stay inside this pocket, and if he moves anywhere to throw, it should be up into the pocket. This movement gives him maximum protection.

As shown in Diagram 6-1, the backs step up, using short steps (fullback left, then right—tailback right, then left), and they are responsible for the area outside the offensive tackles. The short step gives them a good angle from which to block their assigned areas. In this type of protection, the backs usually take on the defensive ends.

One of the weakest parts of any drop-back series is that many of the offensive backs will not or cannot handle the pass protection necessary for success. There are many

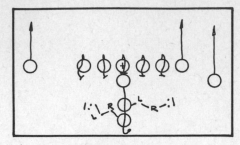

Diagram 6-1

theories which may be used to teach the backs to block. It has been our experience that the best method is to have them assume a good football position. A back's feet should be spread shoulder width, knees slightly flexed, and head in a rigid position with the pressure on the back of the neck. The head should be tucked in the shoulders. His arms should be spread in a wide position.

The back's rule is to look to the outside and then inside. If no one is rushing from the outside, he should look for linebackers who are rushing from the inside. The back will use a cross-body block, which will cut the man down, bringing the opponent's hands out of the quarterback's line of vision.

A drill we have used to teach this maneuver is shown in Diagram 6-2.

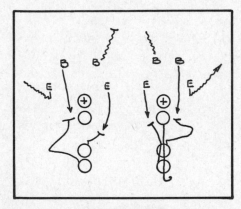

Diagram 6-2

The other widely used protection has each lineman blocking out and the fullback and tailback stepping up and blocking the linebackers in case they rush. If the linebackers do not rush them, then the fullback and tailback help the linemen (Diagram 6-3).

As shown in Diagram 6-3, the guards block the No. 1 man from the center on the line of scrimmage. The tackles take the No. 2 man, and the backs take the linebackers. The center blocks over or drops back, and then area blocks. The backs use the same technique and type block described for the cup protection.

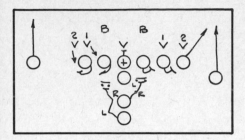
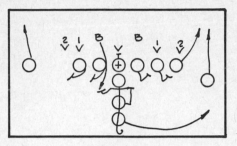

Diagram 6-3   **Diagram 6-4**

This type of protection is also good when the team is going to flare a back, split both ends, and needs maximum protection (Diagram 6-4).

Now that the quarterback is protected, work must be done on the receivers and their routes and patterns.

Some of the individual routes are shown in Diagram 6-5.

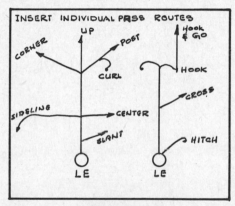

Diagram 6-5

When the receivers are on the left side, the definitions for their moves are as follows:

1. Slant—Take two steps at the defender, break at a 45° angle, and look for the ball.

2. Center—Three-quarters speed directly at the defender, 10 or 12 yards deep. Use a head and shoulder fake out, and break in at a 90° angle.

3. Sideline—Charge directly at the defender, 10 or 12 yards deep. Use a head and shoulder fake inside, plant the inside foot, and break out at a 90° angle. Give 2 yards back toward the quarterback on the break.

4. Post—Go directly at the defender, approximately 15 yards, fake out, and break in at a 45° angle. Make the defender turn his body out.

5. Corner—Charge directly at the defender, approximately 15 yards, fake in, and break out at a 45° angle. Make the defender turn his body in.

6. Up—Use a straight line pattern directly up the field.

7. Hitch—Take two quick steps, stop suddenly, and face the passer.

8. Cross—Go up the field 4 yards, and then break diagonally across the field for a point 12 to 14 yards beyond the line of scrimmage.

9. Hook—Go up the field 10 yards, stop quickly, turn, and face the passer. Always hook away from the linebackers. The depth of the hook can be called, that is, hook at 13, hook at 8, etc.

10. Hook-and-Go—Execute a hook, make a complete turn, and then go up the field.

11. Curl—Go directly at the defender. Make him turn out, and then curl in (approximately 12 yards).

In a discussion of the hook pass, we have found one point that might help receivers get open. Most coaches instruct their receivers to drive the defenders deep and then hook. Our method of teaching the basic hook is to have the end release, drive deep, and glance over his inside shoulder, looking for the linebacker. He should watch the linebacker and move away from him. When a hook is called in the huddle, neither the quarterback nor the end will know exactly where he is going to hook. As the quarterback drops back, he should look for the linebacker. If the linebacker moves inside, he knows his end will hook outside and vice versa. Most linebackers are instructed to watch the quarterback. This is why we work on the hook as described. The halfbacks are instructed to loosen up on the drive deep by the end, so we do not worry about the defensive halfback breaking up the hook. If the halfback does try to break up the hook, then the hook-and-go should work.

Many teams develop a fine passing game around the split ends and flankers but neglect a fine weapon in the tight end. In addition to the basic hook pattern described previously, we have a pattern called the tight delay. This is an excellent maneuver to use against a team that blitzes linebackers or has linebackers who really fly back into their hook areas. The tight end should drop-step a short distance to his outside with his outside foot. Then he should use a shoulder block on the defensive end and immediately look for the linebacker in his area. He should stay with the block for a count of one thousand, one, pause, one thousand, two, and then move into the area left open by the linebacker. The key to this play is the delay of the end and his looking for the linebacker. If the linebacker is plugging, the end should go immediately into the area and look for the ball. If a coach is having trouble with shooting linebackers, especially if they rush 80 percent of the time, he could try the tight delay on drop-back passes. If the linebackers blitz, the tight end will be hit. If not, use the regular pattern which was called (Diagram 6-6).

As mentioned previously, protection and individual routes are important to a passing team. After the receivers have learned their individual routes, then they can combine a few of these routes and form a unit pattern.

As an example, if a coach wants the flanker to run a cross route, the tight end an up route, and the split end a sideline, instead of calling each route for each player give the entire pattern a name.

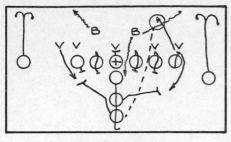

Diagram 6-6   **Diagram 6-7**

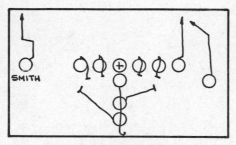

Diagram 6-8

Diagram 6-7 shows the drag-in. Every player on the team knows what to do on a drag-in call. This is only one of many patterns which can be drawn up. The principle is the same, give a name to a group of individual routes, turning them into a unit call.

If, after a time, the coach feels that his team has progressed sufficiently to give them an additional weapon, he can use a unit pattern with an individual change. Diagram 6-8 shows the drag-in—Smith—sideline and go.

There are many ways to call individual routes, but the best method we have found is to call the receiver by his name. Then the quarterback never gets X-Y-Z or 1-2-3 mixed up. He says, *Jones—hook* and Jones will never make a mistake. In addition, everyone likes to hear his name. Perhaps he will run a little better if he knows everyone has his eyes and hopes on him.

Now that the quarterback is protected, all the receivers know their individual routes, and the team knows the unit calls, we have some tips for the receiver.

We feel the following is the most important page of the receiver's notebook which we have assembled, and should be gone over periodically by the receivers and the coaching staff.

Receiver's Guide

1. Any football player can run patterns—only receivers find open spots and get free. Teach the receivers to look around for open areas and use their eyes.

2. Every player in a 3-, 4-, or 5-man pass play is eligible. We do not want any

decoys. Do not stop running or break the pattern. In a player's mind, he should always be the intended receiver.

3. Always know the yardage needed for a first down. Every complete pass should result in a first down (unless it is a flare control or delay pattern).

4. As soon as a pass is caught, all remaining receivers become blockers. Go to the ball and block for the pass receiver.

5. If the receiver sees a blitz coming, he should look for the ball in a hurry.

6. Come to the passer when he is in trouble. The receiver should raise his hand so the passer can find him in a hurry.

7. Always know where the sideline is. Run the pattern accordingly. Never run out of bounds.

8. Get off the ball as quickly as possible. The first three steps in football are the most important. Make the defender retreat.

9. When running a unit pattern, make sure one defender cannot cover two men.

10. Learn all types of defenses. A receiver should know when he is zoned, single-, or double-covered. The defense can alter the routes. Speed is more important than faking against a zone. Find the open spot in a zone.

11. When running against single coverage, make the defender move and then go opposite. A change of pace and faking are more important than speed against single coverage.

12. The only time a receiver is ever a decoy is when a screen or a draw is called. Run the best patterns. A basic rule we have used is that receivers run opposite a screen call. For example, screen right—the receivers go left to make the defensive backs and the linebackers go with them. This is called negative blocking.

COACHING THE PASSER

by Paul Bryant

Paul "Bear" Bryant
University of Alabama

Because there are certain things that cannot be taught a passer, we like to find a boy with the natural ability to throw. However, there are some things that may be taught which will be helpful.

The first thing to teach is the grip. We prefer that the passer grip the ball with the point of his little finger touching the lace almost in the center of the lace. If the point of any of his other fingers touches the lace, he will be gripping the ball in the center or the roundest part. We do not believe the ball may be thrown as well if it is gripped with the point of the forefinger, middle, or ring finger touching the lace. Our passer is also told not to grip the ball as tightly in inclement weather as he does under ordinary weather conditions.

The next thing to teach the boy is how and where to hold the ball. We like to have the quarterback do some faking before he sets up to throw. After each fake the ball should be brought back to the quarterback's stomach. His forearms should be touching his hips in a relaxed position. This relaxed position helps keep the ball closer to his body and makes it easier to hide. During the faking of the ball, the quarterback should shift his entire weight toward the back rather than toward the extension of his arm and the ball. We like the quarterback to set up ready to throw, and he should hold the ball with both hands until he is ready to release it, thus giving the quarterback a relaxed position. The ball should be in a cocked position right along the passer's ear, thus no time will be wasted in releasing it.

This brings us to the next point—the release and delivery. We feel that if the passer has learned the grip, the release and delivery will come easier. Our passer is instructed to release the ball with a snap of the wrist. Very few passers have a good wrist snap; therefore, there are very few good passers. This wrist snap may be developed by drills. In delivering the ball, which is actually part of the release, the passer, except in rare cases, is told to step toward the receiver as he throws. Not only will the passer be more accurate if he steps toward the receiver, but he will also be going in the right direction to cover in case of an interception. By stepping toward the receiver as he throws, the passer will not be throwing from an awkward position—across his body or against his own weight.

In our opinion, the footwork of the quarterback is very important. He should know where he is going to be when he throws. The receivers should also know the spot from where the passer is going to throw. It is also necessary for the line to know where the passer will be on a straight back-up pass since the team might be using pocket protection. Our passer is instructed to retreat straight back on any pass where the line will be forming a pocket. The passer is told to set up in a hurry and stay in the pocket. He is also instructed to retreat straight back on screen passes. The quarterback should make one or more fakes to the other backs on any type of pass where the line is using aggressive pass protection.

The running or optional pass, we feel, is one of the best passes in football because of the element of surprise. No particular footwork is designated for the running pass because we feel that the passer would overact his part. Instead, he is told to throw only when he cannot run. With these instructions, the passer is expecting to run, and he throws only when forced to do so by the defense.

In summary, the points listed below should be very helpful in teaching a passer some of the important phases of passing: 1. Push off. 2. Hide the ball on the way back. 3. Set up fast. 4. Get at least seven yards deep on most passes. 5. The passer should be under control when he lands with the ball in a position to be thrown. 6. He should look straight down the field. 7. Hop back in the pocket before throwing. 8. The passer should step in the direction he is throwing. He should not throw against his body or off balance. 9. He should call to teammates to cover up and cover himself. 10. The passer should throw the ball out of bounds or hold it if no one is open. 11. He should know his pass routes. 12. The passer should know his receivers. 13. He should know his defenders, both weak and strong. 14. The passer should know when to throw a hard or soft pass. 15. He should not throw interceptions. By that we mean the passer should not get rid of the ball just to be getting rid of it.

COACHING THE RECEIVER

by Paul Lanham

Paul Lanham
Washington Redskins

With the increased emphasis on the passing game and the pro style offense, it seems appropriate that we devote a proportional amount of time to the development of those skills associated with being a receiver. The following material is the result of securing information on this subject from a distinguished group of players and coaches. This material has been integrated into our system over the past three seasons, and is presented here in the same manner that it is given to our players.

Stance. A split receiver's stance should be three-point, which facilitates a quick release. If he is doubled, then he may use a two-point stance. A two-point stance makes it easier for him to release and avoid the double. Also, if he is the flanker and doubled, he may back off the line of scrimmage to facilitate his release.

Alignment. There are three general variables that determine a split receiver's alignment: 1) the offensive play called, 2) the defense facing him, and 3) his position on the field.

The Play Called. The width of the split certainly is determined to a great extent by the receiver's play assignment. There are five general situations that prevail when he is in a split assignment: 1. On crack-back blocking, use a minimum split, 5 to 8 yards. 2. On pass patterns to the outside or a hitch, take a minimum to normal split, 8 yards. 3. On pass patterns to the inside, take a normal to maximum split, 8 to 12 yards. 4. In case of isolation of a defender, take a maximum split, 12 to 15 yards. 5. Experiment with the defender when not involved directly in the play called. Use any reasonable split in order to learn how the defender will react and to mask the split when directly involved in a play.

The Defense. There are five general coverages which the defense will use for covering a split man. They are as follows: 1) man, 2) zone, 3) tiger (cornerback tight), 4) double, and 5) walk away.

1) Man coverage should not influence the width of a split receiver's split. 2) Zone coverage—usually a team cannot play zone if the split receiver's split is greater than 10 yards. From 10 yards a distinct weakness of the defense is the safety covering deep outside. If he splits more than 10 yards, the split receiver will force the defense out of zone into man coverage unless they cheat the safety to the outside to compensate. 3) Tiger coverage should not influence the width of a defender to get him into a nose-up position. When the defender is playing the split receiver loose, very few fakes will be needed to beat him.

However, if the defender plays him tight and the split receiver is not fast or quick enough to make him loose, then he must concentrate on beating him by getting him to turn his hips or cross his feet.

If the defender's position is nose-up and the split receiver is running an out pattern, release two steps straight up the field. Then shade to the inside to try to turn the defender to the inside. Depending upon his position, fake and make the break. In reality, this will appear to be a weave to the defender.

When the defender's position is inside and the split receiver is running an out pattern, or the defender is outside and the receiver is running an inside pattern, explode off the line of scrimmage slightly away from the defender to get him into his back-up quickly. Then, when he is retreating at full speed, break the pattern short.

If the defender is inside and the split receiver is running an inside pattern, or the defender is outside and the receiver is running an outside pattern, release two steps up the field. Then the split receiver should shade away from the defender to try to turn the defender toward him. When he does this, turn into him, and then, depending upon his position, fake and make the break.

Under the same circumstances, release directly toward the defender four or five steps. The split receiver should plant and break away from the defender to try to turn the defender toward him. Then, depending upon his position, fake and make the break.

In general, if the split receiver is not sure of his approach, he should try to get the defender nose-up regardless of his position or the pattern that is being run. Of all the approaches, the weave is probably the most difficult to read.

On deep patterns, if the split receiver is going deep, he should try to convince the defender he is going to run a short route. This can be done by giving a poor fake on the fake short route. If the split receiver gives the defender his best fake, he may fool him to the extent that he will not cover him on his short route. Second, use a change-of-speed approach. Try to deceive the defender by having him misread the speed. Then, when the defender is fooled, open up and beat him deep.

The Breaking Point. On short patterns, as the split receiver approaches the proper depth for the pattern, he will find the defender in two basic positions. He will either be playing tight, 1 to 3 yards, or loose, 4 to 6 yards. If he is on the split receiver tight, about 4 yards before he reaches his breaking point, then the split receiver must reduce his speed to gather himself in order to fake and make a sharp break. As he approaches the breaking point and the defender is playing him loose, 4 to 6 yards, the split receiver should run his break at top speed because the defender is too far away to be affected by any fakes. To insure getting open when the defender is that deep, sometimes the split receiver may cut the depth of his pattern a couple of yards short.

Faking. This is done any time between alignment and the catch. However, most of the time it is done during the approach or during the break. Faking is designed to convince the defender that the split receiver is going one place when he is going somewhere else. Faking is usually done by stepping, reaching, turning, looking, varying speeds, or any combination of these or other body maneuvers that can be used to fool the defender. The split receiver should study his opponent and continually vary his fakes. Run the routes with no fake, one fake, two fakes, or sometimes even three fakes, be in the game mentally, and work the opponent. A split receiver should practice his faking until he has control of his body. He should become an expert. A common fault for a beginner is to try to fake with too much speed. He should slow down on some routes because the fake must be deliberate in order to be effective. Faking, like the other phases of the receiving game, requires practice. It does differ in this respect in that a split receiver does not have to be smooth in order to be effective. He should develop his own style.

Tips on How to Get Open. 1. A split receiver should familiarize himself with pass defense. Learn the weak and strong spots of different coverages. Many completed passes just beat the defense, not the individual defender. 2. Learn the strengths and weaknesses of the man who is guarding. Vary the method of running the same pattern. Vary the number of fakes. 3. He should do his best to get open on every play, whether he is the first choice receiver or not. 4. Watch the defender's feet while making the moves. Try to get him to cross his feet, turn his hips, or get off balance. 5. On a play-away, experiment on the defender to find out what he will do. 6. Never show the best move when it is being used. 7. If a split receiver breaks and gets open, he should keep moving. Hook and then break out or in. 8. Being in too big a hurry in the approach and fakes is a common mistake made by most pass receivers. 9. Make several routes or patterns come off the same type of fake or move. 10. Practice, practice, and practice is the best way to become proficient at getting open. 11. Remember, there are four basic ways to work the defender to get open. The split receiver should use speed to make the defender play him loose, off 4 to 6 yards, to provide the short patterns. Make him cross his feet. Have him turn his hips. Get him off balance.

Diagrams 6-9 through 6-22 show the basic pass routes, and are diagramed for a player split to the left.

On the comeback (Diagram 6-9), the split receiver should explode off the line of scrimmage, sprint to a depth of 12 yards to make the defender think he is going deep, pivot to the inside, and come directly back toward the quarterback.

The hook is shown in Diagram 6-10. Approach fast and just stop and turn for the ball. The split receiver should make sure he has enough yardage for a first down. After he hooks, he should come toward the passer. After the catch, his best chance for getting free is to fake in, pivot, and run to the outside.

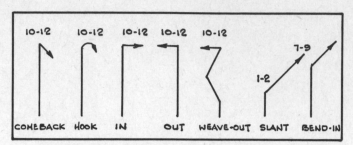

Diagrams 6-9 through 6-15

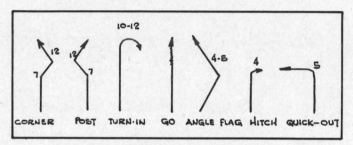

Diagrams 6-16 through 6-22

On the in (Diagram 6-11), he should explode off the line of scrimmage, work the defender, break to the inside, and continue running across.

When running the out (Diagram 6-12), he should explode off the line of scrimmage, work the defender, break to the sideline, and come back toward the line of scrimmage if the defender is tight on him. Also, if the split receiver runs out of room on the sideline, he should come back toward the line of scrimmage.

On a weave-out (Diagram 6-13), he should explode off the line of scrimmage, break three steps to the outside, plant and turn into the defender, read him, make the fake, and then break.

Diagram 6-14 shows the slant. Take one or two steps up the field, or just a quick fake, and break 45 degrees to the inside.

The bend-in is shown in Diagram 6-15. The split receiver should explode off the line of scrimmage, give the defender the impression that he is going deep, plant about 7 yards, and break 45 degrees to the inside.

On a corner (Diagram 6-16), use a sprint release, shade to the inside, and break at 12 yards for the corner.

For the post (Diagram 6-17), use a sprint release, shade to the outside, and break at 12 yards for the goal post.

On the turn-in (Diagram 6-18), explode off the line of scrimmage, pivot, and roll to the inside, clearing any defender in the zone in front. Come toward the passer.

Diagram 6-19 shows the go pattern. Use a sprint release, shade to the inside, break to the outside, and up the sideline. The split receiver must get close to the defender by faking, varying his speed, etc., before he can blow by him deep.

On an angle flag (Diagram 6-20), use a sprint release four to five steps to the inside, plant, and break for the flag.

Diagram 6-21 shows the hitch. Use a sprint release for four steps, and then turn the shoulder toward the quarterback.

On a quick-out (Diagram 6-22), speed out, run as fast as possible, and round the breaking point.

On a long pass, the split receiver must concentrate on moving at top speed after the break and watch the ball into his hands. He should practice catching over both the right and left shoulders. Practice stopping and coming back for a pass that is underthrown. He should not stand and wait for the ball to come to him. Practice fighting for the ball.

On two break patterns, do not make such a good fake that the defender will not take it. The split receiver wants the defender to be able to read his first fake and to think that it is his final move.

Scramble Rules. When the quarterback is in trouble due to a rush, the following rules will prevail: 1. If he is running a deep pattern, the split receiver should come back toward the quarterback. 2. If he is running a short pattern, he should go deep. 3. If he is running a pattern to the off-side of the field, he should come back across.

Catching the Ball. 1. When he looks back, the receiver should not lose his speed, but should keep sprinting. 2. When looking for the ball, avoid turning the body. Try to turn only the head. 3. Even though it appears as if the passer may not get the pass away, keep running. 4. As the pass approaches him, the receiver should keep moving at top speed. He should not slow down unless the ball is underthrown. 5. Do not reach for the ball too soon, because this will slow the receiver's speed and impair his balance.

Concentration. 1. This is the most important quality, essential to being an exceptional receiver. 2. A receiver must be completely oblivious to everything except catching the ball. 3. He knows he is going to be hit, but he does not know when or how hard.

The Catch. 1. Always catch the ball in the hands. 2. In catching the ball, the receiver should always have his thumbs or little fingers touching each other. 3. Look the ball all the way into the hands. 4. Be confident in catching. Eliminate fear of missing the ball. 5. A split receiver should develop the attitude that the ball is his when it is thrown. Go after it and battle for it. He should dominate the ball and not let it dominate him. 6. He should never jump for the ball unless it is over his head and out of reach.

Footwork—Body Control. 1. Having control of his body is essential to being a good pass receiver. 2. Proper footwork provides the necessary balance and body control for catching. 3. Adjusting for the bad pass and turning himself to make the necessary catch require footwork. 4. It is extremely important for a receiver to remember that repetition is the key to learning and mastering this technique. 5. Put the ball away immediately. This must become instinctive after each catch. Once he has made the catch, the receiver should explode for the goal line.

Practice. A receiver must catch hundreds and hundreds of passes in order to learn how to really use his hands.

Carrying the Ball. This is the most important responsibility of the offensive team. A receiver cannot play if he cannot handle the ball without fumbling. The ball should be held between the web of the fingers and the elbow. The elbow must be held in, close to the body, in order to avoid fumbling. Fundamentals of running with the ball are: balance, strength, cutting, and toughness. The receiver must think in terms of inches, feet, and yards. There are times when he must drive for inches and feet; other times, the risk should be taken for yards.

Downfield Blocking. This is a difficult technique for most players. A great deal of desire and practice are necessary in order to become proficient. A capable downfield blocker is a great asset, since often this is the block that springs the ball-carrier for the long run. Discipline and hustle are essential, and a player must assume on every play that this is the play on which the ball-carrier will need his block to go all the way. Do not try to block the defender in a certain direction for the ball-carrier, merely deliver the block.

Two downfield blocking techniques are employed. Our procedure is to stalk a defender or actually block him. In stalking a defender, we will take him as deep as we can on our pattern, and then, when he reacts to the run, we keep front face position between the defender and the ball-carrier. Do not throw a block, merely keep in his face and shield him.

In actually blocking downfield, it is necessary that a player run through on his block. Step on the defender's toes and avoid throwing too soon. Either a shoulder or a cross-body block can be used. Probably a combination of the two is best. Use the shoulder block when he is retreating, and just keep running through. The cross-body block is probably best when the defender is trying to side-step.

Passer-Receiver Relationship. Completing passes requires close cooperation between two players. Developing timing and familiarity with each other is imperative. Establishing communication with each other is invaluable. The passer must practice with the receiver until he knows his every move. They must be able to anticipate the actions of each other under certain game conditions. The key to completing passes is getting the ball to the receiver on the break. This understanding, knowledge, and relationship must be developed off the practice field as well as on it. Coordination between the thrower and the catcher is essential to the success of the passing game. Confidence between the two is necessary for efficient operation. A great amount of dedicated work is the only way to develop this confidence.

Recognizing Coverage. Five general coverages are used by the defense for covering a split man—man, zone, tiger, double, and walk-away.

The various coverages do affect a split receiver's patterns. A general discussion of each coverage follows.

Man coverage (Diagram 6-23) has little effect on the basic routes. It is simply the receiver's ability to run a pattern versus the opponent's ability to defend. Most defenders

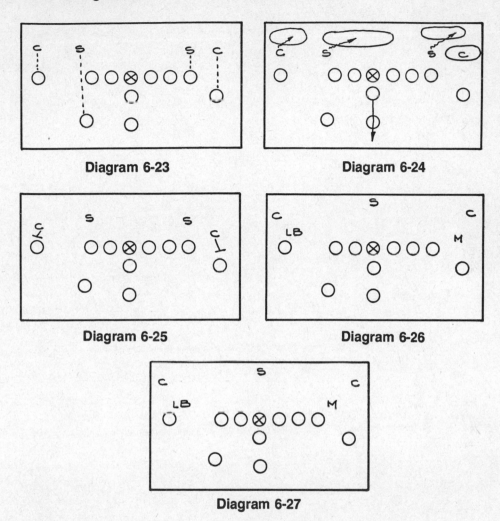

Diagram 6-23

Diagram 6-24

Diagram 6-25

Diagram 6-26

Diagram 6-27

will give the short pass, hitch, out, hook, etc., to make sure they are not defeated deep. Crossing patterns such as the pick are usually quite effective versus a man defense.

Three kinds of zone coverage are used—corner support and safety support from a seven-man front, and three-deep zones from an eight-man front. From a seven-man front, the zone will rotate to the action side. However, from corner support, they cannot rotate if the split of the wide receiver is greater than 10 yards, because the safety cannot cover the wide man deep outside (Diagram 6-24). From safety support when the receiver is split, the safety has trouble covering the wide flat. From an eight-man front with a three-deep zone, they also have a problem covering the flat if the ball is brought to the corner in a sprint-out, because the man who is responsible for defending the flat short is also responsible for the contain.

In general, versus corner support, the receiver should run inside patterns. If it is safety support, he should attack outside. If it is an eight-man front, he should run outside patterns with the ball coming to him. Finally, to split the zone and make the defense play the man on the corner, the receiver can take a maximum split.

In order to beat the cornerback who is playing tight on the line of scrimmage in tiger coverage (Diagram 6-25), we like to have the receiver do the following: 1. Test him deep first with speed. 2. Fake going deep, and then run a comeback to the sideline. 3. Use the quick-out. 4. Hit into him first and then use the quick-out. 5. Release wide several times to make him go outside and then fake out and beat him to the inside.

Faking is an important aspect of beating tiger coverage. Since the defender is playing so close, he must read the receiver's look and reach for the ball in order to know when to play the ball himself. Thus, a good fake will cause him to turn his back on the receiver to play the fake.

Double coverage (Diagram 6-26) will dictate a change in the receiver's stance. He should change from a three-point to a two-point. It will also necessitate a change in some patterns such as from an out to a turn-in.

Generally, the walk-away (Diagram 6-27) should not cause any concern.

Training a Receiver. In order to develop touch, the following drills are used.

1. Grip the ball in one hand, then in the other. Repeat for one minute. 2. Throw the ball in a hand drill. Do not look at the ball. Repeat for one minute. Rotate a plate weighing 25 to 30 pounds between the fingers. Repeat for one minute.

Concentration. 1. Pass a ball to the receiver underhand with a stiff elbow. It will twist, float, and turn. Look the ball into the hands. 2. Place a bag 3 yards from the goal post. Go between the bag and the post. Deliver the ball so that the receiver runs past the post while the ball is in flight. 3. Flip a towel across the path of the ball in front of the receiver. 4. The receiver catches the ball as he runs between two stand-up dummies. Bump the receiver as he makes the catch. 5. Place four stand-up dummies on the ground. As the receiver steps over the dummies, throw the pass to him. 6. Place a defender in front of the receiver. As the passer delivers the ball, spread the hands and let it pass through to the receiver. 7. As the receiver is preparing to make a catch, have him pushed from the back or side. 8. Deliver the ball just as the receiver regains his feet and looks for it.

Catching. In catching a ball, the receiver must have his thumbs or little fingers touching each other. He should always put the ball away. 2. Intentionally throw the ball high, low, behind, and in front of the receiver. Use a net to field missed passes. 3. Toss the ball between two receivers, and have them fight for it. 4. With the receiver's back to the passer, toss the ball over the receiver's head. Then toss it over his left and right shoulders. 5. With his back to the passer, have him signal and turn around in ready position. Deliver the ball just as the receiver turns. 6. Use six receivers per passer. Each receiver catches four passes on the passer's left side and then four on his right side. The patterns are short, and are look-in, overhead, out-in, and out. 7. Six receivers start with one ball and then increase to five balls. Pass the ball within the circle. 8. Catch the ball, lower the shoulder, drive through the dummy, and score. 9. The receiver should practice catching the ball near the sideline, but in bounds. He should use chop steps. 10. Have the receiver turn his back to the thrower. The thrower tosses the ball underhand, the receiver sprints to the ball, leaps in the air, and catches the ball as high as he can. 11. Place four receivers at the corners of a 5-yard square. Toss the ball up in the middle, and have them fight for it. 12. Throw the ball to the side of the receiver. Have him move to receive it, but make certain he does not reach for the ball too soon. 13. Have the receiver run through the "Blaster." Throw the ball and notice how quickly the receiver is able to refocus.

Part II
DEFENSE

7 / The 5-2 Defense

5-2 DEFENSE

by Andrew Grieve

Andrew Grieve
Morgan State University

A military strategist once stated, *the best defense is a good offense*. This may apply to football, to a degree, but a military campaign does have characteristics that permit the offense to be a continuous process, or at least that is the hope of the generals. However, in football, a successful offense must eventually lead to a team shifting to defense. For this reason, the football coach must have a philosophy of defense other than just depending upon his offense. Since every football team will be on defense, it is imperative for a coach to develop some semblance of organization in this phase of the game.

There has been a tendency for coaches to spend more time on the offensive phase of the game because they feel more teaching is required to develop the skills necessary for a successful offense. This is probably the reason for the increase in the number of high-scoring games during the past few years. Conversely, it is possible that a coach will be carried away with defensive emphasis and permit the offense to slide. An intelligent coach will review his practice plans constantly to verify that he is spending an equal amount of time on both phases of the game.

Before deciding on a particular defense, a coach should review the basic objectives of defense. The perfect defense, which is naturally idealistic, will achieve the following: 1. Stop the opponents from scoring. 2. Stop the long gain. 3. Stop the first down. 4. Stop short yardage. 5. Keep the opponents in poor field position. 6. Gain possession of the ball. 7. Gain possession in good field position. 8. Score while on defense.

Obviously, any defense that fulfills all of the previously mentioned objectives would be perfect. In certain games the team might well play the perfect defense, while in others the players might exhibit degrees of perfection. If the team attains the first objective, at least games will not be lost. The coach might well finish the season with some ties, but he is not losing.

As is true in any undertaking, whether it be that of a coach, a salesman, or an engineer, the individual must be sold on his product. No one can expect to sell a theory or an item if he is not completely sold on it. After a thorough study of the 5-2, our staff decided that it would fulfill all of the basic objectives of a good defense. Over a period of several years our optimistic outlook became even stronger as the 5-2 proved to be effective for us.

We felt the effectiveness of this defense was the result of two factors. The first was the false look that it gave to the opponents. The basic alignment (Diagram 7-1) appeared as a 5-2-4. It ended with a seven-man spacing on one side and a five-man spacing on the other, with a corner man supporting. Second, due to the variations of responsibilities, a team that was able to analyze every defensive move would find it difficult to adjust their blocking, since we did not have the defense move in the same direction each play. If the offense assumed there would be a crashing end with a supporting corner on the right and blocked accordingly, it might well turn out to be a containing end with a tackle supporting from the inside.

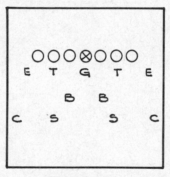

Diagram 7-1

Before moving into the individual responsibilities, it must be stated that this is highly disciplined defense. There can be little variation on the part of the individual defensive players from the basic movements. Once the play is underway, then there will be normal defensive reaction, but the original movement must be synchronized. Any player who decides he should not move in the predetermined pattern will cause a complete breakdown in the defense. This becomes obvious when a player makes a mistake and moves in the wrong direction. It might be wise to indicate during a practice session what can occur if any one of the defenders does make the wrong move. The results will be quite obvious to the players.

With the defense in the proper alignment, the coordinated individual movements which make this defense effective must be indicated. Diagram 7-2 shows the individual movements and responsibilities on a loop left call. A loop right is shown in Diagram 7-3.

Looping End—Line up on the outside shoulder of the defensive end and loop out.

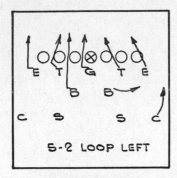

Diagram 7-2

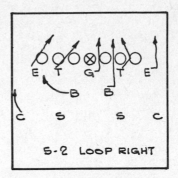

Diagram 7-3

He must never allow himself to be blocked in. He should keep the play inside but give ground grudgingly.

Looping Tackle—Shade the outside shoulder of the tackle and drive into the end smartly unless he is split so far that he cannot block, then check back to the inside. Deliver a forearm lift from the inside out. This will defeat the cross-block as the looping tackle takes the initiative away from the end. It will also help to counter a double-team. It will also slow up the end if he is an intended pass receiver.

Middle Guard—Line up head-on with the middle man on the offensive line. He should be slightly off the line so he cannot be cut off. Loop to the left and never permit the middle man to hook. Drive into the backfield and search.

Slanting Tackle—Line up head-on with the offensive tackle, pointing slightly to the inside. Slant directly into the guard, using a forearm lift from the outside in. Attempt to drive him into the hole to his inside. Penetrate and search.

Slanting End—Line up on the outside shoulder of the offensive end and crack through his outside shoulder. The offensive end should never take the slanting end in. If the play comes his way, the slanting end must force it deep.

Looping Linebacker—Line up 1 yard off the offensive guard, loop to the left, and shoot through the gap hard. Penetrate and search.

Off-Side Linebacker—Line up 1 yard off the guard. Slide to the right slightly to check the tackle hole, but key the near-side back. Play the football. The tackle hole is the off-side linebacker's first responsibility, but he should be ready to pursue.

Looping Corner Man—Line up 5 to 6 yards deep, off the outside foot of the defensive end. He should be pass conscious, as he has the outer third. Key the offensive end for a block on the tackle. If the play develops in his direction, he should come up to support the defensive end.

Off Side Corner Man—Line up 5 to 6 yards deep off the outside foot of the defensive end. The corner man's responsibility is the outside on a play run toward him. He should come up fast and contain, and no one should get outside him. Think reverse, pass defense, and pursuit when the flow is away. His pass responsibility is flat coverage to his side.

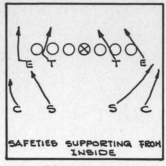

Diagram 7-4

Safety Man—Line up six yards back, off the inside foot of the defensive tackle. Be pass conscious but ready to come up fast on a play through the line. On wide plays, the safety on that side should move up to make the tackle from the inside out (Diagram 7-4).

Keying

The off-side linebacker, both corner men, and the safeties should be concerned about keys. As mentioned previously, the off-side linebacker must key the setback on his side. If the halfback is missing, he should key the fullback. He must be ready to protect the off-tackle hole first. However, the movement of the back will indicate to him the direction of the play.

A looping corner man should key the end and/or wingback. If the end blocks down on the tackle, he should be ready to come up and support. If the end and/or wingback releases, the looping corner man must be ready to cover the deep outer third.

Because he has probably one of the toughest responsibilities on the field, the off-side corner man must key the end and/or wingback. A block down on the tackle will indicate a play his way, and he must support from the outside as the end is crashing in. On a pass pattern, he should cover the flat area.

The safeties should key the setback on their side. If he is missing, they should key the nearest setback to their side, who will usually be the fullback.

Variations

We keep our variations to a minimum, but they provide a change of pace. Two variations involve the off-side tackle and the off-side linebacker, while the other involves the off-side end and the cornerback.

On the tackle switch, the off-side linebacker and off-side tackle vary their positions to confuse the defense. This decision can be left to these two players if they feel it will prove effective. It would not concern the movements of the other defensive players because no other defensive adjustment would be necessary. If the call is *tackle in*, the tackle should slide to the gap to his inside. He should slam into the guard and attempt to plug up the holes on both sides of the guard. Then the linebacker should shoot through the off-tackle hole. The spacing on this side would be an Eagle defense with the linebacker rushing, and it has proved to be an excellent pass defense rush (Diagram 7-5).

When the call is *tackle out*, the tackle should crash through the tackle hole while the linebacker should drive into the guard, plugging the middle. These two variations tend to confuse the blocking assignments if the offense picks up the standard 5-2 movement (Diagram 7-6).

The final variation is the monster call. This is a standard type of adjustment used by many five-man fronts. Prior to the snap, the tackle should slide to the inside gap, the end should move to the off-tackle gap, and the corner man should move up on the line of scrimmage. From this adjustment, the tackle should crack into the guard and plug up the middle. The end should smash inside the offensive end and concern himself with the off-tackle hole. Then the corner man should contain as he normally would in this alignment, but he should be doing so from the line of scrimmage rather than from his deep position. In this variation, the linebacker is usually free due to the plugging of the interior offensive linemen, and he should be free to play the football and go with the flow (Diagram 7-7).

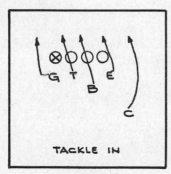

Diagram 7-5

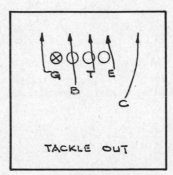

Diagram 7-6

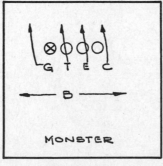

Diagram 7-7

5-2 Versus Formations

In some situations, slight adjustments may be necessary due to the type of offensive formation. Most of these are minor variations, but the defense should be prepared. The scouting reports should prepare a team for these adjustments.

Versus a Wingback

In looping to the wingback, no adjustment is needed. The looping end must be certain he is not caught in by the wingback. The monster and the tackle switch can be used on the off-side (Diagram 7-8).

In looping away from the wingback, only minor adjustments are necessary. The slanting end should go inside the wingback and the corner man should cover the outside as usual. The monster man and the tackle switch may be used on the off-side (Diagram 7-9).

Versus a Flanker

With a loop to the flanker, the corner man must be far enough out so he cannot take the end in. If he is close enough to take the end, he should be played as a wingback. The end will usually move out a maximum of 4 to 5 yards from his normal position. If this is the situation, the corner man must be ready to come up and support to the inside. From a true flanker position, the corner man should key the flanker and cover him man-for-man if necessary. Otherwise, he should cover his outside third. The monster should be avoided due to the pass defense. However, the tackle switch would be effective (Diagram 7-10).

On a loop away from the flanker, regular line play may be used. The tackle switch would be appropriate, but the monster would not. The corner man should cover the flanker from the inside out. The remainder of the secondary should rotate slightly so the safety man can support outside the slanting end. The loop protects the outside away from the flanker. Rotation also aids on pass defense (Diagram 7-11).

Versus a Split End

The offense is weakened to the split end side, and looping to the split end will provide a strong defense. A tackle switch may be used, but the monster is not advisable. The looping end must be certain he cannot be blocked in by the split end. On the loop to the split end, the defensive end can move out with the end up to 4 yards. He must be able to contain. The corner man must cover the split end from the inside out and force him to the sideline (Diagram 7-12).

On the loop away from the split end, the tackle switch may be used but not the monster. The corner man covers the split end as he did in the loop to the split end. There should be a slight rotation by the secondary to the split end. The off-side safety man should be ready for a run to the split end, as the corner man may be pulled deep by the split end. The slanting end need not concern himself with the split end but should crash

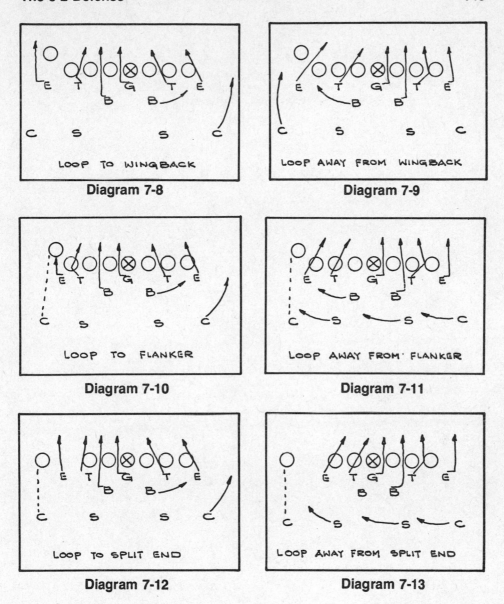

Diagram 7-8   LOOP TO WINGBACK

Diagram 7-9   LOOP AWAY FROM WINGBACK

Diagram 7-10   LOOP TO FLANKER

Diagram 7-11   LOOP AWAY FROM FLANKER

Diagram 7-12   LOOP TO SPLIT END

Diagram 7-13   LOOP AWAY FROM SPLIT END

in. The off-side linebacker should be free to support on any run to his side due to the inside adjustment of the defensive line (Diagram 7-13).

Versus a Slotback

On a loop to the slotback, he should be handled as the end. The looping end must never be taken in by the slotback. The on-side corner man should cover the split end from inside out. The on-side safety man must be ready to support from inside out. Both the monster and the tackle switch may be used (Diagram 7-14).

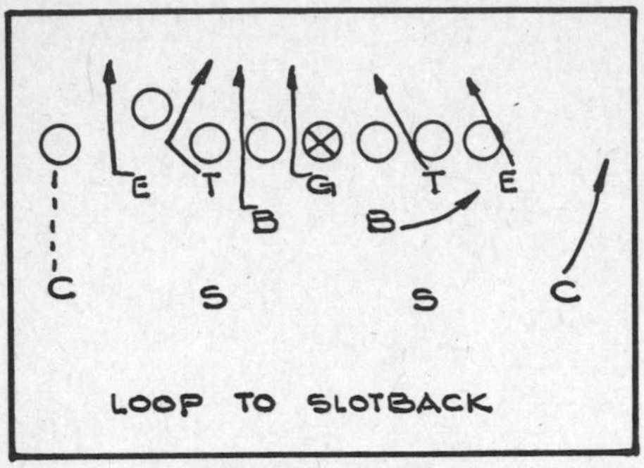

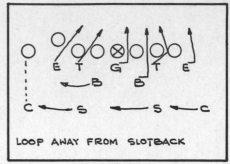

LOOP TO SLOTBACK

Diagram 7-14

LOOP AWAY FROM SLOTBACK

Diagram 7-15

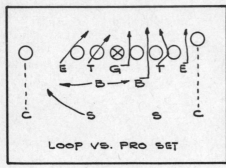

LOOP VS. PRO SET

Diagram 7-16

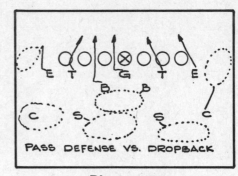

PASS DEFENSE VS. DROPBACK

Diagram 7-17

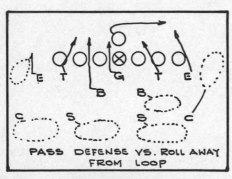

PASS DEFENSE VS. ROLL AWAY FROM LOOP

Diagram 7-18

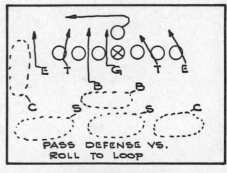

PASS DEFENSE VS. ROLL TO LOOP

Diagram 7-19

In looping away from the slotback, the off-side end should crack inside the slotback. The off-side corner man must cover the split end as he did in the loop to him. The secondary should rotate and the off-side safety should be ready to support outside. The off-side linebacker can support on any plays to his side. Neither the monster nor the tackle switch would be advisable (Diagram 7-15).

Versus a Pro Set

The defense should always loop away from the split end. The corner man should cover the wide men from the inside out. The off-side linebacker should play the football and be free to support on any play to his side, and support on the outside as well. The tackle switch can be used, but not the monster. The safety man away from the loop must be ready to come up and support to the outside in case of a run to the open end (Diagram 7-16).

Pass Defense

In order to be effective, any defense must protect as well against the pass as against the run. We found that the 5-2 was as effective as any we had ever used. In fact, with the four-deep look, a quarterback is going to be wary of putting the ball in the air. Even with a corner man coming up to contain, the deep coverage is still effective.

Versus the Dropback

The 5-2 provides coverage as adequate as any other type of defense. Diagram 7-17 shows the zone coverage. The on-side corner man and the two safety men will be covering the three deep zones. The off-side corner man will have little difficulty in covering the flat to his side, while the looping end will be in good position to cover the flat on his side. Although there are divergent theories on the hook zone, we like the carry-through with the stunt by the on-side linebacker to provide an added pass rush. The off-side linebacker should drop into the middle and be ready to slide to either side. The loop of the on-side tackle into the offensive end will slow his release considerably and add to the pass defense.

Versus the Roll

The roll to the slanting end should not develop too much of a problem as his slant path should place him in good position to force the passer deep and the corner man should still be able to cover the flat. We instruct the end never to permit himself to be hooked, and he should apply outside pressure on the quarterback. The shooting linebacker will also develop another problem for the passer on a roll to the loop. If there is a problem on a roll-out away from the looping end, then a simple rotation in the secondary should alleviate the difficulty. The looping end would have to drop back quickly, but his area of responsibility would be most difficult in which to throw (Diagram 7-18).

On a roll to the looping end, a rotation of the backfield will be necessary. The on-side corner man should cover the flat on his side, and the safeties should be responsible for the outer and middle thirds. The off-side corner man should check for the reverse and then cover the deep outer third. Once again, this area would be the most difficult in which to complete a pass due to the nature of the movement (Diagram 7-19).

Prevent

The coach's attitude toward a prevent defense will determine the adjustment in the 5-2. The purist may drop both linebackers away from the line and have a four-man rush with seven pass defenders (Diagram 7-20). We have always received adequate coverage from our standard defense and would rather have a fairly good rush. If a coach's philosophy is that a stronger pass rush is more effective, then Diagram 7-21 shows how shooting both linebackers may provide this added pressure.

In conclusion, we would like to state that the versatility of this defense is one of its strengths. In addition to using the 5-2 as a standard defense, we have also used it as a goal line defense, with suitable variations, for a punt rush and as a punt return. Over the years this defense has been good to us, and we always felt it was not wise to argue with success.

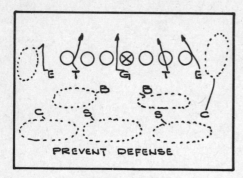

Diagram 7-20

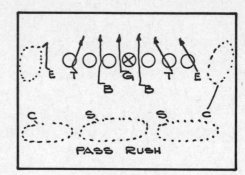

Diagram 7-21

SHIFTING 5-2

by Myron Tarkanian

Myron Tarkanian
Pasadena City College

The shifting 5-2 is based primarily on an Oklahoma 5-4 defense used in conjunction with variations that proved successful for the University of Arkansas teams.

It is our feeling that the shifting or sliding portion of the defense is valuable for the following reasons: 1. Athletes enjoy it. 2. The offensive blockers are confused. 3. Defensive players are allowed to become attackers instead of waiters. 4. Very little time is necessary to teach the 5-2. 5. A basic defense is able to have a variety of looks. 6. A flexible secondary is permitted, as a monstered three-deep or a four-deep can be used in conjunction with each variation. 7. This defense attempts to free the linebacker completely.

Working on the assumption that our players would be meeting teams with one tight end and the other split, it was determined that different types of individuals would be required to play the two defensive end positions. We decided to flip-flop the two, depending on the offensive tight end. This idea worked well, and we ended up flip-flopping everyone to meet the strengths of the offense and prevent a possible mismatch which a flip-flopped offensive line attempts to create.

As shown in Diagram 7-22, each player is designated by position.

Strong End—We look for the larger, stronger man who can handle the double-team and off-tackle hole for this position.

Strong Tackle—This position requires the larger, stronger man who can play the double-team and hold the area.

Middle Guard—Our quickest down lineman who can hit and pursue is given this assignment. When he is in a gap situation, he must be able to penetrate. Size is not important, but quickness is necessary.

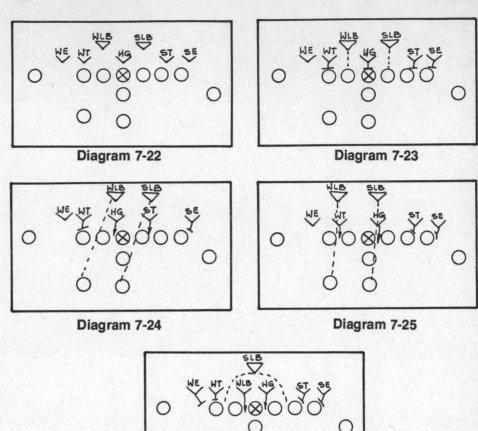

Diagram 7-22

Diagram 7-23

Diagram 7-24

Diagram 7-25

Diagram 7-26

Wild Tackle—This player must be quick and able to handle short-side plays such as options. Ability to pursue is necessary.

Wild End—He must have the agility of a linebacker, be able to double cover, and get into pass defense on occasion.

Strong Linebacker—This player should be the stronger and bigger of the linebackers, and will usually key the opponent's fullback.

Wild Linebacker—He should be the quicker of the two linebackers, be able to play quick tosses, and key the offensive halfback.

The basic defense that is taught first is the 5-2 Okie (Diagram 7-23). Considerable time is spent teaching the usual techniques and reads of this defense.

The stack defense (Diagram 7-24) is used a great deal, especially with a monstered three-deep secondary, because it is well balanced.

The responsibilities of the strong end and the wild end remain the same throughout the entire defense. They play tough Okie techniques.

Strong End—A. Assume a three-point stance. B. Go to the outside shoulder of the offensive end. C. Deliver a blow and read. D. His first responsibility is off-tackle and then he should work out.

Wild End—A. He should assume a two-point stance, and his alignment will vary. B. Up tight on the line of scrimmage. C. Walk away. D. Double cover.

Strong Tackle—A. Four-point stance. B. His alignment is in the gap between the offensive guard and tackle. C. Penetrate hard. D. Attempt to occupy both blockers in order to free the linebackers.

Strong Linebacker—A. He should be tandemed directly behind the strong tackle. B. Feet parallel. C. Key one of the remaining backs, usually the fullback.

Middle Guard—A. Four-point stance. B. His alignment is in the gap between the offensive center and the short-side guard. C. Penetrate to the near leg of the quarterback. D. Attempt to occupy both blockers in order to free the linebacker.

Wild Linebacker—A. He should be tandemed directly behind the middle guard. B. Feet parallel. C. He should key one of the remaining backs, usually the set halfback.

Wild Tackle—A. Three-point stance, 12 inches off the ball. B. Outside shoulder of the short-side tackle. C. Deliver the blow and read. D. Do not allow the tackle to block down on the linebacker.

In appearance, the wildcat alignment (Diagram 7-25) is similar to the stack. However, this alignment causes many problems. Its strength lies towards the tight end side although it can be run at any point on the field, and it is equally as strong from a four-deep secondary alignment.

The strong end's and wild end's responsibilities remain the same.

Strong Tackle—A. Three-point stance, 12 inches off the ball. B. Outside shoulder of the tackle. C. Deliver the blow, read, and play the off-tackle hole. D. Do not allow the tackle to block down on the linebacker.

Middle Guard—A. Four-point stance. B. Align in the gap between the center and strong guard. C. Penetrate to the near leg of the quarterback. D. Attempt to occupy the blockers.

Wild Tackle—A. Four-point stance. B. Align in the gap between the guard and the tackle on the short side. C. Penetrate hard. D. Attempt to occupy both blockers.

Strong Linebacker—A. He should tandemed directly behind the middle guard. B. Feet parallel. C. Key one of the remaining backs, usually the fullback.

Wild Linebacker—A. He should be tandemed directly behind the wild tackle. B. Feet parallel. C. Key one of the remaining backs, usually the halfback.

The pinch defense is our only six-man front (Diagram 7-26). It is effective on short yardage situations or as a change-up, because men are placed in the gaps on either side of the center, and they penetrate hard and often. One player could come through without being blocked and cause serious problems in the offensive backfield. If both men are blocked, our middle linebacker will be freed because the offensive center is prevented by the gap guards from coming out on him.

The strong end's and wild end's responsibilities remain the same.

Strong Tackle and Wild Tackle—A. Three-point stance, 12 inches off the ball. B. Go to the outside shoulder of the tackle. C. Deliver a blow and read. D. Do not allow the tackle to block down on the middle linebacker.

Middle Guard and Wild Linebacker—A. These players become the gap guards. B. Four-point stance. C. Penetrate hard through the offensive center. D. Go for the near leg of the quarterback.

Strong Linebacker—A. He becomes the middle linebacker. B. Feet parallel. C. Align 12 inches behind the heels of the gap guards. D. Keep ahead of the offensive center. E. Cover the guard-tackle hole opposite the block of the center.

These four fronts are run during every game. Of course, the percentage of time they are used depends on the opposing team's tendencies, scouting reports, and field position.

As mentioned previously, our team always lines up in a 5-2 regular and shifts to the desired front on the command of the strong linebacker, who is our defensive signal caller. Our players attempt to shift at the latest possible moment prior to the snap of the ball. We must know the opposing team's get-off count and prepare for it the entire week prior to the game.

In our opinion, the shifting 5-2 has a tremendous potential and is worth consideration.

8 / The 4-4 Defense

4-4 DEFENSE

by Drew Tallman

Drew Tallman
Dartmouth College

The 4-4 defense is not used extensively by many teams at the present time. However, some teams utilize it as a basic defense. A few coaches employ this defense as a preventive measure for the passing game. Two defensive guards are aligned over the offensive guards. Two linebackers are positioned over the offensive tackles. The defensive tackles are positioned on the offensive ends. The defensive ends are off the line of scrimmage and three yards outside the offensive end.

Diagram 8-1 shows the 4-4 even-diamond defense.

As will be noticed, a defensive man is not positioned on the offensive center. Therefore, it is an even defense. The 4-4 utilizes the three-deep diamond secondary for its pass coverage and an eight-man front for the running game. This is one of the advantages of the four-man line—only four defensive linemen are needed. The alignment calls for versatile linebackers who can get to the ball fast, fill the running holes,

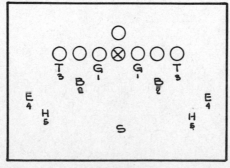

Diagram 8-1

especially inside, and retreat to their respective hook areas. Since there are four defensive linemen, two linebackers, and two defensive ends in a stunting position, a multitude of stunting and blitzing can be performed.

The 4-4 defense is employed mainly for passing teams, passing situations, and for teams that consistently run the ball to the outside. The defense can rush four defensive linemen and have the hook and flat areas well covered. The three-deep can rotate if required, giving added strength to the outside on passes. If stunting and blitzing are needed when the offense is passing, they can be easily utilized at any time. Stunts are used for the running game when it is essential. The 4-4 is usually used for this purpose.

The 4-4 defense is versatile. It can easily adjust to any offense, whether tight or spread. This defense can easily change its alignment for different defensive looks.

Following is the alignment, stance, initial movement, execution, and responsibility of the defensive guards, tackles, ends, linebackers, halfbacks, and safety in the 4-4 defense.

Defensive Guards (Number 1 Men)

Alignment: Line up in nose-up position. On wider splits, start aligning to the inside. On less yardage, play close; on long yardage, play loose.

Stance: Three- or four-point stance.

Initial Movement and Execution: The guard should step, deliver a blow, and control the offensive guard, being aware of the inside. He should move to the inside to stop any play in that area. Be aware of the center's block.

Responsibility: Key the guard's head. If the guard pulls away from the center, look for the trap from the inside, and then pursue. If the guard pulls behind the center, release and pursue. 1. On play toward them, the defensive guards should guard their area and go to the inside. 2. On play away, they should pursue, and should not run around. 3. On a drop-back, they should rush to the inside. The guards are responsible for the draw and screens. They should be alert for the trap play.

Coaching Points: The defensive guards must protect to the inside and shut off the middle area.

Defensive Tackles (Number 3 Men)

Alignment: Line up in nose-up position. This will vary according to the line splits.

Stance: Three-point stance.

Initial Movement and Execution: Key the end's head. Strike a blow to the end and do not offer resistance.

Responsibility: The tackle must close and protect to the inside, and be aware of the dive play. However, if the play goes to the outside, the tackle must not be blocked in. 1. On play toward him, the defensive tackle should play the offensive end area and to the inside. 2. On play away, he should chase the man, staying as deep as the ball and being aware of the reverse, counter, and bootleg play coming back. 3. On a drop-back, he should attempt to hold the end up and not let him release. Rush from the outside-in.

Coaching Points: Strike a good blow into the head of the end. Do not let him release easily downfield. Play the inside, but be ready to go outside. He should not penetrate across the line unless the play goes away from him.

Defensive Linebackers (Number 2 Men)

Alignment: Line up in nose-up position approximately 1½ yards off the line (this will vary).

Stance: Two-point stance.

Initial Movement and Execution: Key the offensive tackle. Play his head and react to his block.

Responsibility: If the tackle blocks down, fill, and watch for the trapper. Do not be hooked. If the tackle fires out, deliver a forearm blow. Play his head and read the backfield. If the tackle pulls, they can fire the gap or pursue. 1. On play toward them, the defensive linebackers should play the offensive tackle area and the inside dive man. Look to the inside. Be able to support to the outside. Never be blocked in. 2. On play away, they should pursue the ball-carrier. Keep the tackle off the defensive halfbacks. 3. On a drop-back, go to the required hook area.

Coaching Points: Change the depth of alignment when necessary. If the tackle is big, play closer. If the linebacker can handle the tackle, he can loosen off the line. Also, change alignment to down and distance, time of game, score, etc. Cover the dive, off-tackle area, and support to the outside.

Defensive Ends (Number 4 Men)

Alignment: Line up 3 yards outside the end and approximately 3 yards off the line of scrimmage.

Stance: Two-point stance, outside leg back.

Initial Movement and Execution: Watch the movement of the quarterback. React from there.

Responsibility: The end should turn everything to the inside. He is the contain man. He should never let any blocker turn him in. 1. On play toward them, they should come up quickly and contain. Be aggressive. Turn everything inside for pursuit. Be responsible for the option-pitch men. 2. On play away, cover the flat and then drop back deep. Go on pursuit only when the ball crosses the line of scrimmage. 3. On a drop-back, play the flat unless involved in a stunt or blitz.

Coaching Points: When containing, do not float. Hold ground and turn everything inside. Know the tactical situation. Support to the inside only when the ball-carrier commits.

Defensive Halfbacks (Number 5 Men)

Alignment: Line up 3 to 4 yards outside the offensive end and 7 to 10 yards deep. Line up as wide as the widest receiver.

Stance: Two-point stance with the outside leg back.

Initial Movement and Execution: Watch the required key. On the snap of the ball, the weight should be shifted back to the outside foot on reading the key.

Responsibility: React to the run if the end blocks. Approach the ball-carrier from an outside-in position. On plays away, look for a pass and then pursue. They must watch for the fake block. If the offensive end pass protects or releases downfield, play the pass first and then react to the run. 1. On play toward them, they should take the deep outside one-third unless indicated otherwise. 2. On play away, they should take the deep outside one-third unless indicated otherwise. 3. On a drop-back, take the deep outside one-third unless indicated otherwise.

Coaching Points: Play the man when he is in the zone. Be as deep as the deepest receiver. When the ball is thrown, go quickly and play the ball at its highest point.

Safety Man

Alignment: Directly over the center, 9 to 12 yards deep.

Stance: Two-point stance.

Initial Movement and Execution: Watch the required key. On the snap of the ball, the first step should be back.

Responsibility: On any play, the safety must think pass first and run second. The safety only assists on runs when it is definitely a run and not a pass. 1. On play toward him, the safety man should take the deep middle one-third of the field unless indicated otherwise. 2. On play away, he should take the deep middle one-third of the field unless indicated otherwise. 3. On a drop-back, he should take the deep middle one-third of the field unless indicated otherwise.

Coaching Points: The safety man must think pass first and run second. Play as deep as the deepest receiver. Sprint to the ball and go through the receiver to the ball.

As can be seen in this situation, the three-deep does not rotate. There are coverages, however, which employ the 4-4 and rotate the three-deep secondary. If the quarterback rolls out to the defense's right, the right defensive end comes up and contains the run or pass. The right defensive halfback moves to the flat area. The safety revolves over to cover the deep one-third of the field. The away halfback rotates and covers the deep middle third of the field. The defensive end away from the flow retreats and takes the deep one-third of the field.

Another method utilized by a few teams is the rotation of the deep safety as an invert man. If the ball goes straight back, the safety will cover the deep middle as usual. If the ball flows in one direction, the safety will fill as an invert in that direction. The defensive halfback toward the flow remains in his respective one-third of the field. The halfback away from the flow again rotates to the deep middle of the field, and the away defensive end retreats to the deep one-third. The safety has no pass responsibilities, and can be used for end runs or for any play executed off-tackle and up the middle.

Stunting, Blitzing, and Angling of the 4-4

The 4-4 defense can utilize stunting a great deal because of the linebackers and the alignments of the defensive ends. It can be utilized as a surprise element or as a basic defensive weapon. The stunts shown are only a few—a multitude of others could be incorporated by the defense.

Diagram 8-2 shows a stunt between the defensive guard and the linebacker. The guard penetrates the guard-tackle gap or goes head-up to the offensive tackle, and the linebacker fires through the guard-center gap or over the offensive guard. Diagram 8-3 shows the defensive tackle driving down on the offensive tackle while the linebacker loops out over the end. A cross-charge between the defensive tackle and end is shown in Diagram 8-4. The tackle loops to the outside, while the end fires through the tackle-end gap attempting to get penetration. A combination of these stunts can easily be employed.

Looping or slanting of the 4-4 line can be accomplished. The right defensive tackle loops to the outside. The right guard angles in the guard-tackle gap or onto the tackle. The left defensive guard angles into the guard-center gap or onto the center. The left defensive tackle loops into the end-tackle gap or plays straight on the offensive end. The linebackers can either pursue or execute various stunts off the loop of the forward four linemen.

Blitzing can be done against the passing game. Diagrams 8-5 and 8-6 show two that can be used in the 4-4. Numerous others can be employed.

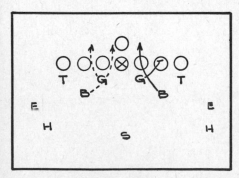

Diagram 8-2

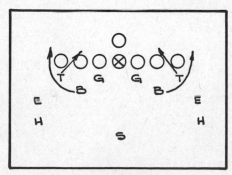

Diagram 8-3

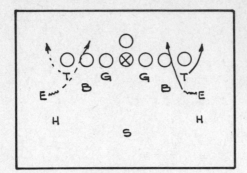

Diagram 8-4

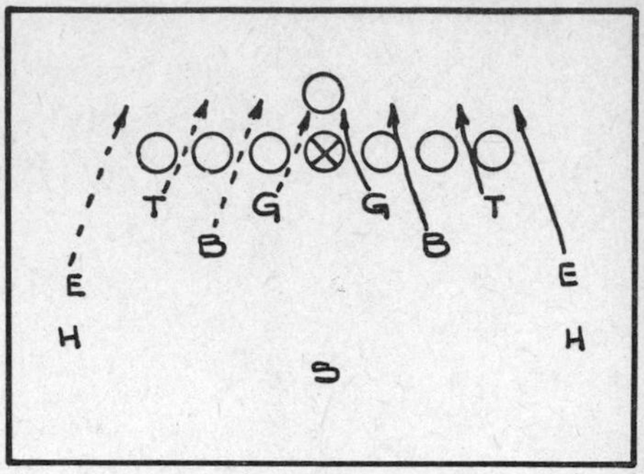

Diagram 8-5

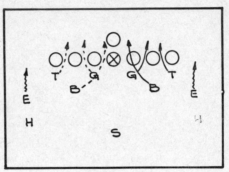

Diagram 8-6

THE SPLIT-4 DEFENSE

by Robbie Franklin

Robbie Franklin
University of Tennessee

If a coach is using a 5-2, 6-1, or any type of read and react defense, the philosophy of the 44 is different from what he is teaching. The success or failure of the 44 depends to a great extent upon how aggressively the defensive players react on the snap of the ball. It is our belief that penetration by a defensive player can cause enough confusion on the line of scrimmage and in the backfield to make the defense effective. Many coaches believe when a team penetrates with reckless abandon, it will develop a weakness that an offensive back can run through for long gains. This may be true when a team penetrates with only two or three men. However, a four- or six-man rush makes our defense effective against the run.

Our basic 44 alignment is unusual, because the four down linemen are lined up in angles (Diagram 8-7).

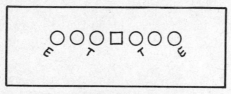

Diagram 8-7

The defensive tackles (Diagram 8-8) line up in a three-point stance at a 15° angle, with their heads on the outside shoulder of the guards. On the snap of the ball, they are responsible for closing the guard-center gap. They may do so by coming across the face of the guard, coming through the guard, or by coming behind the guard. The technique the tackle uses depends upon how tough the guard is to handle. Our reason for using the angle alignment is that it provides good backside penetration and pursuit. The offensive

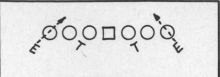

Diagram 8-8   **Diagram 8-9**

guard and tackle do not have a good blocking angle on the defensive tackle, and the angle penetration by both tackles eliminates the inside trap.

The two players in this position must have good size, because they cannot be blocked out by the guards, and, of course, the more speed they have, the better off they will be.

The defensive ends (Diagram 8-9) use the same 45° angle and three-point stance the tackles use, with the exception that they line up 1½ yards outside the last tight lineman on the line of scrimmage. This player will always be a tackle or an end. The ends are responsible for penetration to the ball as quickly as possible. Our ends are not given responsibility for containment, except on a special stunt. Therefore, they are kept aggressive. If they are coming hard enough, our ends should meet any quick-hitting play on their side on the line of scrimmage. The backside end provides good pressure from behind. The only key that the defensive end has is the tight end. If the tight end turns out, the defensive end plays through him to gain penetration. The angle alignment is used with our ends, because we believe it makes them quicker on their penetration. Angle penetration makes them more difficult to block and provides a good, aggressive pass rush. The end must close on the ball, getting as much depth as the ball.

A defensive end must be aggressive and enjoy mixing-it-up on every play. Speed is the most important quality for this position. The defensive end need only be of average size, because 90 percent of the time offensive backs will be blocking on him.

The inside linebackers (Diagram 8-10) use a parallel, two-point stance with their outside foot lined up on the offensive guard's inside foot. They line up about 6 inches behind the back foot of the angle tackle, and must be able to clear the tackle on their scrape. The on-side linebacker is responsible for scraping the tackle-guard gap and gaining penetration as he hits the gap. The linebacker away from flow must drag to the nose of the center, check for a counter, and then pursue. Both linebackers key the quarterback.

Linebackers enjoy playing this defense because they do not have to read several keys before they can react. The inside linebackers are used a great deal for penetration.

The linebackers do not have to be great football players, but they must have the speed and ability to get to the ball. These players will seldom have to take on a blocker one-on-one and make the tackle.

Our outside linebackers, or bandits, as we call them, are the most versatile players on the defensive unit. Their basic alignment (Diagram 8-11) is a low, two-point stance, nose-up on the tight end. The bandits' first responsibility is delaying the release of the

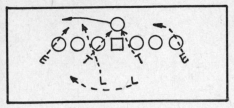
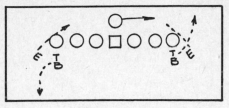

Diagram 8-10   **Diagram 8-11**

tight end. This is a difficult technique to teach because after two or three good licks on the
tight end, the bandits tend to become lazy and merely bump him. The bandits must
understand the importance of their position and take pride in punishing receivers. On the
snap of the ball, the bandit must strike the tight end, then carry out his second
responsibility, which is containment if the ball comes to him, and cover the backside
one-third if the ball goes away. If there is a split end, the bandit will be either nose-up on
him or stacked behind the defensive end, depending on the down and the distance.

The bandit must be a player who can stand on the line of scrimmage and whip a
blocker, run with backs out of the backfield, and make adjustments to the opponent's
offensive formations. Actually, this player is the quarterback of the defense.

With our fronts, a three-deep zone pass coverage, man-for-man, and a combination
of the two are used.

Diagram 8-12 shows the 44 basic alignment and responsibility.

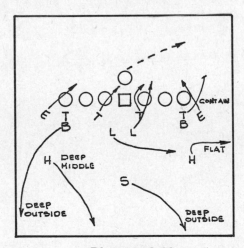

Diagram 8-12

The basic stunts that we use are shown in Diagrams 8-13, 8-14, 8-15, 8-16, and
8-17. In our opinion, they are what make the defense so confusing, especially to
offensive linemen.

This defense is simple to teach and the players enjoy playing it because it is easy to learn. The most important teaching point is to keep them aggressive and hungry to get to the ball-carrier.

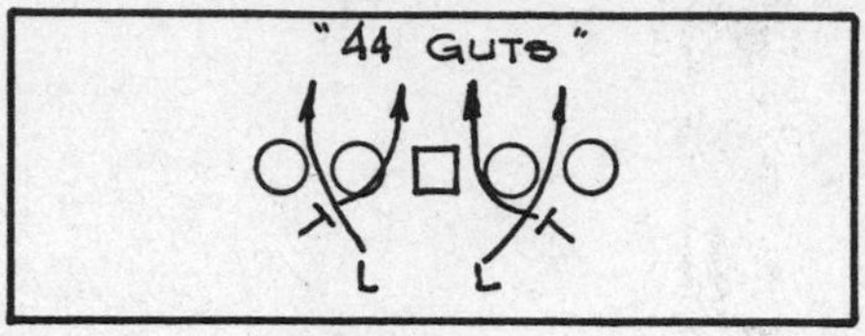

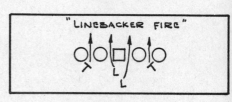

Diagram 8-13

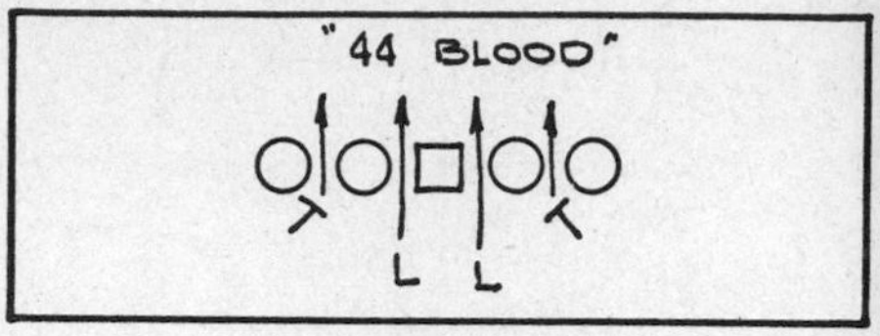

Diagram 8-14

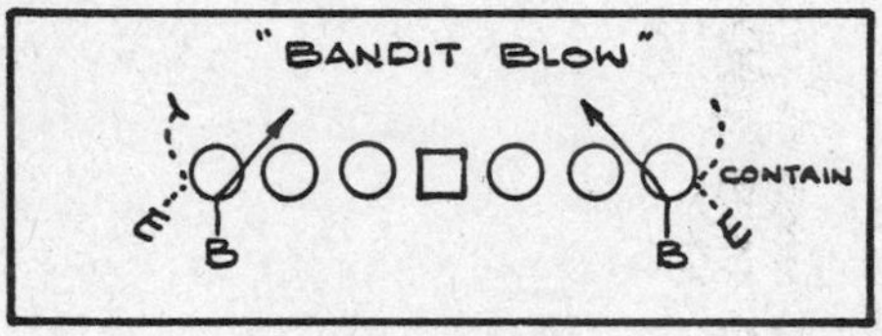

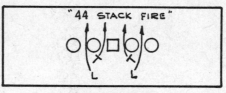

Diagram 8-15

Diagram 8-16

Diagram 8-17

9/ The 4-3 Defense

STUNTING PRO 4-3

by Nick S. Voris

Nick Voris
Clark High School
Hammond, Indiana

When considering the pro-type defense, we decided: 1. It was a fundamentally sound defense. 2. It adjusted easily to flankers, split ends, and spreads. 3. It made good use of better than average linebackers. 4. It offered the advantages of a four-spoke defense.

Diagram 9-1 shows the alignment against a full house backfield.

The guards assume a three-point stance, with the outside foot back, two feet off the ball, and head-up on the offensive guards. On the movement of the hand, they strike a stunning hand shiver to the offensive guard's head, taking a short step with their outside foot at the same time, remaining low and keeping their shoulders and feet parallel to the line of scrimmage. They key the offensive guards and the ball. The guards are responsible for the inside area, and should never be blocked out. They should pursue to both sides of the line and must keep inside leverage.

We instruct the tackles to assume a three-point stance, with their inside foot back,

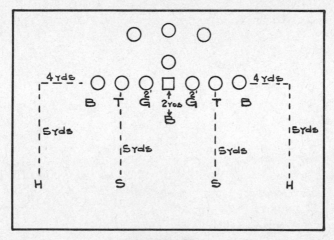

Diagram 9-1

and line up on the outside shoulder of the offensive tackle. On movement of the offensive player's hand, they strike the opposing player with their inside arm, bringing up their inside foot at the same time. They must keep outside position at all times, with feet and shoulders parallel to the line of scrimmage. They key the down hand of the offensive tackles and the ball. The tackles are responsible for the off-tackle area and must force all outside and inside plays. They should never be blocked in by the tackle.

The outside linebackers assume a two-point stance, with their outside foot back, and their inside leg on the outside ear of the offensive end. They key the head of the offensive end, the near back, and the ball. Outside linebackers are responsible for the outside, off-tackle, and hook zones. When the action is towards them, they should keep leverage on the ball and force the play. They take the quarterback on the option. On action away, they should keep leverage on the ball in case of a cutback.

The middle linebacker assumes a ready position, feet parallel, head-on the center, and 2 yards off the ball. He should key the center, quarterback, and fullback. He must never be blocked alone by the center. He is responsible for the inside area, pursuit, outside, and the hook zones. The middle linebacker must think run first, pass second.

The defensive halfbacks are 4 yards outside the end and 5 yards from the ball. They are turned in at a 45° angle so they can view the quarterback. They key the ball through the receivers on their side.

The defensive safeties line up 5 yards from the ball and on the outside shoulder of the offensive tackle, in a square stance. They key the ball through the receivers on their side.

Diagram 9-2 shows the stunt that is used to counter off-tackle or outside plays which are penetrating our defense. On this stunt, the outside linebacker fires to a position 1 yard behind the offensive tackle, and the tackle loops behind the linebacker, assuming the outside coverage.

Two stunts used to stop inside plays and to aid in a pass rush are shown in Diagrams 9-3 and 9-4. The defensive guard charges through the inside shoulder of the offensive guard, and the middle linebacker fires behind the guard and between the offensive guard and tackle. The defensive guard attacks the inside shoulder of the offensive guard. The defensive tackle goes through the outside shoulder of the tackle, and the outside linebacker will fire behind the defensive tackle and between the offensive guard and tackle to the ball.

Diagram 9-5 shows how we stunt to put an end to the opponent's trap and center plays. The guards slant hard to the heels of the center, giving the area outside the men stunting to the middle linebacker to cover.

Diagram 9-6 shows one more way that we pass rush the opponents. The guard attacks the outside shoulder of the offensive tackle, and after making contact, rushes the passer. Our defensive tackle loops around our guard and rushes the passer between the offensive center and guard.

We are sure that the information contained in this article and some individual imagination on the part of the coach could mean success for the team.

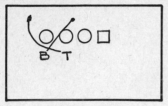

Diagram 9-2

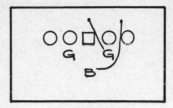

Diagram 9-3

Diagram 9-4

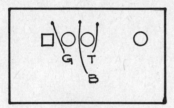

Diagram 9-5

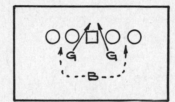

Diagram 9-6

THE READING FRONT FOUR

by Ron Marciniak

Ron Marciniak
University of Miami

We feel defensive line play must dictate to the opposing team's offense and that it can change the complexion of a football game. In offensive line play, the lineman blocks a defensive alignment or stunt. The offensive lineman adjusts his techniques according to the defensive maneuver. Therefore, we believe the defensive lineman must react to the offensive blocker's key or movement. We term this technique *reading*. The defensive line cannot be in a *reading* assignment all the time; they must also be in an all-out *Go* defensive technique some of the time. This change of pace will aid the defensive linemen and make the offensive line hesitant and unsure. But keep in mind the *reading* defense is aggressive after the *read* or *key*.

First, we will explain the alignment, stance, key, technique, and responsibility for each of the two defensive line positions. Then we will cover the *reading* technique and principles. The 43 defense is shown in Diagram 9-7.

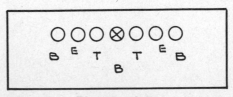

Diagram 9-7

Defensive Inside Tackle Play

1. *Alignment:* Head-up on a normal split of 2 feet, but relative distance from the

tackle versus big offensive splits. 2 to 3 feet off the ball and adjustable to down and distance.

2. *Stance:* Three-point stance.

3. *Key:* The defensive tackle should key the offensive guard in front of him first, and then the tackle on his side.

4. *Technique: Read technique* in a *read* defense, deliver a shoulder forearm blow opposite the guard's head key, keeping the arm and leg toward the play, free. *Go technique* in an aggressive call, be up on the ball and deliver a vicious inside shoulder/forearm blow into the guard.

5. *Responsibility: Read*—The man over and to either side. *Go*—The man over and outside, then inside. Pursue to the ball. Pass rush. Draw.

Defensive End Play

1. *Alignment:* Inside foot to outside foot of the offensive tackle. On the ball or 12 inches off the line of scrimmage, but adjustable.

2. *Stance:* Three-point stance.

3. *Key:* The defensive end should key the offensive tackle in front of him first, then the end on his side.

4. *Technique: Read technique* in a *read* defense—Deliver a shoulder/forearm blow opposite the tackle's head key, keeping the arm and leg toward the play free. *Go technique*—An aggressive call. Be up on the ball and deliver a vicious inside shoulder/forearm blow into the tackle.

5. *Responsibility: Read*—The man over and outside (work against the inside-out block of the tackle). *Go*—Over the defensive end and outside. Pursue. Backside chase and trail the ball for a cutback. Rush the passer. Contain the dropback pass. Draw.

Spring and pre-season practice are the times when repeated *reading* drills and fundamentals must be covered, scrimmaged, and accomplished. After the five basics of this defense have been established, then recognition of offensive blocking patterns should be taught. We believe in teaching the whole thing first and then breaking it down in later or subsequent practices. Bear in mind that teaching linemen to *read* on defense demands patience and time. The defensive lineman must know *how* he will be blocked and *who* will be blocking him. In his study and mastery of offensive blocking patterns, he will come to see the whole picture according to what is happening to him at his area.

The defensive lineman must see the man in front of him first. Simple as this may sound, the technique must be worked on. Be sure the linemen are in a stance that affords them good vision, balance, and movement. The two down tackles have the advantage of being able to see the movement of the ball as well as the man on their nose. The defensive end does not have this advantage of seeing the ball most of the time. Linemen should realize that the offensive man's down hand and head, while he is in his offensive stance, are the first objects to move. The defensive lineman in this type of defense must *read* first and then react to the *key*. We do not believe a defensive lineman can *key* on the move without guessing some of the time. Guessing will place him in a position to be blocked and break down the overall defensive scheme.

Keep in mind that there is a similarity in the initial key movement of the offensive lineman for different blocking patterns. Therefore, the tackle must concentrate on his offensive guard, but be conscious of the guard-tackle *key*, just as the defensive end must concentrate initially on his offensive tackle, but be conscious of the tackle-end *key*. The object of this type of line play is to recognize the block by the patterns of movement and defeat it as quickly as possible in the proper direction with correct techniques. Stress quickness of the feet and body position. We must remember that the players' big hearts, their desire, and second effort cause the eventual outcome of successful line play.

As the defensive lineman sees movement, he *reads* the blocker's headgear. The defensive man must always strive to neutralize the blocker and gain leverage. In accomplishing this objective, he must maneuver to keep his outside arm and leg toward the playside or headgear direction free. This means he is delivering a shoulder blow and a step through the headgear with the opposite or farthest shoulder arm pad. Taking away leverage is the initial goal of the defensive lineman. As he carries out these techniques, the defensive lineman must strive to keep his knees bent. He should get his shoulder pads under the blocker's shoulder pads. It is necessary for him to keep his head up, knees bent, maintain a wide base, and fight to keep his feet parallel to the line of scrimmage. We tell our linemen to *fight to keep the hips square*. Quick movements of the feet with a good base are essential in destroying the blocker and/or fighting to get free to move into the proper lane of pursuit. In today's game, the cutback play and reverse are more prominent on offense. Therefore, it is important that the front four do not overread or overpursue. We tell our linemen to check each hole as they slide along the line of scrimmage in pursuit.

Now, should the man opposite a defensive lineman go away from him, then the defensive man can expect to be blocked by another man using another offensive technique. These movements and techniques are called blocking patterns.

The inside tackle is confronted with different blocking patterns from those encountered by the defensive end. After the five basics are covered for each position, then we teach the mastery of blocking patterns for each particular area or position in the defensive line. Blocking patterns must be mastered on paper, in the mind, and on the field. Defensive linemen should be able to diagram all blocking patterns pertinent to their position. They should then see opponents' films to study particular blocking patterns. Finally, and most important, they should work against these patterns for recognition, both dummy and live on the practice field.

Diagram 9-8 shows the blocking patterns that are most common or basic to the inside tackle.

The blocking patterns (Diagrams 9-9 to 9-16) are shown from one side only. Of course, the same patterns would be mirrored from the other side.

Diagram 9-17 shows blocking patterns that are most common or basic to the defensive end.

Again (Diagrams 9-18 to 9-24) we are showing the patterns from one side, and, as in the case of the tackles, the patterns would be mirrored to the other side.

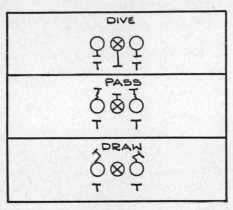

Diagram 9-8

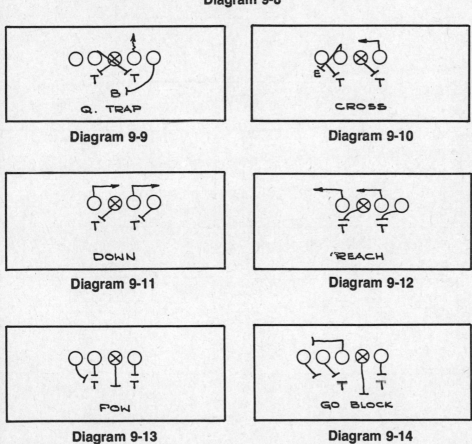

Diagram 9-9   **Diagram 9-10**

Diagram 9-11   **Diagram 9-12**

Diagram 9-13   **Diagram 9-14**

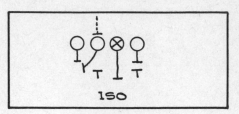

Diagram 9-15

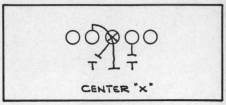

Diagram 9-16

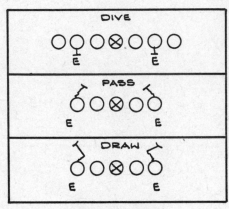

Diagram 9-17

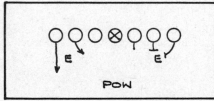

Diagram 9-18

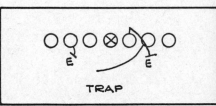

Diagram 9-19

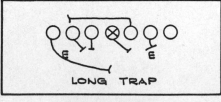

Diagram 9-20

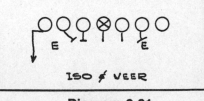

Diagram 9-21

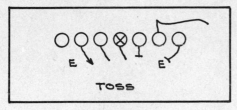

Diagram 9-22

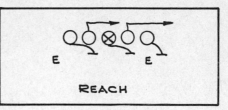

Diagram 9-23

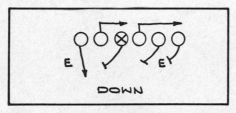

Diagram 9-24

10 / Goal Line Defense

THE 6-5 GOAL LINE DEFENSE

by Drew Tallman

Drew Tallman
Dartmouth College

The 6-5 goal line defense has an even-man line with six defensive linemen and one linebacker. The four-deep secondary usually adjusts close to the line of scrimmage, giving the appearance of a 6-5 defense. Diagram 10-1 shows the alignments of the 6-5 goal line defense.

The defense is a nine-man front, but could be considered an eleven-man front, due to the position of the defensive halfbacks. In many instances, the defensive halfbacks and cornerbacks could be replaced by four defensive linebackers. The defensive guards could be removed, with the two tackles also being positioned over the middle area. While the 6-5 is mainly utilized on the goal line, the defense can be employed any place on the field. This defense is excellent on third and one, fourth and a foot, or any other short yardage situation. The 6-5 defense is excellent when the opponent's offense is backed up on the 1-, 2-, 5-, or even the 15-yard line. Many coaches employ the 6-5 as their

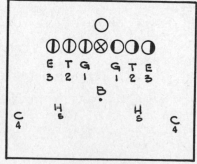

Diagram 10-1

basic alignment and do not utilize any other defense. These coaches use it any place on the field and do not have to adjust when a defense is essential on the goal line or in short yardage situations.

Coaches believe that in order to win, the team must win on the goal line or on third or fourth down situations. Therefore, this defense must be played tough. The 6-5 is not a hit and pursue, but is a penetration defense that must stop the offense to no gain or even a loss. Each defensive lineman should charge low and hard to get across the line of scrimmage and make the tackle.

The defensive guards should align on the inside eye or gap position between the offensive center and guard. In a few situations, the defensive No. 1 men will align head-up on the offensive guards if certain slanting or angling maneuvers are being executed. If the offensive guards split more than usual, the defensive guards should adjust closer to the center and drive for penetration across the neutral zone. They must protect against the quarterback sneak and the inside running game, but should keep the middle linebacker free to make tackles wider. Both the defensive tackles and ends can align on the outside shoulder, outside eye, or head-on position on their offensive opponents and drive for penetration across the line. The defensive linemen must be tough and aggressive ball players up front to stop the running game of the offensive team. The middle linebacker must protect the area over the offensive guards and then pursue outside.

Following are the alignments, stances, initial movements and executions, responsibilities, and coaching points for each position in the 6-5 goal line defense.

Defensive Guards (No. 1 Men)

Alignment: Align on the inside eye or the gap between the offensive center and guard, approximately 6 to 12 inches off the ball. A defensive guard must maintain position with himself and the other defensive guard. He can position on the outside shoulder of the offensive center if inches are needed for a touchdown.

Stance: A low, four-point stance with the inside foot forward should be used. The elbows and knees can be bent from this position to explode across the line of scrimmage.

Initial Movement and Execution: On the snap of the ball, the defensive guards should spring off the forward inside foot, dropping the outside shoulder and going for penetration in the center-guard gap. They should attempt to get their heads and shoulders across the line of scrimmage. While going for penetration, the defensive guards go for the center's near hip. The charge should be hard and low (submarine movement).

Responsibilities: 1. Play Toward—The center-guard gap. Protect against the sneak and any play in that area. Keep the offensive center off the middle linebacker. 2. Play Away—Pursue to the ball. 3. Dropback—Rush the passer hard from the inside. The defensive guards are responsible for the draw play.

Coaching Points: The defensive guard should aim for a spot approximately 1 yard across the line of scrimmage. On penetration, he should remain low, then bring his head and shoulders up and look for the ball. Keep the shoulders square to the line of scrimmage.

Defensive Tackles (No. 2 Men)

Alignment: Align either on the outside shoulder, outside eye, or head-up position on the offensive tackle. If the split of the offensive tackle is wider than usual, the defensive tackle can position on the inside shoulder of the offensive tackle or in the guard-tackle gap. They should be approximately 6 to 12 inches off the line of scrimmage.

Stance: A low, four-point stance with the inside leg forward should be used. The defensive tackles should be in a good explosive position.

Initial Movement and Execution: Spring off the inside foot and drive through the offensive tackle, going for approximately a 1-yard depth into the backfield. Keep the outside arm free.

Responsibilities: 1. Play Toward—Responsible for the off-tackle area and the dive play. Force the dive man to the inside. A defensive tackle should not be blocked in by the offensive tackle. 2. Play Away—Pursue to the ball. 3. Dropback—Rush the passer from the inside.

Coaching Points: If the defensive tackle is expecting a trap, he should stay low and meet the trapper with his inside shoulder and forearm. On penetration, he should execute a low, hard submarine charge. He should deliver a hard blow into the offensive tackle.

Defensive Ends (No. 3 Men)

Alignment: Align on the outside shoulder, outside eye, or head-up position on the offensive end. If the end takes an abnormal split, the defensive end can play either on the inside shoulder or align in the tackle-end gap.

Stance: A two-, three-, or four-point stance can be employed. If penetration is desired, usually the stance will be four-point when a defensive end is aligned head-up on the end, or two-point if he is positioned on the outside shoulder.

Initial Movement and Execution: On the snap of the ball, drive through the offensive end to approximately a 1-yard depth. If the defensive end is on the offensive end's outside shoulder, he should drive through the offensive end's outside hip.

Responsibilities: 1. Play Toward—Do not let the end release for a pass. Protect the offensive end area. The defensive end is the contain man. He should not be driven in or hooked by the offensive end. He should contain on roll-out passes. On the option play, he should take the quarterback. 2. Play Away—Chase the ball-carrier, looking for the reverse, bootleg, etc. 3. Dropback—Rush the passer from the outside-in. Do not let the passer get outside.

Coaching Points: Drive tough through the offensive end. Go to the ball aggressively. Jam the offensive end hard.

Defensive Middle Linebacker (0 Man)

Alignment: Line up 1 to 2 yards off the line of scrimmage. Be at least as deep as the heels of the defensive guards. Down, distance, and field position will determine the alignment.

Stance: An upright, two-point stance should be used. The defensive middle linebacker should be low with his head up.

Initial Movement and Execution: On the snap of the ball, he should look for the sneak. He may key the quarterback or another back. On flow, step toward the required areas of protection from offensive tackle to tackle.

Responsibilities: 1. Play Toward—The quarterback sneak or anything over the middle area. 2. Play Away—The primary responsibilities are the areas over and outside the offensive guards to the offensive tackles. If the play goes to the outside, the linebacker should pursue the ball-carrier from the inside-out. If there is an action pass, he should go to the on-side hook zone. 3. Dropback—Cover the middle one-fifth of the field.

Coaching Points: Look for the dive play coming inside the offensive tackle. Step up and meet the ball-carrier, staying low. Play the quarterback sneak aggressively.

Diagram 10-2 shows the coverage of the defensive guard, tackle, end, and middle linebacker. The defensive linemen should come across hard, while the middle linebacker protects the guard-tackle gap and then pursues wide to the outside. Many times the defensive guards charge into the knees or groin of the offensive center, as shown in Diagram 10-3. This is usually necessary when inches are needed for the touchdown or first down and the defense wants to stop the quarterback sneak.

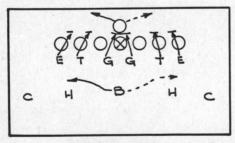

Diagram 10-2

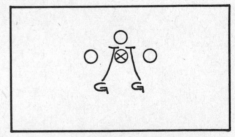

Diagram 10-3

Defensive Cornerbacks or Outside Linebackers (No. 4 Men)

Alignment: Line up approximately 2 yards wide and 2 yards off the line of scrimmage.

Stance: Upright, two-point stance with the inside foot forward.

Initial Movement and Execution: Key the ball, the offensive back or end.

Responsibilities: 1. Play Toward—Contain play as executed in regular cornerback play. 2. Play Away—Rotate to the deep outside. 3. Dropback—Cover the deep outside one-fifth of the field. These players can rotate.

Coaching Points: The defensive cornerbacks or outside linebackers must force everything to the inside. They should play tough and aggressive.

Defensive Halfbacks or Inside Linebackers (No. 5 Men)

Alignment: Line up on the inside shoulder of the offensive end, approximately 2 yards off the line of scrimmage. This will be determined by the down and distance, field position, etc.

Stance: An upright, two-point stance with the inside foot forward should be used.

Initial Movement and Execution: They can key the ball, the nearside halfback, etc.

Responsibilities: 1. Play Toward—Protect the off-tackle area first. Support quickly. Contain the quarterback on the option and take the quarterback on the outside belly play. If play goes outside, go to the flat and assist in containment. 2. Play Away—Pursue to the ball. Check for counters, reverses, and bootlegs. 3. Dropback—Go to the required one-fifth of the field. These players can rotate.

Coaching Points: The defensive halfback or linebacker must stay with shoulders square when supporting the off-tackle hole.

The five defensive linebackers or secondary can employ zone, rotational zone, invert zone, man-for-man coverage, etc. Diagram 10-4 shows one of the defensive coverages versus the back-up pass, and Diagram 10-5 shows a rotational coverage when the ball flows to the right. In many instances, man-for-man coverage is employed on the goal line because passes are quick and short. Probably more teams use man-for-man than zone coverage. With man-for-man, the defensive man must play the offensive receiver tight, if any type of defensive play is going to be made. Diagram 10-6 shows man-for-man coverage on the goal line.

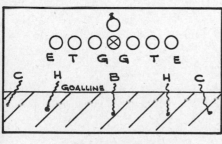

Diagram 10-4

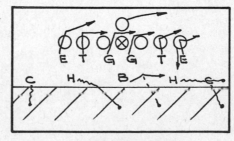

Diagram 10-5

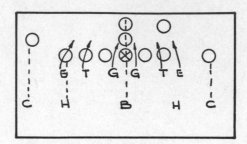

Diagram 10-6

Adjustments to Offensive Formations

Many coaches agree that in order for a goal line defense to be successful, the defense must be able to cover any offensive formation with simplicity and flexibility. With the 6-5 goal line, the adjustments are usually made with the five linebackers or the middle linebacker and the defensive secondary. The defensive line will not shift unless unusual situations occur.

If the offensive line takes wider than usual splits, the defensive guards are aligned in the center-guard gaps, while the defensive tackles should station on the offensive tackle's inside shoulder or in the gap between the offensive guard and the tackle. The defensive ends should align on the inside shoulder of the offensive end or in the tackle-end gap, while the cornerbacks or outside linebackers should position themselves on the outside shoulder of the offensive end. This defensive alignment then becomes a gap-8 with either three linebackers or a middle linebacker and two defensive halfbacks.

If the offense splits an end, the outside linebacker or corner man goes out and usually plays man-for-man defensive coverage. The defensive end usually plays tight or stacks behind the defensive tackle. However, he could position in a double-up or possible walkaway alignment.

Versus a wingback alignment directly outside the offensive end, the defensive alignment can remain the same. The defensive end may position on the outside eye of the offensive end if he is not stationed there in the first alignment. The defensive end could maneuver out, position in the end-wing gap, and shoot that seam for penetration. It is possible for the inside linebacker or defensive halfback to adjust outside the position head-up on the wingback while remaining with his same responsibilities. The away inside linebacker could also tandem directly behind the defensive tackle. Another method is for the middle linebacker to tandem behind either the defensive guard or the defensive tackle nearest the wingback. While not all of these methods can be utilized at one time, Diagram 10-7 shows the defensive positions mentioned. The assignments and responsibilities of these players remain relatively the same.

Against a flanker formation, the defensive corner will cover the flanker similar to that of a split end adjustment, and align approximately 3 to 5 yards in depth, executing man-for-man coverage. The remaining defensive players play their positions the same, or the middle linebacker and the two defensive halfbacks could make similar adjustments as is done versus the wingback formation.

Against a slot formation, the defensive end plays the slot as if he were an end. The cornerman covers the split end, while the defensive halfback adjusts over the slot and keys him man-for-man. The defensive middle linebacker and the away defensive halfback adjust in the manner described for the wingback. A wide slot formation is shown in Diagram 10-8, and indicates one of the methods in which it can be covered. If a zone was being used, the defensive inside halfback would not have to cover the wide slot man-for-man, but would align in his original position on the field in the zone coverage.

If the offense puts a man in motion, the defense could either play zone or execute man-for-man, defensive coverage. Diagram 10-9 shows the tailback going in motion toward the wingback side with the defensive linebackers playing man-for-man coverage. In this situation, the defensive corner man maneuvers out and covers the wide motion man. The inside halfback or linebacker adjusts out to take the place of the corner, and covers the wing, man-for-man. The middle linebacker shuffles over and takes the responsibility of the inside halfback, while the away inside linebacker, or halfback, plays the middle linebacker's position. A simpler method is the shifting of only one linebacker (Diagram 10-10).

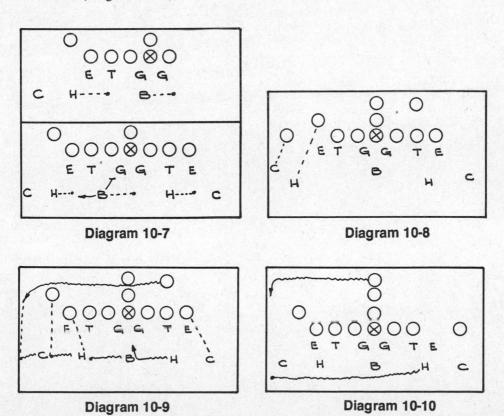

Diagram 10-7

Diagram 10-8

Diagram 10-9

Diagram 10-10

BASICS OF THE 6-5 DEFENSE

by A. James Krayeske, Jr.

A. James Krayeske
Wilby High School
Waterbury, Connecticut

The 6-5 goal line defense (Diagram 10-11), like any other defense in our repertoire, includes the nose man, the slant and loop tackles, and the anchor and boom ends as the front five, the two linebackers, the Indian, better known as the monster man, and the three-deep secondary. First of all, the 6-5 goal line defense must be sold to the defensive unit, and, secondly, it must be approached with pride as a motivating factor. This defense must be played with a great deal of what we call authority, confidence, and the enthusiastic, determined conviction that no one will cross our goal line. This is the area of the field where the word *pride* has played so large a part in our defensive plan.

When an opponent gets inside the 10-yard line, this area is called our pride zone. This is the point where the team should be mentally and physically prepared to meet the challenge because of the pride and mental attitude instilled in them by the coaches. They

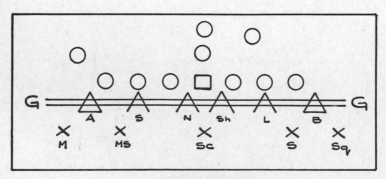

Diagram 10-11

186

must believe that the 6-5 goal line defense is the only thing that can be used to stop the on-rushing enemy. This idea must be sold to the players as a team and as individuals on a personal basis or this defense will not accomplish its basic objectives.

In coaching the front six with our regular five-man front plus the shuffle linebacker, the most important factor is penetration. The front six must form a new line of scrimmage, grasp the advantage from the offense, attack on the snap of the ball, and get 1 yard into the backfield. To assist in getting penetration into the opponent's backfield, the goal line stances of the linemen are adjusted. The linemen should bend their elbows so their heads and shoulders are lowered to a point where the chin is approximately 7 to 9 inches off the ground.

This fundamental technique will assist a defensive player in exploding up and under the offensive blocker, breaking his charge, and when he brings up his hands and feet quickly from under him, he has a good football position, with his feet under, knees slightly flexed, butt down, and shoulders parallel to the line of scrimmage. With his head up, he should search for the ball and pursue it until he has completely annihilated the ball-carrier. We want to make our players believe that they cannot be scored upon when the opponents have the ball inside our 5-yard line or in the pride zone.

The basic responsibilities of the 6-5 goal line defense are as follows:

1. *Guards:* Their alignment varies from the inside eye of the guard to the gap. They should charge and entertain three men, the guards and the captain. They should not allow the center or the guard to block the middle linebacker.

2. *Tackles:* Line up on the outside, with the shoulder facing in slightly. Charge with the inside shoulder on the offensive tackle's outside knee and drive to the backfield. Drive on an inward angle, not straight across. If the offensive tackle oversplits, then the defensive tackle may go for the inside with his outside shoulder.

3. *Ends:* Line up the inside eye on the offensive end's outside eye. Use tough Oklahoma technique and eliminate the off-tackle play. They must never be blocked out or hooked. No one should run between the defensive end and the tackle. If the pass is toward him, the defensive end should hit the offensive end and contain. Back up the pass, outside rush, flow away, and trail from behind. On a belly option, take the fullback.

4. *Middle Linebacker:* He must be the best tackler, and line up facing the center. His depth varies. He should not be caught up between the guards. Read the quarterback. Fill the dive hole on the side of flow. On an action pass, take the strong hook zone. On a drop-back pass, he has the middle one-fifth of the field.

5. *Cornerbacks:* They should line up 2 to 3 yards wide. Their depth varies. They should play cautiously. Versus a run, the cornerback is the outside contain man. Nothing should ever get around him. On an action pass toward him, he has the deep outside zone. On flow away, he should revolve slowly and watch the ends. On a dropback pass, he has the outside one-fifth zone.

6. *Safeties:* Straddle the end's inside leg. Key the football. On flow coming, take

the first man outside the end. The safety has inside-out leverage on the run. On flow away, watch the dive hole for the counter and pursue. Take the quarterback on the belly. On an action pass toward him, the safety should go to the flat zone. On an action pass away, take the middle. On a dropback pass, the safety has one-fifth of the field.

7. *Coaching Points:* The cornerbacks, safeties, and the middle linebacker should adjust to different sets or motion. On a dropback pass, they should never go deeper than 5 yards and then zone.

A good coaching point to remember, especially for the cornerbacks, middle linebackers, and safeties, is the adjustment to different sets or motion. Diagrams 10-12 and 10-13 show reactions to the left and right on running plays. Diagrams 10-14 through 10-16 indicate pass coverage on a straight dropback pass and a roll-out or sprint-out action.

On a dropback pass, the five secondary men play a zone of one-fifth of the field each (Diagram 10-17). On an action pass, they play man-for-man. A coaching point would be emphasizing the distance to be covered by the defender in a goal line defense. Remember, the end zone is only 10 yards deep.

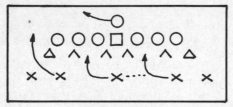

Diagram 10-12

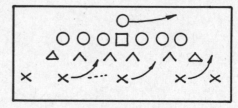

Diagram 10-13

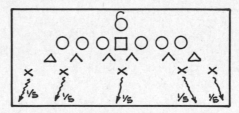

Diagram 10-14

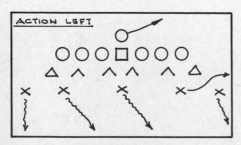

Diagram 10-15

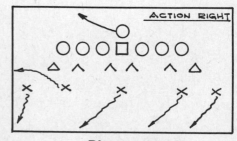

Diagram 10-16

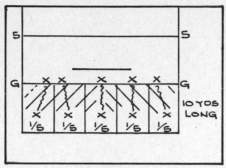

Diagram 10-17

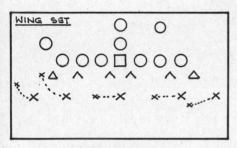

Diagram 10-18

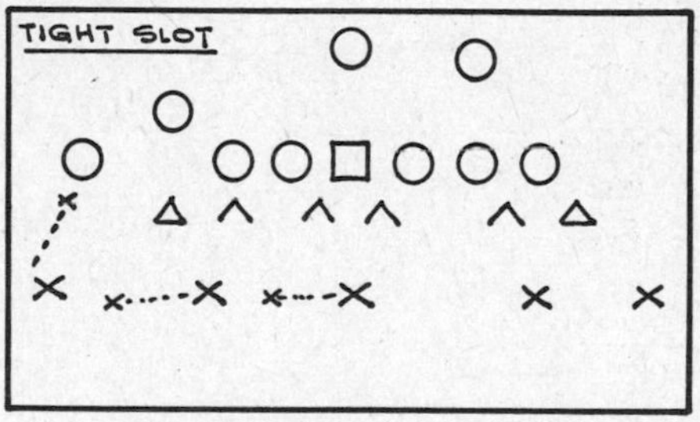

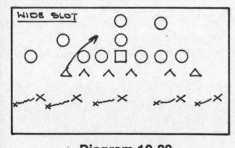

Diagram 10-20

Diagram 10-19

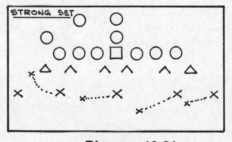

Diagram 10-21

Diagrams 10-18 through 10-21 show the basic adjustments of the 6-5 goal line defense. These seem to be the most widely used formations in this area of the field.

The adjustment for a wing set would be to move the safety men (monster safety and safety) on the side of the wing man from normal alignment to an outside shoulder position of the wing man in a two-point stance on the line of scrimmage. The middle linebacker and the other safety men should move over about half a man.

The corner man (monster) on the side of the slot should move to an outside shoulder position on the end, and play at his normal depth. The anchor end should move on the slot if he is tight, and if he is wide (Diagram 10-20), he should move inside, blow the gap, and get to the ball. The safety (monster safety and safety) on the side of the slot should stack in back of the end on a tight slot, and play the slot himself if he is wide. The other remaining defensive secondary men should move over about half a man on a tight slot, and a full man on a wide slot.

On the strong set, the monster safety man on the strong side should play the wing man on his outside shoulder on the line of scrimmage. The scrape linebacker should move over into the area between the offensive tackle and the guard, and have his outside leg split the crotch of the defensive tackle. The regular safety man should move into an area between the offensive guard and the tackle away from the strength (Diagram 10-21).

The monster man should go and keep to the outside of the widest receiver until he can cover him into the sideline by moving to the inside. Position dictates this move in most cases. If the monster is on the short side, he should play the wide man to his inside. If he is on the wide side, he should play the wide man to his outside.

The monster safety should move outside of our defensive end (Diagram 10-22).

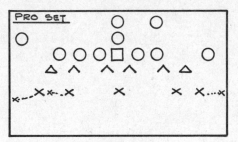

Diagram 10-22

An unbalanced line would also be played with a similar adjustment by moving everyone to cover (Diagram 10-23).

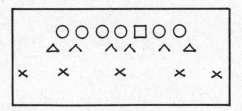

Diagram 10-23

Diagrams 10-24 through 10-29 show some of the variations that we have used in the 6-5 goal line defense on different occasions. These variations are a necessary part of the defense because they provide the same alignment but different looks and games to offset the offensive patterns of the opponents.

Alignment/Responsibility: Ends: Gap to the inside and blow in. Tackles: Gap the inside and blow in. Safety: Adjusts by moving to the outside shoulder of the end. All Other Players: Play the same as in the 6-5 regular.

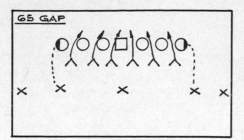

Diagram 10-24

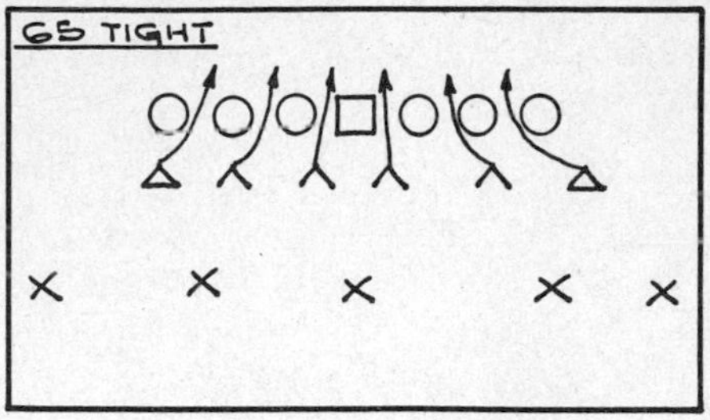

Diagram 10-25

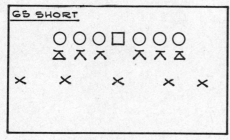

Diagram 10-26

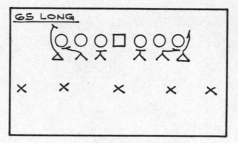

Diagram 10-27

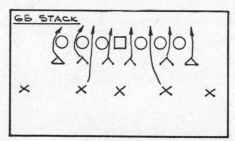

Diagram 10-28

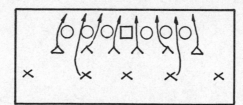

Diagram 10-29

Alignment/Responsibility: Ends: Gap the inside and blow in. Line up the head and charge through the inside gap. Tackles: Gap to the inside and blow in. Line up the head and charge through the inside gap. All Other Players: Play the same as in the 6-5 regular.

Alignment/Responsibility: Ends: Line up head-on their man and use a control charge. Tackles: Line up head-on their man and use a control charge. Guards: Line up head-on their man and use a control charge. All Other Players: Play the same as in the 6-5 regular defense.

Alignment/Responsibility: Ends: Line up in a loose Oklahoma technique. Tackles: Loop to the head of the offensive end and control him. Do not let him out. Guards: Play the same as they would in the 6-5 short. Secondary: Play the 6-5 regular but looser.

Diagrams 10-28 and 10-29 show two ways of playing the 6-5 stack.

Alignment/Responsibility: Ends: Loosen slightly and blow straight into the backfield. Tear things up. Tackles: Loop to the outside gap. They have off-tackle responsibility. Safeties: Cheat in until they are almost stacked behind the tackle. Shoot the dive hole on the snap of the ball and get into the back hook. All Other Players: Play the same as in the 6-5 regular defense.

The 6-5 goal line defense must meet the basic needs of a coach's philosophy and his personnel, and he must be able to sell this defense to the players.

Part III
THE KICKING GAME

11 / Kick-Offs and Extra Points

THE CONVENTIONAL KICK

by George Allen and Don Weiskopf

George Allen
Los Angeles Rams

Don Weiskopf
Sports Editor

No play in football wins or loses as much yardage as the kicking game. This is the reason we work every day on kicking, and include such fundamentals as protecting, covering, and returning, as well as the actual kick itself.

According to statistics, the kicking game accounts for over 60 percent of the lost yardage and 25 percent of the scoring in a football game, which shows how important kicking is. Frankly, we do not think a team can win a championship without a sound kicking game. A problem we have in professional football is that many players do not take a deep interest in kicking organization and practice.

In our opinion, we can win two games each year on our kicking game, and those two might win us a championship. Therefore, we work on it every day, all through the training camp and throughout the season. Next to passing, if a team has a defense and a kicking game, it is going to win a number of football games because the kicking game can be used as an offense.

Place Kicking

Field goal or extra point kicking demands a team effort. A successful place kick depends not only on the kicker and the holder, but also on the center and blockers working together. In order to be an outstanding place kicker, an individual must have good leg power. He should also be well coordinated because kicking requires good timing and coordination.

We break down the place kick into a four-part machine:

1. The center must get the ball to the holder low and over the spot without wasting time.

2. The holder must get the ball on the spot, and if he can put the laces in front, it

makes for an easier kick. However, if he cannot, he should get the ball on the spot so the kicker can kick through it.

3. Of course, the kicking team must have blocking first in order to make the four-part machine work.

4. Last, but not the least important, the kicker must kick the ball through the uprights.

In place kicking, a square-toed shoe is more effective than the normal round-toed shoe that is used in punting.

A kicker should try to kick extra points and 40-yard field goals the same way. He should try to kick straight and let the distance take care of itself. The worst thing a place kicker can do is try and overpower the ball. Usually a kicker will try to kick too hard on long field goals. It is still a natural swing and follow-through, whether 30 yards or 50 yards. Every kick should be executed the same way, with the same rhythm. If he hits it right, the distance will take care of itself. The important thing is to hit it straight.

All the best kickers are talented. When a kicker goes sour, it is usually because he has lost his confidence and concentration. When this occurs, everything is lost, especially timing and rhythm, which are musts.

Holding the Ball. The holder and the center are important in the execution of a successful field goal. The snap must be perfect, the holder must get the ball down, and he must have the laces turned toward the goal posts. If they are on the side, the ball will go to the side the laces are on.

Many holders like to kneel and place their left knee approximately 1 foot from the kicking tee and to the right side. They may extend their right leg forward, bending it at the knee, to allow the right foot to be flat on the ground. Then they are able to move up, down, or to the side if the snap is poor. His hands, which actually reach for the ball, form a good target for the center. His eyes are fixed on the ball.

After catching the ball, the holder focuses his eyes on the spot where he wants to place it. The tip of the ball toward the center should be placed on the tee. The ball is set in an erect position and held on the proper spot with one finger. Then the kicker boots the ball from under the finger.

The Approach. Just before the holder receives the ball, the kicker makes his initial step with the kicking foot. The second step is a lunging power step, which comes to a point about 6 inches behind the ball and straight ahead.

Contact. With the knee flexed, the kicker finishes with a snap of the lower leg. Immediately after contact, his knee joint is locked and his toe is pulled up.

Follow-Through. After making the kick, the kicker must continue to keep his head down and follow through. The right foot must be brought straight through on a line with the goal posts.

Kicking Off

Essentially, the kick-off is the same kick that is used for the extra point and field goal. The main difference is that the kick-off man has a longer approach to kick the ball. He usually takes a 10-yard run at the ball to get a little more power behind him.

The Run. The kicker's first step should be with the left foot. Using a 2-inch tee from which to kick off, he paces off the exact approach distance in strides. The last two or three steps prior to contact are a little longer so he can put more power into the kick.

Approach. The kicker must start from the same spot each time and learn to approach in a straight line. He increases his run to three-quarters speed up to the actual kicking action, when full speed should be started.

Contact. The kicking foot should move in an easy, relaxed swing that reaches maximum velocity on contact, with the lower leg snapping forward from the knee. The right ankle and knee should lock just prior to contact.

Follow-Through. Keeping the eyes continually on the ball, the kicking foot should follow through after the ball, never deviating from the line of the kick. Most kickers will land on the kicking foot (right).

Protecting the Kicker

Strong protection is important to the man who is kicking. Even when a kick is not blocked, his effectiveness is hindered if he is hurried.

Field Goal and Extra Point Protection. Team protection used in the field goal and extra point kick is identical. The kicking team will line up in a tight line from end to end. The responsibilities of the linemen are to protect inside. The offensive backs will line up tight behind, and slightly outside of, each end. Although they are primarily concerned with inside protection, they have a basic responsibility to bump any rush man who is going to their outside. The holder lines up 7 to 8 yards behind the center.

Rushing the Kicker

Rushing the kicker is important to the defense. Indeed, a blocked and recovered punt can be a great builder of morale for any football team.

The Place Kick. The eight-man rushing line is generally used in attempting to block the field goal or extra point. As in blocking the punt, overloading and pulling stunts are used.

Kick-Off Defense

The kick-off team must not only have speed, but it must have size in the middle to meet a wedge. The third men in from either sideline have to be speedy since they are the ones who have to force the action.

The two outside men have to be strong and active enough to keep the play to the inside. These outside men must stay on their feet and protect the sidelines.

THE SOCCER STYLE KICK

by Ron Marciniak

Ron Marciniak
University of Miami

The Holder is an integral part of the kicking game. He assumes a stance on his left knee and places his right foot in front. His left forefinger spots the tee for the kicker, and his right fist, which is in front of his jersey numbers, spots the target for the center. He turns to his kicker and says, *Are you ready?* While maintaining this stance, he provides a target for the center and the place-kicker. Then the holder turns to the offensive line and calls, *get set*. On this command the front nine must freeze. Then the holder places both fists in front of his jersey as an added target for the center.

He opens the fingers on both hands wide, and any time after his hands are open, the center is free to snap the ball. The ball is snapped at the holder's numbers. On the way back, he tries to position the ball so that the laces will be placed to the front, away from the point of impact.

The holder concentrates on the ball and places it on the tee in an upright position. Most soccer-style kickers prefer to have the football straight up and down on the tee. Holding the ball with his left index finger, the holder balances it with his right hand then pulls his hand under his crotch. He concentrates on the football throughout the kick and keeps his eye on the spot. The holder's concentration prevents the ball from moving prematurely.

Using the same holder builds confidence in the place-kicker. We try to have a No. 1 holder and a back-up holder. The holder must have good hands, and is usually a quarterback. After the kick is away, the holder covers to his right and the kicker is required to be the safety valve to his left. This is important, especially on field goal attempts.

In order to develop a place-kicker, the perfect place-kick must be broken down into as many fundamentals as possible. Then an attempt should be made to develop these fundamentals to a high degree of perfection. A kicker should try to develop a rhythm. The basic fundamentals are as follows: 1. Tee up. 2. Alignment. 3. Stance. 4. Concentration. 5. Approach. 6. Foot contact. 7. Follow-through.

Tee Up: After he leaves the huddle, the kicker's first duty is to set the tee. He is responsible for setting the tee at 7 yards from the ball. It should not be deeper or shorter than 7 yards. If the tee is not placed at the proper depth, the kicker loses the angle of protection provided by alignment of the front nine players. Align the tee flat, straight, and on the target. Next, the kicker should place his plant or left foot firmly in the direction of the target, alongside the tee, approximately 3 to 6 inches to the left. Then he should step with his right or kicking foot to size up the proper stride for the impact step. The next distance step to the rear is taken with the left or plant foot.

Alignment: The kicker must determine what the line of flight must be in order for the ball to split the uprights. He must also set up his angle of approach. When a right-footed kicker kicks from the right side, he must decrease his alignment angle to the line of the ball. When he kicks from the left side, he must increase his angle to more than 30°. The kicker must compensate his aim for wind conditions and weather, realizing that the wind, particularly a cross-wind, will affect the flight of the ball.

Stance: The kicker's stance should be comfortable, well balanced, and his body should lean forward slightly at the waist. He should assume a relaxed running position. It is necessary for him to be confident and deliberate as he assumes his stance. He should face the ball and stand with his left foot forward of his right foot. The distance of the stance from the ball depends on the length of the kicker's steps. The holder checks with the kicker to see if he is ready.

Concentration: This could easily be considered the No. 1 fundamental in kicking. The kicker should concentrate on his center first, then the holder's hands, and finally the spot on the tee. Concentration should cover kicking through the ball, keeping the eyes on the point of impact, and follow-through.

Approach: If the first body movements of the approach are correct, the balance of the kicking techniques will be easy. The approach for a soccer-style kicker is more difficult than it is for a conventional place-kicker. A soccer-style kicker must be concerned with angles. He should start his first step as the holder places the ball on the tee. As he prepares to take his first step, he should lean forward. The weight of his body should be shifted to his left leg as he steps first with his right foot. As the second step is taken, the kicker's right leg is cocked to kick.

Foot Contact: The point of impact on the ball is made with the middle high instep of the kicker's right foot. His foot meets the lower third of the football. From the snap of the ball by the center, to the impact of the kicker's foot, the ball is away in one second. The maximum time is never more than 1.4 seconds from snap to impact. When working with the kicker, the coach should use a stop watch.

Follow-Through: The terrific acceleration with which the kicker goes into his kick makes a great contribution to the success of the distance and accuracy of the kick. It is important to use the same step and swing each time. The kicking foot should start its swing about a foot or so behind the ball and extend as far beyond the ball as possible. Developing a kicking rhythm is necessary because the style must become mechanical. Without good follow-through with the kicking leg, the ball will fall short of its target. Remember, the follow-through helps keep all the other actions in the kick under control. The kicker should try to be comfortably balanced on his left foot after impact as his right leg swings through to the left of the target.

On kick-offs, the ball is slightly tilted back, but in placements that are held, the ball will be straight up and down. Keep in mind that faster acceleration is necessary in the approach technique for the kick-off in the soccer-style. On the second step, the kicker's entire body is off the ground as he increases his acceleration near the point of impact. The definite plant of the left foot alongside the ball before impact is straight and firm. The kicker's hips are rotated into the ball. His foot and leg are turned to form the wedge of the driver. The point of impact occurs when the inside high instep of the right foot scoops the ball. His eyes are focused on the point of impact. In the follow-through, the kicker's hips are rotated fully to the front, and the kicking zone is extended beyond the tee.

If the kicker is not hitting the ball well on a practice day, he should not continue to kick that day. Continuing to kick may cause him to develop bad habits.

The amount of in-season kicking should be left up to the individual, but he should not tire his leg. It is not unusual to take 50 to 60 kicks a day, three days per week.

During the summer months and off-season, our place-kickers train with a weighted rubber ball.

Being a good place-kicker requires desire and endless practice. Size and weight are not important ingredients in becoming a good place-kicker. The qualities of a great kicker are attitude and personality. Kickers must be able to practice by themselves. The coach should provide enthusiasm for the kicker, but the kicker must set goals for himself. Following these suggested techniques could lead to great results.

12 / The Punt

WINNING WITH THE PUNT

by Dr. Edward J. Storey

Dr. Edward J. Storey
Mamaroneck High School
Mamaroneck, New York

If every kicking situation is controlled, a team's season will be successful. Statistics show that two-thirds of all games are won or lost by a kick. Teams that are successful with their kicking games work at it from a team standpoint as well as individually with the personnel directly involved. There is no substitute for a kicker, punter, or place kicker who is well trained for the job he must perform. This training must be well planned and not consist merely of sending the kicker to the other end of the field to practice on his own without a plan.

An analysis of the game of football shows that it is made up of kicking, offense, and defense. Rarely do we observe football coaches dividing their practice time into the three parts equally.

Center and Kicker Coordination

In our coaching career, we never had a punt blocked. This, we believe, was due to the fact that we had a definite method of handling the ball by the kicker and considerable practice was conducted with the center doing his part to achieve this smooth handling.

The football will rotate one and one-half times per 5 yards when centered by the average center. When we had our kickers stand 10 yards back, it would rotate so that if the center placed the ball laces up for passing, the ball would come to the kicker laces up, ready for placing on the foot.

We had our punters receive the ball from the center with the right hand under it, middle finger on the under seam, and hold it that way. The left hand should be placed on top of the ball in a position that is comfortable for the kicker. As his weight shifts to the right foot on his first step, the ball is moving from a position on his hip. When the balance foot is planted, the ball is placed on the kicking or the right foot. For most kickers, maximum impact can be achieved if the foot strokes the ball about 1½ feet from the ground. Our kickers kicked with a step and a half.

Every day some time should be spent with the center passing the ball to the kickers. Only in this way can this center-to-kicker coordination be developed.

Probably the kicking game of most teams that do poorly can be traced to lack of practice in centering the ball to a kicker. Professional kickers tell us that they have great difficulty because few coaches allow them time with their centers. One kicker told us that there were times when he would not know who would be centering for him at game time. We have all seen kickers who *fiddle* around with the ball when it comes to them and use so much time that a poor kick results or it is blocked.

Punting—Offensive or Defensive?

The punt is a kick in which the ball is dropped from a hand and is kicked before it hits the ground. It may be used for a free kick, from scrimmage, or at almost any time a player has the ball in his hand.

There are two types of punts—the end-over-end and spiral. The spiral kick results when the long axis of the ball is placed *across* the long axis of the foot. The end-over-end results when the long axis of the ball is placed *along* the long axis of the foot.

Actually, there are two types of spirals. There is one that comes off the right foot naturally, which we call a left spiral, because when the ball is laid on the foot, the front point of the ball points to the left. Then there is the spiral that comes off a left foot when the ball is placed on the foot with the front point of the ball pointing to the right. This we call a right spiral. A right-footed kicker can kick this type of spiral with special coaching and practice.

At some time we expect to see an unusual kicker who will develop the ability to kick all three types of kicks—the end-over-end, the left spiral, and the right spiral.

When it is bouncing, the left spiral kick will cut out to the right of the kicker. Conversely, the right spiral will bounce to the left, and the end-over-end will continue its bounce in a direct line with the balance foot, the left, if the kicker kicks on balance. We instructed our punters to use an end-over-end kick to their left. If a right-footed kicker kicks a left spiral to the left, it will bounce back on the field of play.

It seems to us that kicking a ball straight downfield to a highly skilled safety man is scoring suicide. This is what the safety man would like to see happen, and he is prepared. He is not prepared or highly skilled in chasing a bounding ball with the many possible crazy bounces. For offensive reasons, coaches should teach their kickers to kick to the left of a right-handed safety man and make him chase the ball on the ground.

We believe in position, not possession. Many, many times we placed our opponents in a defensive position when our punters put the ball out of bounds inside the 5-yard line. When the opposing kicker in subsequent plays has to kick out from behind the goal line, he is in a tension build-up and the chances are that a poor kick out or a blocked kick will result if the coach has prepared his team for this possibility.

When in position behind their line waiting for the ball, we had our punters assume a stance with the kicking foot in front of the balance foot. Their arms were extended forward with the palms down. The palms down position gives the center a target. We told the center to place the ball under the roof of the kicker's hands. If the hands are palms up, many passes from the center go to the kicker's head. This is an important skill in the handling of the ball from the center to the kicker.

The kicker gains momentum with his steps. Of course, this is linear momentum and it should be used for the impact on the ball. This is accomplished by the lean back when his right leg comes through. His foot is planted and the lean backward helps the right foot get maximum impact under the ball. The push for the kick comes from the planted left foot. This starts in motion the linkage that brings the right leg into kicking position. Of course, the left foot for the right-footed kicker is his balance foot, directional foot, and anchor foot to the ground. When a kicker's left foot leaves the ground, he loses pushing power. He also uses foot pounds of energy that are not used for propelling the ball, merely lifting himself off the ground.

The ball rolls off his foot into the pattern of a perfect spiral. It will go to the height of its trajectory and turn over. When a punt does not turn over, it is generally due to the contact of the toes on the ball. Depressing the toes is necessary for the ball to roll off the foot and start to spiral.

No kicker will ever achieve maximum success until he develops a sensitive kinesthetic sense. This is the feel of the ball on his foot when punting the ball.

To achieve this feeling, we had our punters pass the ball from their foot every day at least 50 times. If at any time during the season they seemed to be going stale, we went back to this fundamental for additional times. We used to have a manager assigned to catch these balls from the kicker and also had him report to us the results. In the routine, the kicker passed ten balls to the manager's belly. Then he passed to the right shoulder, followed by passing to the left shoulder, and repeated. This is an effective way for the kicker to learn to balance the ball on his foot while also achieving balance on his left foot.

When the kickers first attempt to execute this kick, they will slice balls and fall off balance. By continuing practice, they will become quite skilled and will be able to target the ball to hit a hand held in various positions by the receiver.

Teach the kickers to pass the ball off their foot with an easy motion much like the motion of the golfer with his driver. Some young kickers try to kick and pass the ball from their feet as though they were using their foot for a nine iron.

Most kickers do not kick enough. The leg muscles are the largest and the most powerful in the body. Coaches should expect their kickers to kick a minimum of 200 kicks per day, except the day before a game. During the summer and early practice sessions, push for the maximum. The kickers' legs will become fatigued, but they will regain their flexibility with a night's rest. Unfortunately for them, most kickers are given little supervision. If coaches will follow these basic kicking plans, they will succeed where it is necessary. They will win with a kick.

THE QUICK KICK

by Alex Agase

Alex Agase
Formerly, Purdue University

In talking to a number of football coaches, we have learned that the use of the quick kick is controversial. Some coaches feel they would rather not give up the football on a second or third down and thereby give up an opportunity to make a first down.

We have employed the quick kick and have used it quite extensively. Our personal feelings are that it is an instrumental play and important to the outcome of a game. In every game in which we have had success, the quick kick has played a prominent role.

Almost every coach readily admits that field position is an important factor in any football game. Our feeling is that we utilize the quick kick to gain field position advantage. On many occasions we have had the ball inside our 10-yard line, kicked on second or third down, and the opponents took over, with no return, inside their own 25-yard line. Generally speaking, our players will quick kick anywhere from their own goal line to the 30-yard line. Any time they have possession of the ball beyond that area they will not quick kick, but take the full amount of downs in order to make the first down. If a kicking situation arises, then they will punt using the conventional style, because from that area they will still gain a certain amount of field position.

Psychologically, we feel that a well-executed quick kick is beneficial to the kicking team and also serves as a negative effect on the opponent.

Rarely will the players quick kick against the wind. The reason, of course, is obvious in that against the wind the advantage being sought is lost. When our players kick with the wind, the kick is almost assured of a long roll after it hits the ground.

Diagram 12-1 shows the quick kick.

The most important point as far as protection is concerned is that the linemen have to block aggressively at the line of scrimmage and not give ground. If the linemen give

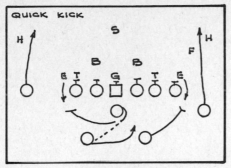

Diagram 12-1

ground, there is a chance the kick may be blocked, because it is being kicked four yards from the original line of scrimmage and is on a low trajectory.

The formation we use is as described with a split end and a flanker who release downfield immediately to cover the kick. The play starts out similar to one of our favorite running plays, the power sweep. The halfback receives the pitch from the quarterback, and takes an open step with his right foot. Then he crosses with his left foot, steps with his right, and steps with his left foot toward the line of scrimmage to kick. He tries to make it appear to be a power sweep and kicks with a sidewind motion. The objective is to kick the ball low and get the long roll.

Two years ago we used the quick kick, with the quick-kicker lined up in the I back position in the I formation. The center would drop his head at the last instant and snap the ball directly to him as he was backing up and then coming forward to kick. We changed to kicking the ball off the power sweep action, and it worked better for the following reasons: 1. The kicker was able to get more distance on the ball by kicking it in this manner than he was when dropping straight back and then stepping forward to kick. 2. The defense did not know when the quick kick was coming, because the center did not drop his head to snap the ball as he did the previous year, which was a last-second tip that the quick kick was coming and the safety was able to get back in reasonable position to field the ball.

The following are the blocking rules and assignments for the quick kick:

The ball should be snapped on the first sound—*go*.
LINE: Minimum Splits.
    Center—Over, gap man, hold.
    Guards—Inside gap, over, hold.
    Inside Tackle—Inside gap, over, hold.
    Outside Tackle—Inside, over, outside.
    Tight End—Inside gap, over, hold.
    Split End—Spot the ball—spring.
    Flanker—Spot the ball—spring.

BACKS:

Right Halfback—Block the man outside the tight end aggressively.

Left Halfback—Quick kick technique.

Quarterback—After the toss to the left halfback, use the power sweep technique. Block the first man outside the left tackle aggressively.

COVERAGE:

Line—Hold blocks until the ball has been kicked, and then release downfield in lanes.

Backs—Hold blocks until the ball has been kicked, and then release to the outside and downfield.

Kicker—Call the direction of the kick and act as the safety.

We believe in this play, and our players also believe in it. When it is executed well, it is an exciting play.

Two other maneuvers are employed off the quick kick. The statue from a fake quick kick is shown in Diagram 12-2. Our flanker back lines up ten yards from the tight end, and on the snap of the ball, races as fast as he can toward and behind the quick kicker. The quick kicker actually goes through the entire motions of the quick kick. Instead of kicking, he hands the ball off to the flanker back, who continues wide around the left end. The quarterback has an important block in this play in that he will block the first man on the line of scrimmage outside of his tackle. The balance of the line blocks their regular rule and then releases downfield in the area where the ball is being run.

Diagram 12-3 shows the forward pass off the quick kick. This play starts out exactly like the statue except the quarterback does not block, but continues downfield, deep and to the sidelines, looking for the pass from the flanker back. No one is blocking the defensive right end, but he usually will take care of himself by trying to get to the quick kick in order to block it. Both of these plays have been used in games and have been effective, but they are only supplemental to the basic play, the quick kick.

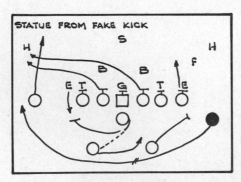

Diagram 12-2

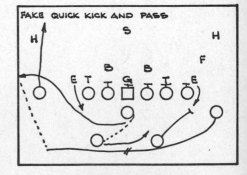

Diagram 12-3

13 / Punt and Kick-Off Returns

DEFENSE AGAINST THE KICKING GAME

by Bobby Dodd

Bobby Dodd
Formerly, Georgia Tech

This is a rather unusual title in these days of offense, but it is certainly one of the most important, and sometimes the most neglected, of all phases of the game. In all close ball games, we think, it will be found that the break or turning point will be centered around the kicking game. How does this come about? A blocked kick, a short kick, a punt return, a mishandled punt, a kick-off return, all center around the kicking game.

First of all, we will take up a defense against the punting game. Fundamentally, there are two ways to defense this phase of the kicking game: 1. Block or put pressure on the kicker. 2. Return the punt. We try to do both at various times. This pressure on the kicker, and returning the punt, does not give the opposition a chance to gamble by overloading the protection of the kicker or the coverage of the kick.

There are two major types of punt protection—the tight and the spread. It is easier, in our opinion, to block a kick from the tight formation, but we try both methods.

Diagram 13-1 shows what we consider our best maneuver, and we have blocked several punts with it. We believe the quickest and easiest way to block a punt is from the strong side. The reason is that the kicker, if he is right-footed, is kicking into the defense rather than away from it.

In the maneuver that is shown in Diagram 13-1, the left end drives hard over the outside shoulder of the outside man in the tandem and forces him to work to the outside. The left end should be aggressive and deliver a good initial blow to the outside man.

The left tackle drives hard into the gap between the No. 2 back and the offensive tackle, forcing the back to help the offensive tackle. This drive by the left tackle is the key to the action.

The left guard lines up in the gap between the tackle and the end, and "bulls" his way into the kicking lane. Usually, the tackle is forced to heap on him to the inside.

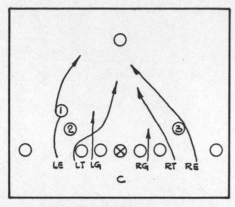

Diagram 13-1   **Diagram 13-2**

The right guard lines up in the gap between the weak tackle and the guard, and "bulls" his way into the backfield.

The right tackle charges the gap between the No. 3 back and the weak tackle.

The right end charges hard over the outside shoulder of the No. 3 back, and goes for the kicking zone.

In this play, the fullback tries to conceal his position a little to the outside of his left end. Being in this position, he masks his charge just long enough to let the other man start trying to maneuver the protection, and open the lane into the kicking zone.

The center lines up about five yards deep, and is ready for a run or a pass in case of a bad snap.

The average tactic calls for the fullback to block the kick, but as it turns out, anyone may block it, depending on the reaction of the protection. We have had four different positions block a punt from this maneuver. The players should be sold on the idea that everyone must think and try to block the kick, and this is extremely important. Every defensive man who is in any position at all to see the kicker, should, as he kicks, raise his arms and drive for as much height as possible, across the kicker's foot, 2 yards in front. The defense never knows where the ball is coming off the kicker's foot. Sometimes they may get the one they never thought they had a chance to get.

Diagram 13-2 shows spread punt protection. We feel it is difficult to block a kick from this type of protection. In fact, we have tried to stunt and block a kick without protection, and have found it impossible if the kicker kicks in two seconds. We do try to put pressure on the kicker from the spread because, when kicking from 13 to 14 yards deep, about one out of three times the snap is a little off, and this affords the necessary opportunity to try to block the kick.

The left end and the right end play slow and are ready for a run in case of a bad snap, or a pass.

The left tackle drives hard over the outside shoulder of the right offensive tackle for the No. 1 back's outside shoulder.

The fullback drives from the outside shoulder of the right offensive guard for the inside shoulder of the No. 1 back.

The center lines up head-on the right guard and works to the middle.

The left guard and the right guard line up on the outside shoulder of the center, drive hard to the inside, and make the No. 2 and No. 3 backs take them.

The right tackle drives hard over the left offensive guard for the kicking zone.

This play will always put pressure on the kicker, and give the left tackle, fullback, or center a good chance to break clean.

The most important factor involved in blocking a kick of any kind is to find the boy who has a particular knack and desire for finding the ball. He may be a third-stringer, but if he has this ability, we put him in in this situation and exploit him. We are always on the lookout for a boy who has this important ability.

The other method of defensing the punting game is to return the punt. We have a good sideline return and a middle return from the double safety. Because we do not want any punt ever to hit the ground, we like using the double safety on a kicking down.

In the right sideline return, which is shown in Diagram 13-3, we line up in an odd defense for one reason—we want someone on the center's nose. This worries him since very few centers are adept at snapping the ball with their heads down. A bad snap is the quickest way to get the kicker in trouble. In this play, we are trying to form a sideline wall, and if we hit the sideline with this wall, we ought to go all the way. Obviously, the same play can be run to the left sideline by reversing the positions of the players and the blocks.

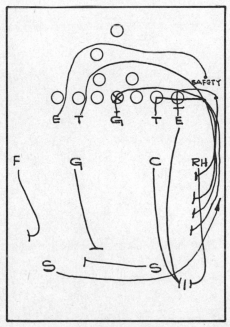

Diagram 13-3

The left end and the left tackle line up on the inside shoulder of the offensive end and tackle, and rush the kick hard to force the offensive end to kick down the middle. The left end stops on the line of scrimmage on the opposite side and is the last man. He is coached to look for the most dangerous last man. Sometimes it is a man inside the wall, but the left end must come up and take him out.

The left tackle goes on around the corner and becomes part of the wall.

The right guard explodes with all his force on the center, and takes the center as far in the backfield as he can on his initial charge. Then the right guard comes down the line to become part of the wall. For this assignment we choose the biggest, swiftest, toughest man on the team.

The right tackle and right end hold up the left offensive end and tackle as long as possible, then spread to the sideline to form the wall. In coaching this return, it is very important that the line does not get down the field too fast. The wall should be approximately 10 yards from the sideline. In order to keep the players honest we put dummies on the line of scrimmage, 10 yards from the sideline, and have the boys go around these. This keeps them from cutting the corner and improves the timing. As the boys come around the dummies, we have them space themselves some 5 to 7 yards apart and look to the inside to pick off the defense. Naturally, the first man around the corner goes down the field to pick up the ball-carrier. His distance varies each time, directly with the distance of the punt.

The fullback blocks the right offensive end out on his side.

The left guard comes back in the middle and takes the first man down to protect the hand-off.

The center and the right halfback are responsible for the left offensive end. We coach the right halfback to keep on the end's outside and maintain his attention from this position all the way down the field, acting as if he were trying to block the end in. The center times his block and blocks the left offensive end out, and we run inside this man to hit the sideline wall.

A great deal of work is necessary on the part of the two safeties in handling punts and exchanging the ball or faking an exchange. It is of the utmost importance that these two men have width when the ball is caught; otherwise, there will be no fake. The defense will know too soon which way the ball is coming. This exchange is a bit of acting; the safety who does not have the ball must carry out his fake to the extreme by faking to carry the ball on his hip. Another coaching point is for the safeties to retreat, if necessary, five or ten yards in order to hit the sideline wall. We feel this retreat is justified, because once inside the wall we have a good chance to go all the way. There are, of course, certan high, short kicks that should require a fair catch, and low sideline punts that should never be exchanged.

The middle return is shown in Diagram 13-4. Any return that is as good as the sideline return must have a complement to make it stand. The middle return is not as good as the sideline return, but when the opponents are playing the sideline return,

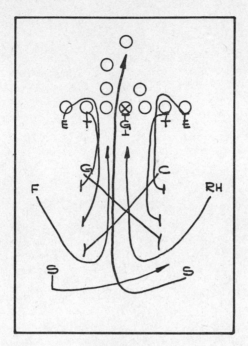

Diagram 13-4

certainly we are prepared to run the middle. Conversely, knowing we will also run the middle, the sideline return is improved.

The ends hold up and force the offensive ends to the outside, and swing inside as second men in a middle lane.

The defensive tackles hold up the offensive tackles, then swing to the inside to become the third men in the lane.

The left guard and the center drop back and cross over, taking the first man down on the opposite side.

The right guard's play is the same in the middle return as it is in the sideline return, except that he drops back and is the last man to pick off the safety man.

The fullback and the right halfback swing back to the inside, and time it so they are leading the ball-carrier up to the middle. Then they take the first man who shows.

The two safeties operate the same as they do in the sideline return, except that they cut sharply up and into the middle of the line.

Handling punts is certainly a most vital phase, and has probably caused the coaches as many heart attacks and gray hair as any other thing in football. Natural individual differences will give varying form, but there are still certain fundamentals that will always hold.

HANDLING THE PUNT

by Robert Ford

Robert Ford
New York State University

Receiving and returning punts is a critical phase of the kicking game. Most punts, if allowed to bounce, will favor the punting team. Therefore, it is necessary for the receiving team to field the punt. Since field position is so important to most offensive units, returning the punt is imperative after the catching is done.

The players who will return punts are selected during pre-season practice. In making these selections, we look for a variety of abilities. The first ability is that of catching the ball. We look for soft hands, good hand-eye coordination, and the ability to judge the flight of a ball. Obviously, this eliminates a majority of the players. Then we like to have some speed in these positions. Even though a young man possesses the previously mentioned qualities, he might not be able to return a punt satisfactorily. The last ingredient is by far the most important, and that is the ability to think, react, and to catch the ball under pressure.

On the average, 10 minutes a day are spent working with the players who will return punts. Usually 15 minutes are spent with them during the pre-practice specialist period, plus 10 minutes every other day when work is done on the punt return.

Instructional time is spent on catching the ball prior to working on the return. We try to sell these players on catching every ball that can be caught safely. They are instructed not to try to catch every ball at all costs, but they should want to catch every ball that will not result in a fumble.

The player who is going to return a punt should always sprint to the area that the ball is going to come down in and then be set for it, rather than floating or jogging and trying to catch the ball on the run. In running, we have found that running on the balls of the feet rather than hitting on the heels will make the ball easier to follow in the air. Landing on the heels makes the ball appear to bounce in the air.

Once the player who is going to return the punt has positioned himself, he should prepare to make the catch. His hands should be extended upward with the little fingers together and the palms up. Contact should be made with the ball at approximately head height. The ball should be looked into the hands. Contact with the ball should be made with the pads of the fingers. Then the ball should be cradled down into the stomach area. The ball should not be allowed to bounce on the shoulder pads or come into initial contact with the forearms or the upper arms. This causes the ball to bounce and makes it difficult to control.

When the ball has reached its peak, the player returning the punt must determine if the point has turned over or if it has not. If it has turned over and is coming at him nose down, he can figure that the ball will continue to come toward him in its downward flight. Then he can extend his arms up and away from his body, make contact with the ball, and cushion it down. If the nose has not turned over and it is coming down nose up, the player who is returning should expect the ball to slide away from him (back toward the punter) as it descends. Therefore, he should position himself so that the kick is coming down on his nose. Then the flight of the ball will bring it in front of him, where he can make contact and cushion it down.

Should the ball be fumbled, our backs are instructed to fall on it immediately rather than trying to advance the ball. More kicks seem to be lost due to neglecting this rule than through any other.

Should the ball bounce by the player who is returning, he should approach it from an angle so that he can evaluate the rush as he picks the ball up. As he approaches the ball, if he decides he cannot field it safely, he should get away from the ball.

Our players who are to return punts work in pairs. The scouting report dictates the depth they should be from the kicker. We prefer lining them up slightly less than the punter normally averages. In our opinion, this enables the players to drift back for the one the punter gets a hold of, but it still permits them to field the short kicks safely. The scouting report also indicates whether the punter is left- or right-footed, the height he gets, as well as the chances for a block. This information is covered with the players who return punts.

The players designated to return punts position themselves on a straight line parallel with the line of scrimmage. They attempt to keep 10 yards between them until the ball is caught. To avoid confusion as to who will catch the ball, the man on the right will make the call. He will make the call as the ball reaches its peak in flight. He will call, *Me, Me, Me,* or *You, You, You.* Once the call is made, it is irrevocable. The man called to make the catch makes it unless there is extreme danger of fumbling due to the sun, a gusty wind or a long run to get to the ball.

The man who is not making the catch is responsible for analyzing the height and depth of the kick as well as the downfield coverage. Should he decide that the kick is exceptionally high or the coverage will arrive at about the time of the catch, he should call, *Fair Catch,* and close in on his partner to watch for a fumble. Should the kick be short, he should call, *Go,* attempt to get in front of his partner, and act as a blocker because the kick will be returned straight up the field.

Should neither the fair catch nor the go call be made, the kick will be exchanged or the exchange will be faked. In setting up the exchange, it is the responsibility of the man who is not catching the ball to position himself on the same line as the man who is making the catch. We have found that unless the two men approach each other on a straight line, the defense is given a definite advantage in reading the exchange area. It is also the responsibility of the man who is not making the catch to maintain the 10-yard spread. Too large a spread reduces the chances of the two backs getting to the exchange area, as the coverage will get to them. Too small a spread will not enable the defense to get close enough to the exchange, and will therefore allow them to start in pursuit. We want to freeze them for a moment at the right depth downfield.

Once the catch is made, the two backs start toward each other, with the man with the ball going on the up the field side. As they approach, the man with the ball extends it toward his partner. He should keep both hands on the ball and aim it at his partner's stomach. The receiver should make a pocket for the ball by having his close elbow up and his wrist under his chin, with the palm of his hand turned out. We have found that this position forces the elbow to stay up. The far arm should be placed at a right angle across the waist, with the palm up.

The ball should be inserted into the pocket sideways. It should not be shoved in point first, because then the receiver has trouble handling the ball. Instead, it should be held out and the receiver should run through the ball. Upon placing the ball into the pocket of his partner, the hand-off man should immediately pull his hands back in toward his own body. He should not allow them to trail behind, as this gives the coverage a clue as to who has the ball. The ball should always be extended with both hands because this causes a rotation of the shoulders, which hides the ball. We have also noticed that if the player with the ball will break his elbows at the point of contact with his partner, he is less likely to let his hands trail past the hand-off area.

After the hand-off is made, the man who has handed off should carry out the fake. He should give ground and pretend that he has the ball and is trying to get around the corner.

The back who has the ball should dip his downfield shoulder as he accepts the ball. This hides the ball from the coverage coming downfield. Then he should give ground as he attempts to get to the wall.

The sideline return requires catching the football, freezing the defense with a good fake, and then getting behind the wall. Surprisingly, it is the latter item that is most difficult to get from a coaching standpoint. Backs do not want to lose ground yet ground must be lost if the back is to get behind the wall. The lead man in the wall must turn in, set his block, and then wait for the back to run the coverage into the wall.

One of the most exciting plays in the game of football is the sideline return. It requires countless hours of preparation, but the results make it worthwhile.

A hold-up return dictates a different strategy for the players who return punts. We are attempting to stop the kicking team from getting downfield by holding them up at the line of scrimmage. Therefore, the back who is not making the catch should get in front of the other back and lead him directly up the field.

Diligent work on returning punts is rewarding. It places tremendous pressure on the opponent's defense and will allow the offense to go to work in good field position.

THE SIDELINE PUNT RETURN

by Glen F. Goode

Glen Goode
Bentley High School
Livonia, Michigan

Football is like many other things in that the rewards and benefits will correlate with the sacrifices and efforts that are expended. Kicking, a very important phase of the game, is controlled by the same principle. We emphasize this fact to our players, and try to impress upon them that a team which has a tendency to loaf occasionally will reveal itself in this area. With this approach in mind, we try to eliminate technical errors and mental lapses.

When a team parlays any area of the kicking game into a game-breaker, usually an element of luck is involved. But this good fortune is frequently overestimated by the spectators and almost always exaggerated by the opponent. We believe that the old cliche, *a good team makes its own breaks,* is appropriate here. The team that capitalizes on the kicking game may be fortunate the setting is right, but luck is not a factor in the execution of the assignments.

Our specialty teams practice every day. All phases of the kicking game are worked on each day for 20 minutes. During the pre-school drills, a third 45-minute practice in T-shirts and shorts is added, working exclusively on the kicking game. An attempt is made to develop pride in the specialty teams by appointing a captain just for these squads. The boy who captained all of the specialty squads one year was second-string on offense and defense, but as specialty captain he contributed vitally to our total team effort. In our opinion, success in this area of specialty teams is the trademark of a champion.

The team starts in the huddle by determining in what direction the punt will be returned. A defense is also called in case the opponents elect not to kick. When this is done, the signal-caller reviews the four essentials of a punt return: 1. Do not be off-side. 2. Do not rough the kicker. 3. Do not clip. 4. Catch the punt.

As the opposition lines up for the punt, our players up front call out to each other to

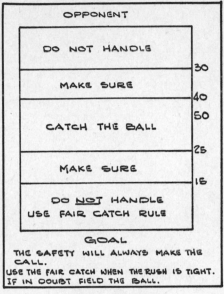

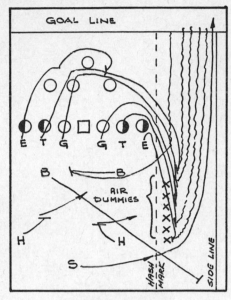

Diagram 13-5   **Diagram 13-6**

be alert for the fake punt. This call will also serve as a reminder for a bad pass from center, or any other breakdown that may cause the opponents to do something other than kick.

Diagram 13-5 is mimeographed and given to all our players so they will understand exactly what to do. If a player has this in his hands three weeks before the first game and is reminded of it repeatedly during the season, confusion will be eliminated or greatly reduced, and full concentration can be given to catching the ball.

In our opinion, young athletes are placed in a losing situation too often before stands full of classmates, faculty, and parents. By this we mean a boy is asked to perform a skill he has only practiced a few times because a dedicated coach wanted to spend more time on offensive or defensive skills and neglected the kicking game. One of the most difficult situations we can imagine in high school athletics is placement as a deep receiver on a punt in a close game, with only minimal coaching and practice in the skill prior to the game.

We have found the drill shown in Diagram 13-6 to be helpful in setting up our punt return. The players holding air dummies line up between the hash marks and the sideline. Other than getting the linemen to hustle, the biggest factor is getting them wide and deep. When the safety catches the ball, he runs for the wall. As he passes the linemen who are blocking air dummies, they are instructed to turn and run with him to the goal. Another point is emphasized. Once the linemen are running for the goal line, we want their heads turning so they are looking for the next player to block. The safety runs the length of the field, escorted by everyone right to the end zone. We think a dedicated football player is necessary to run down the field to set up the wall and then turn and run back in the direction from which he came, looking for another block.

KICK-OFF RETURNS

by Paul Dietzel

Paul Dietzel
Formerly, University of South Carolina

One of the most overlooked phases of football is returning the kick-off, and perhaps there is a reason. Many coaches feel that inasmuch as their teams actually have few opportunities during a game to return a kick-off, possibly much of the time spent on it is wasted. However, in order for a team to become *grooved*, it is certainly necessary for the players to know how to return a kick-off. It is definitely a mistake for a coach to wait until Thursday night of the week of the opening game and then suddenly realize that no work has been done on the kicking game. Certainly, it is much better for him to have taught it during the earlier practices so that the final practice sessions can be devoted to emphasizing the things which must be done frequently in a game such as the plays from scrimmage, both offensive and defensive. We will probably teach the kick-off return during the second or third practice early in September.

Basically, since starting to coach we have used four kick-off returns. For the past few years three or four returns other than those we shall discuss have been used. However, the original four seem to be sound, and certainly are quite simple to teach.

Diagram 13-7 shows the first return to be covered. This return is one of the easiest to teach and one of the most effective kick-off returns in football. We call the wedge return, and set up the wedge on the football where it is caught. The front man must be alert for an on-side kick and be sure he is not hit by the ball in case it is a hard, line-drive kick. After the kicker approaches the ball, the entire team comes to a ready position. As soon as the kicker's foot hits the ball, the five front men turn their backs on their opponents and sprint for the ball as hard as they can go. As they are going back, they ascertain the direction in which the ball has gone and try to get to it as quickly as possible. As soon as they are about 15 to 20 yards from the ball, they slow down, get under control,

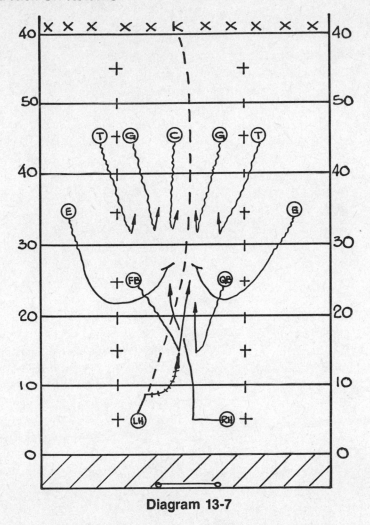

Diagram 13-7

turn back, and face their opponents in a formation that actually resembles the manner in which they would come out of the huddle.

The guards are a couple of yards from the center and the tackles are a couple of yards from the guards in a wide wedge pattern. As they start up the field, they tighten up closer to each other. The ends have more or less drifted to a position where they now protect the flanks of the wedge, and are in a position to keep any player from breaking into the wedge from the sides.

Our fullback sets the position in the wedge because he and the quarterback drop back and form the apex of the second wedge about five or six yards in front of the receiver. The fullback will be the point of the second wedge, and he should wait until the ball is in the receiver's hands. After the ball hits the receiver's hands, the fullback will call *go* as loudly as he can because that will start both wedges up the field.

As shown in the diagram, the non-receiving halfback will form to the left of the fullback and the quarterback will always form to the right of the fullback. We always designate which receiver will carry the ball if it is kicked in the middle, and he will call for the ball if there is a questionable kick. The non-receiver should keep his distance from the other receiver, that is, approximately 10 yards, and should watch the receiver so that in the event he should drop the ball, the non-receiver will be in a position to help him recover it.

When the ball is caught by either receiver, both players will start toward each other to fake the reverse. However, the non-receiver will break off a little sooner than the ball-carrier so that he can get into the wedge. The ball-carrier tries to stay in behind the wedge as long as he can, and any time he sees daylight he may break off to the outside. It is a serious mistake for the ball-carrier to get out of the wedge too soon and it is also a mistake for him to stay in until he falls over the front runners.

Obviously, it is very important for the members of the wedge to keep their feet as long as possible so that the wedge will be maintained. Ideally speaking, the idea of the wedge is to force everyone outside of it by sheer numbers. This has been a very fine return and it is the easiest one we have tried to teach.

For a change of pace, the kick-off return right and left as shown in Diagram 13-8 has been used. When a kick-off return is run to one side or the other, several things must be kept in mind. First of all, the exchange on the fake or reverse is used because we think it will slow down the coverage of approximately half of the defenders. It just means that they must stay at home. For that reason, only the players on the on-side are blocked. Both ends should drop fairly straight back so they show no flow (even though the front line does). We count from the sidelines of the on-side toward the middle of the field.

The rules for this return are fairly simple. The end positions himself by drifting back and timing so that he will set his block on No. 2 only after the receiver has started back up the field. Our on-side tackle sprints hard to get positioned outside of No. 3 and then times himself to set his block late. The on-side guard, center, the off-side guard, and the off-side tackle do exactly the same on Nos. 4, 5, the kicker, and No. 7 (the kicker is No. 6, but we always refer to him as the kicker, so the next man would be No. 7). The off-side end drifts straight back and down until the ball is settling, and then he sprints hard to come across and protect the exchange lane. He will block anyone who is loose.

Our fullback and quarterback drift back to the inside to show the wedge return. Then the quarterback will lead the play and block out on No. 1. The fullback will help on anyone who needs help to the inside. Once again, the halfbacks should use the same judgment in fielding the ball. We designate the man who returns kick-offs best to handle the middle ball, and have the other halfback maintain his distance, which is approximately 8 to 10 yards. As the ball is settling, if the proposed ball-carrier must move toward the other halfback, then the non-receiving halfback must give ground laterally so that the distance between remains relatively the same.

As soon as the receiver catches the ball, he turns and faces in toward the other halfback, and they go toward each other at a rapid pace. We have a rule which certainly helps to avoid embarrassing ties. Nothing is worse than to have two halfbacks collide on

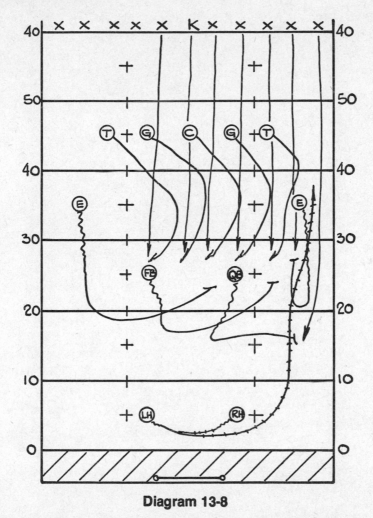

Diagram 13-8

an exchange. That rule is, *The man with the ball always goes in front.* We have already called the return side; therefore, it will either be an exchange or a fake exchange so that the ball will end up on the side designated. The halfback who is the faker must carry the fake out all the way to the sideline and keep both hands on his hip with a shoulder lowered, because he must hold up the backside rushers.

The exchange between the backs can be made in any way the coach decides. However, we have found that the cross-hand exchange (ball handled with the outside arm) may be much more deceptive, but the added danger is too much of a risk. Our players are taught to execute the exchange in the simplest possible manner. This is something that requires considerable practice.

The kick-off return left is merely the opposite direction, but the techniques and rules are the same.

Perhaps the kick-off is a very small part of the game of football, but it is much easier to start a game near mid-field than it is for a team to start it near its own 5-yard line.

KICK-OFF RETURN FUNDAMENTALS

by Don Read

Don Read
Oregon Institute of Technology

While the kick-off return which we shall discuss is not new in football, it is used rarely. However, due to its wide-open nature, it can be a great addition to any offensive attack. Like any other aspect of football, success is dependent upon the time and emphasis placed on it in practice sessions.

When adequate time is devoted, this return will supply the big run and the edge which is the little extra needed by a team. This offensive play features the element of surprise and razzle-dazzle, and is a demoralizing weapon that can provide a team with a good field position or achieve a score with amazing regularity.

Objective of the Return

As mentioned previously, the objective of this kick-off return is to score or obtain good field position. However, unlike some others, concentration is placed on freezing the opposing team in their lanes by the crossing action of the backs. The completed maneuver gives the offense the advantage of blocking only the on-side of the opponent. Of course, this means that it is only necessary for the eleven offensive players to defeat half of the defending team. The opposing team's off-side is forced to stay on the side of the field away from the return. Because of a fake or crossing action, they are unsure where the play is directed.

How the Call Is Made

No doubt, there are several ways to call the return. One effective method is to call *Right—Second Man*. This means the return is to the right with the first man faking to the left, and the second man going to the right is given the ball. A call of *Left—Second Man* would designate the return left and provide the second man with the ball. Returns can allow the first man to get the ball and the second man to fake by calling *Right—First Man* or *Left—First Man* (Diagrams 13-9 and 13-10).

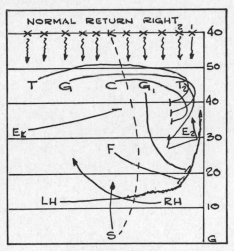

| Diagram 13-9 | Diagram 13-10 |

The Hand-Off

As shown in Diagrams 13-9 and 13-10, the safety in the three-deep will serve as the pivot man, and is responsible for catching as many kicks as he possibly can and making the all-important fake and hand-off. The pivot point is set in accordance with the depth of the kick. The deeper the kick, the farther the safety should run after catching the ball before setting up to make the exchange. As an example, a kick to the goal line might provide for the safety setting up on about the 10- or 15-yard line. On the other hand, a ball kicked to the 15 should be set up right at the 15- or 20-yard line. Height of the kick will also dictate where the pivot point should be. The higher the kick, the closer the exchange should be made from the point where the ball is caught.

After the safety catches the ball, he should sprint to the pivot point, turn his back to the opposition, and bring the ball to his stomach. With his back to the opponents, he should fake to one back and hand to the other, depending upon the call. An open-hand fake should be used with the other hand which is covering the ball held against the stomach.

A good eye fake can be of value in helping make the play go. It is important that the pivot man maintain a good wide base and be in a relatively sound football position. Keeping his shoulders rounded and his head tilted downward slightly will also aid deception.

If the Kick Is Short

A kick that does not reach the 20-yard line is defined as a short kick. It is difficult and extremely hazardous to attempt a return of this nature when the kick is short. Therefore, a short kick should be returned straight up the field for whatever yards can be obtained. In other words, there should be no attempt to carry out the play because a short kick does not allow adequate time to execute the return.

Blocking the Changing Lane Team

One obstacle some teams find difficult when returning kick-offs is blocking men who cross or change lanes while covering on the kick. To overcome this maneuver, a team should not block specific individuals, but rather wall off an area and block any opponent who enters. This insures that the players who are most dangerous to the play will be defeated.

However, at the point of attack, we do believe specific players must be blocked. These players are the two outside men on the kick-off team to the side the return is going. The man closest to the sideline when the return begins to develop should be double-teamed out, and the second man from the sideline double-teamed in. Thus, if a team's two outside men change lanes by crossing, the stunt is picked up.

Setting the Wall

The most important aspect of a kick-off return is the picket line or wall. Three major points should be emphasized with respect to setting the wall.

First, the picket line should be formed in the correct alignment. The wall should be deep or near enough to the depth of the kick to insure that the ball-carrier gets behind the wall. Most returns are stopped before the runner gets to the wall.

A second feature which requires emphasis is appropriate spacing of players along the picket. When the distance between the players along the wall is too great, the probability of leaks is good. It is recommended that the spacing not exceed 5 yards.

Third, the distance the picket should be set from the sideline must never exceed 15 yards. The farther the wall is from the sideline, the more difficult is the job of keeping the running lane open.

When the Ball Is Kicked to a Halfback

If the ball is kicked to one of the halfbacks, the return should be run in the same manner as a normal return, except for the three deep backs. All blocking responsibilities are constant in both the normal and halfback returns. The halfback's task, if the ball is kicked to him, is to make the catch and run a path in front of the other halfback. Whether the ball is kept or handed off depends upon the call. If, for example, the return is right and the right halfback gets the ball, he should hand it to the left halfback, who runs the return as called. The left halfback should execute a one-handed hand-off and offer a good fake, keeping his front shoulder rounded, hips open, and his arms over his stomach (Diagrams 13-11 and 13-12).

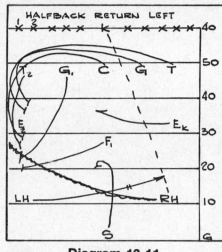

Diagram 13-11   **Diagram 13-12**

The Key Blocks

On a sideline return, the most important blocks are those made where the running lane is formed, more specifically, at the initial point of attack which is at the lip of the wall (Diagrams 13-9 through 13-12). The two double-team blocks made here will open the gate and allow the runner to get inside the picket or prevent the return from setting up.

The technique we recommend is to have the guard on the call side and the fullback double-team the man in the outside lane out. The defender in the second lane on the return side is blocked by the tackle and end to the call side. The combination of these two blocks should provide a wide opening in the defensive alignment.

Both double teams should be executed as close to the receiving position of the ball as possible. An ideal placement is 10 yards in front of the spot where the ball is handed off. The block on the outside defender should take that man out of bounds, while the block on the second defender must take him off his feet or drive him at least 10 yards from the sideline.

Some coaches will feel that the kick-off return play presented in this article is rinky-dink football. We believe it is good, sound football—an offensive weapon not capitalized upon by many. This play furnishes the basic elements of surprise and tremendous explosiveness. When it is executed correctly, it will supply a punch unequaled by any other play in an offensive attack.

Part IV
COACHING THE BACKFIELD

14 / The Offensive Backfield

RUNNING THE FOOTBALL—FOUR BASIC MOVES

by Ara Parseghian

Ara Parseghian
Formerly, University of Notre Dame

The Cross-Over Step

In executing the cross-over step, a ball-carrier should approach the tackler on balance, with his eyes focused squarely on him. The ball-carrier should lead with one foot toward the tackler and then cross over sharply with the other foot. Most players also use a stiff arm in conjunction with the cross-over step. As the right foot crosses over the left, it should be placed down sharply and not hung in the air.

The Side Step

The approach in the side step is the same as it is in the cross-over step. A ball-carrier will lead with his inside foot toward the tackler, with most of his weight on that foot. His knee should be slightly bent and his body should be somewhat forward. As he feels the tackler going for the inside leg, he should spring off that leg in a lateral direction, transferring his weight to the other foot. This motion should also be sharp, and the runner should not hang his foot in the air, but make rapid contact with the ground. Most players will also use a straight arm in conjunction with the side step. The side step could be broken down into the approach, planting the inside foot, side step, and recovering to continue running downfield.

The Straight Arm and Pivot

Again, the approach should be on balance as the ball-carrier nears the tackler. He should straight-arm his opponent, pivot on the near or outside foot, make a three-quarter turn, and drive off in the new direction. When using the straight arm, it is best to place the heel of the hand on the opponent's shoulder pad. We also feel that it is good to come out of the pivot in a low position in order to maintain good balance and be able to continue downfield. The ball-carrier should protect the football as he completes the pivot.

The Shoulder Drive and Pivot

This maneuver is similar to the straight arm and pivot except that the ball-carrier hits with his shoulder. He leads with the far or inside foot, makes contact with the tackler's shoulder, and then pivots off in the new direction. This type of stunt is used mainly by backs, generally fullbacks, who are trying to break through the line. It is imperative for the ball-carrier to stay low in executing the stunt in order to meet the tackler.

DEVELOPING QUARTERBACKS

by Pepper Rodgers

Pepper Rodgers
Georgia Tech

As is done with our quarterbacks, we will start from the basic fundamental of the quarterback's stance, and build from there. The quarterback should be aligned in a parallel stance, with his knees bent slightly and his back straight. From this position it is our feeling he will be able to execute any maneuver that is asked of him regardless of direction or footwork. Executions should come with equal ease for movement left, right, backward, or forward. Many times movement is restricted when coaches instruct the quarterback to stagger his feet. This staggering of the feet will at the same time cause false steps on certain maneuvers, which will in turn necessitate a loss in both time and timing.

Our quarterbacks are taught what is termed a heel-to-heel relationship with their hands when accepting the ball from the center. Whether the quarterback is right- or left-handed, he is taught to accept the ball with his right hand placing pressure on the center's buttocks, and the left hand underneath acting as a guide and clamp once the ball is snapped. The center is taught to give the ball a half-turn, thereby giving the quarterback the meat or the largest part. Our quarterbacks are taught the three P's, which are: pressure, push-off, and pull-back, which mean pressure the center, push him off on the snap, and the always important, pull the ball back to the abdominal area.

On the snap of the ball, the quarterback executes the advantage step, which is used to place maximum pressure on the corners. Teaching the advantage step is actually teaching balance and, at the same time, a disguise of balance. On this step, it is our intention to keep the quarterback from taking false steps when he is sprinting in one direction or the other. In order to accomplish this, we go back to the balance mentioned previously. We found that when the quarterback wanted to sprint to his right, to keep from taking a false step with his left foot, all he had to do was shift his weight to his left foot. It is difficult to false step with a foot that has extra weight on it, but relatively easy to push off. In order to execute this maneuver, the quarterback must have a close, bent arm position to the center.

Considerable time is spent on center-quarterback exchange, because every play must start with this exchange. How many times on crucial plays have we seen either the quarterback or the center move early and stop a play before it is started. This will not happen if coaches do a good job of coaching this particular phase of the game.

The next area that is emphasized is the quarterback's ability to set up or place maximum pressure on the corner when he is passing. Nothing irritates us more than to see a quarterback jog from under the center. By doing so, often he is not set and ready to throw when the play is designed to break down the defense. Second, by jogging from under the center, his chances of throwing the ball before defensive pressure is applied are minimized. This returns us to the area of false steps again. It was found that when the quarterback is pressured to exit from the center with maximum efficiency, he will have a tendency to false step. This loss of effort and time should be watched closely and certainly should be eliminated.

Ours is basically an outside team. We say this mainly because the offense is designed around the quarterback sweep. Therefore, most of our passing game is designed to resemble this sweep as much as possible. Diagram 14-1 shows this basic sweep play, and Diagram 14-2 shows the basic corner pass.

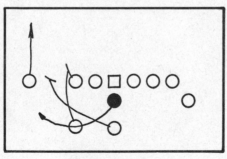 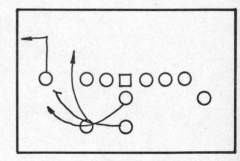

Diagram 14-1   **Diagram 14-2**

Not only do the two plays appear alike, but included is the option to run or pass on the corner pass play. As can be seen, if it is executed properly, the defense should not be able to key run until the line of scrimmage is crossed or until the ball is in the air.

Coaches who are familiar with sprint offenses are aware of the pitfalls brought about by corner-rotating defenses to support the run and at the same time help eliminate the short quick pass. Opportunity many times necessitates *alteration*. Notice we said *alteration* and not *change*. We hesitate to change when alteration will suffice. In an attempt not to give the defense the advantage of knowing where or exactly when the quarterback is going to pass, the alteration is used at times to pull up behind the tackle in order to throw the ball. Pulling up behind the tackle is certainly nothing new in football.

Pulling up behind the tackle still provides the outside run and the sprint look long enough to keep the defense honest, and at the same time, the ability is present to force full field coverage and throw to either side much as would be seen in a dropback type of attack. If he does a good job of executing, there will be very little, if any, difference in the first five steps of the quarterback. This should, theoretically, delay the defense's ability to key our intentions relative to the run, pass, or throwback.

At present, one of the main controversies in football is whether pulling up behind the tackle and throwing back to a wide receiver out on the other side is a safe pass or not. By actual measurement, the basic difference is three and one-half to four yards. Diagram 14-3 shows the overall difference by comparison. True, the quarterback may be a little farther from one receiver, but at the same time he is closer to another, plus the quarterback is moving and the defense has to worry about the corner run, the corner pass, and the pull-up with full field passing ability. Probably the most important aspect of the throwback passing game is that the quarterback knows when *not* to throw as much, or more so, than when to throw. Most passers can hit the wide-open receiver. The problem comes when the receiver is covered. Our quarterbacks are taught that when their receivers are covered, they have two options. First, they should pull the ball away and run. Second, they should throw the ball away from the defender. The receiver might have a chance, but the quarterback should be sure the defender does not get the ball.

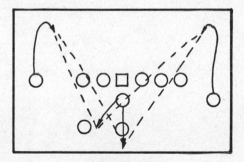

Diagram 14-3

Any good quarterback loves to throw and complete passes; however, the great thing to emphasize in the case of young quarterbacks is when *not* to throw the ball.

When using a moving quarterback who sprints to either side and pulls up behind the tackle, there is another problem which should be discussed. It really is no problem for a right-handed quarterback to set up and throw when he is moving to his right. Also, a left-hander has no problem when he is moving to his left. The difficulty arises when they move away from their throwing arm, i.e., a left-handed quarterback moving to his right to throw back left. We have tried two different techniques. The first was a complete turn at a set point. This worked to some degree, but many times the passers could not pick up the receivers once their back was turned. Now we tell our quarterback to use basically five steps in setting up.

This is not an iron-clad rule, because each boy will differ in physical make-up and cannot possibly duplicate the exact steps and distance to a set point. The quarterback takes four steps and pivots. With the pivot he has not moved the basic five steps to a set point, and after a gathering of the body, he should be able to throw with maximum efficiency and still not have lost sight of the receivers or the defense.

The final area that is stressed in quarterbacking is simplicity. We try to keep the quarterback's decisions on the field at a minimum. This is not to say that he does not have the usual responsibilities before and at the snap of the ball. We try to relieve him of responsibility once the play has started. Our quarterback is not asked to read an entire defense, or the entire secondary, for that matter. He is given a primary and secondary receiver, usually on the same side of the field. As mentioned previously, this helps minimize the chances of a bad play.

To sum up, we approach our quarterbacks and offense in three phases: 1) fundamentals; 2) simplicity; and 3) execution. If quarterbacks are to be successful, they must be outstanding in these areas.

30 RULES FOR THE QUARTERBACK

by Frank Broyles

Frank Broyles
Formerly, University of Arkansas

---

1. Know your offense thoroughly.
2. Know the capabilities of each teammate.
3. Find out as much as you can about every opponent.
4. Know what defenses to expect.
5. Know how to penetrate the various defenses with your offense.
6. Know when to use flankers, wingbacks, and split ends.
7. Know what to call in critical situations.
8. Always call plays with force and confidence.
9. Permit no talking in the huddle.
10. If the opponent is short of reserve strength, play a hard-hitting, bruising game in an effort to wear the team down physically.
11. Every call should be made with a purpose in mind, based on the overall strategy.
12. Special plays may be effective either early in the game against an opponent who has prepared well for the basic attack, or later in the game when the opponent begins limiting the success of the basic attack.
13. When any defensive weakness is spotted, direct the attack at it before it can be corrected.
14. Play faster when the wind is to your back; slower when you are facing the wind.
15. When using flankers, watch the defense. If they shift toward the flanker, run to the opposite side. If they do not shift, run toward the flanker.
16. Avoid running the same play in the same situation every time.
17. If the opposing team has a reckless, hard-charging line, concentrate on traps, counters, reverses, and screen passes.
18. The element of surprise is one of your most useful weapons. Use it wisely. Catching an opponent off guard can often compensate for a lack of offensive strength.

19. When your team is behind, open up your offense with special plays and passes in an effort to catch up. You have nothing to lose by taking chances when behind.

20. Do not have definite rules when to pass.

21. Plays that involve considerable ball-handling or sharp turns should be avoided when the field is wet.

22. When the field is wet or muddy, it is best to kick and let the opponent do the fumbling.

23. Be alert. If you see a defensive back limping during the game, throw a pass in his area. If you see a lineman limping, run a play over him.

24. When your team is backed up to the goal line, do not take chances with passes or slow developing plays, and do not wait until fourth down to kick.

25. Be careful when using special plays. Their failure could have an adverse effect on the team's morale.

26. When facing a strong head wind, it is not safe to throw anything other than short passes. When the wind is to your back, long passes may be very effective.

27. Do not always wait until a *passing down* to pass.

28. Know which defenders stop each play that you call, and then make your calls with those facts in mind. Often when a particular defensive man makes the tackle on a play, the companion play or a check play may be successful.

29. When your team is behind with time running out, play fast and recklessly. When ahead, play a slow, conservative game.

30. Take advantage of the breaks. When one comes your way, score.

DRILLS FOR THE QUARTERBACK

by George H. Allen

George Allen
Los Angeles Rams

Quick Delivery Drill

The purpose of this drill is to speed up the hand, wrist, arm, and footwork actions used by quarterbacks in passing. In addition, it is designed to reduce or eliminate the long-arm action of the passers in throwing. A weighted football which has been developed for passers is ideal for this drill.

1. A drill of this type is needed because so many quarterbacks take too much time palming and fingering the football so that it is properly adjusted to their hands. By eliminating wasted movements before throwing, the quarterback will have more time to spot the receiver and throw.

2. Place two quarterbacks from seven to ten yards apart and give one a football. Since this is not a distance drill, the space between the two quarterbacks should never be more than 20 yards.

3. Have the quarterback who has the ball pass it to the other quarterback, using a fast, short-arm action. The coach should watch him closely to see that there are no unnecessary movements. As soon as the second quarterback receives the ball, he should adjust it to his hands very quickly, without any loss of motion or time. Then he throws it to the first quarterback, using fast-arm action. Insist on little or no windup.

4. The coach should be careful that the quarterbacks do not develop any bad habits. Due to the fact that they are hurrying, there is a tendency to forget footwork, follow-through, and other fundamentals. A coach should be present to watch the drill and offer suggestions until the quarterbacks learn the timing.

5. The coaching points to remember in this drill are as follows: 1) Get the ball away

quickly. 2) Use short-arm action so that the defense cannot read the quarterback's arm. 3) Release the ball above the right ear. 4) Position the ball directly in front of the right shoulder so that no motion is wasted before the release. 5) Throw off the right foot. 6) Face the receiver and step in the direction of the throw. 7) Execute a complete follow-through with the passing arm.

6. As a rule, the quarterbacks will discover they can throw accurately and it is not necessary to grip the ball a certain way every time. On getting rid of the ball quickly, the quarterbacks will realize they have been taking too much time to adjust and throw. Usually, the quarterbacks are not aware of this until this drill is introduced.

7. An essential coaching point is that the quarterback should not have the ball low on his chest, but should place it at shoulder height. Thus, he does not have to raise the ball very much when he is releasing to throw. Wasted movements getting the ball into correct delivery position should be eliminated.

8. We feel it is necessary for the quarterback to set his fingers on the laces if the ball is wet. The extra time involved is essential when throwing a slippery ball.

9. Remember, this drill does not consider the footwork necessary in getting back to throw. Footwork is stressed after the passer is set to throw.

Circle Drill

The purpose of this drill is to provide quarterbacks practice in passing on the run. They attempt to complete a pass to a receiver who is running to their left, while they are running to the right. Quarterbacks must lead the receiver and throw a soft pass. The drill also emphasizes the importance of proper footwork while throwing to the left and right on the run.

1. Have two quarterbacks face each other, approximately 7 yards apart. If only one quarterback is available, use an offensive end or a back as the receiver.

2. The quarterback who has the ball should run in a circle to his right at half speed. Then the receiver starts to run to the quarterback's left. In other words, the receiver is running away from him. Speed should be increased gradually as the players perfect the fundamentals of throwing and footwork.

3. The quarterback forms the ball in his hands, sets himself, and leads the receiver. He comes to a stop and throws off his right foot. We are not interested in having him throw on the dead run, or jump in the air and then throw. Footwork is important and balance is essential.

4. The release of the ball is above the quarterback's ear level, and there is a complete follow-through.

5. The receiver catches the ball with his fingers well-spread and looks the ball into his hands. He receives the ball on the run.

6. Now, the receiver becomes the passer and starts to run to his left, while the other quarterback who is now the receiver runs to his left.

7. The quarterback must stop and reverse his feet and throw to the other player. He is facing the receiver and throwing off his right foot.

8. The ball is released with a complete follow-through of the passing hand.

9. As they warm up, the quarterbacks gradually increase the distance of the circle. Then they reverse directions and run opposite paths.

10. If a coach wishes to teach a quarterback to throw on the run without coming to a stop, this drill will also serve the purpose.

Wrist Drill

This is strictly a wrist drill for the quarterbacks. If a heavy-weighted ball is used, the passer's wrist and arm will be strengthened. Throwing while on one knee forces the quarterback to throw with his wrist and arm because no body movement is possible. This is an excellent drill, and it should be used daily to get snappy wrist action, which is necessary in throwing.

1. Place two quarterbacks five yards apart and have each one kneel on his right knee. If two quarterbacks are not available, then use another player to return the ball. However, when two quarterbacks are used, it is possible for both to warm up at the same time, and the coach can make corrections without repeating.

2. Gradually increase the distance between the quarterbacks to 7, 10, and finally 15 yards. A regulation football will suffice; however, a weighted passing ball which is designed for quarterbacks will give the passer better results. A regulation football should never feel heavy to a quarterback.

3. Essential coaching points in teaching this drill are: 1) Insist on a short-arm action pass. 2) Have the quarterback throw, using only wrist action, because he is attempting to eliminate long-arm action as much as possible. 3) Have the quarterback form his hands to the ball quickly and point his left shoulder in the direction of the throw.

4. The receiver's arms are outstretched and the fingers of both hands are well-spread. His head is down slightly and his eyes are focused on the flight of the ball. These are the essentials of good receiving.

Warm-Up Drill

The purpose of this drill is twofold: first, to teach quarterbacks to throw while running to the right and then to the left; second, to serve as a warm-up conditioning drill. Rather than have the quarterbacks take calisthenics, it is more beneficial for them to acquire a skill and condition their legs by running in the warm-up drill.

1. Place two quarterbacks 5 yards apart. Instruct them to pass to each other while running across the field on the marked lines. After they reach the other side, they should reverse positions so that one quarterback is throwing while running to his right, and the other quarterback is throwing while running to his left.

2. Gradually increase this distance to 10 yards and then to 15 yards. If the proper fundamentals of throwing on the run are taught and mastered, it will not be necessary for the quarterbacks to throw longer.

3. A regulation football is recommended for this drill, rather than a weighted ball. As soon as the quarterbacks reach the practice field, they should start the drill. They should go back and forth, running at half-speed several times.

4. The coaching points to stress in this drill are as follows: Throw off the rear foot, whether running right or left. Throw with the feet on the ground. We do not want any player to throw while he is jumping in the air. Reverse the feet and hesitate before throwing to the left. We also want the quarterback to come to a stop before throwing to his right, assuming that he is right-handed. A lead pass should be thrown so that the receiver can catch it in stride. It is difficult for many quarterbacks to lead a receiver while throwing on the run. They will usually overthrow their target. This type of pass need not be thrown too hard. In fact, the most common fault among young quarterbacks is that when throwing on the run, they throw too hard. They should adjust the ball to their hands quickly, get it in position to throw, and get rid of it in the least amount of time, with the fewest motions. False movements before releasing to throw must be eliminated. The final point is to have the quarterback do the same thing every time, whether he is going to pass or run. In other words, he should not telegraph his intentions.

5. This drill should be performed daily, and need not extend over the calisthenics period. Marked improvement will take place in passing on the run if just five minutes of each practice period are allotted to this simple drill.

Cup Drill

The purpose of this drill is to provide practice for the quarterback in going back to pass. A drill of this type is necessary early in the season to emphasize the fundamentals of setting up to pass.

1. Place a center on offense with the quarterback.

2. When the quarterback calls his cadence, the ball should be snapped on a predetermined number.

3. This is a drill which every quarterback should practice. Receivers are not necessary at this time, but should be added later.

4. The coaching points to stress in this drill are as follows: The quarterback should pivot on his left toe as the ball is received. His knees should be bent and relaxed, and his elbows should be close to his body. The passer pushes off to his left to go back quickly. His body should lean backward, but not so flat that he is not under control. He should go back quickly, but always be well balanced. The passer should come to a stop with hesitation and plant his right foot. Then, his weight should be shifted from the front to the rear foot. The passer must perfect his steps and footwork to the exact distance he is

setting up. He steps forward into the imaginary cup of protection and releases the ball with complete follow-through.

5. Stepping forward is necessary to set up the blocks for the line and the backs. The natural thing for a quarterback to do is to go back farther and farther. If the quarterback does not step up into the cup, the line cannot block.

6. This is a drill which must be repeated until the quarterbacks have mastered all the fundamentals of setting up to pass.

Running-Off Drill

The purpose of this drill is to provide the quarterback with practice in running off. There are times when he is forced to run with the football. Since many quarterbacks will not scramble when rushed, a drill of this type is needed.

1. Place two ends, a quarterback, and a center on offense. The ends should be 12 yards apart. Have the quarterback go through his complete routine of setting the team, calling the defense, and cadence.

2. The center should drop back and set to block according to the call of the quarterback, even though only two men are on offense and a skeletal crew is on defense.

3. Station two linebackers on defense and have them vary their positions. The linebackers may do any of the following: Both may drop back and cover the pass. One may red-dog. Both may red-dog. Both may dog from one side. They may line up in any position and play games to confuse the quarterback.

4. If they do not red-dog, the quarterback should attempt to hit the open man. This maneuver also provides him with practice in looking off.

5. When one linebacker red-dogs, the quarterback may attempt to hit the opposite receiver or he may run off.

6. If both linebackers red-dog, the quarterback should try to adjust and throw quickly or run off and scramble.

7. The coaching points that should be stressed in this drill are: When setting up to pass, the quarterback should be under control and on balance at all times. He should be fluid enough to adjust quickly and change his course according to the tactics employed by the defense. The quarterback cannot eat the ball continually, but must run at times to keep the rushers honest and help his team. He should improve his peripheral vision so that he will be alert and able to throw sooner than he anticipates in emergency situations.

Looking-Off Drill

The purpose of this drill is to provide practice for the quarterbacks in looking off. Since most defenders read the quarterback's eyes, it is necessary to have a drill that is devoted to the improvement of this vital skill.

1. Place a center and a quarterback on offense. Station them in the middle of the field so there will be ample space.

2. Locate two receivers approximately 10 to 12 yards apart. These players represent offensive ends. If necessary, they may be extra linemen, junior varsity, or frosh personnel. As the quarterback retreats to pass, they should remain in that stationary position.

3. Place a defensive player between the two receivers. This man should be a middle linebacker or a deep back. However, any player will suffice, but this drill particularly provides good training for the middle linebacker. He can improve his reactions and footwork, and it is amazing how much more ground a defender will be able to cover by utilizing this drill daily.

4. A passer should not retreat over 6 or 7 yards. If he retreats deeper, the defender will deflect or intercept most of his passes. If he goes deeper, the distance between the two receivers should be increased to 15 yards.

5. The defender should line up from 2 to 4 yards deeper than the receivers. This is necessary so that he can come up at the proper angle and either intercept or knock down the pass.

6. The coaching points to remember in this drill for looking off are as follows: As the quarterback receives the snap from the center and retreats to throw, the coach should make certain that his footwork is correct. When he is moving backward, there should be no false steps or lost motion. The coach should instruct him to retreat quickly so that he has more time to set and locate his open receivers. The quarterback's weight should be on his back foot, and his body should not be too high. Balance is essential in the retreating movements, because the quarterback may have to stop and throw sooner or run off if the protection fails. The coach should insist that his passer always be under control as he retreats. He should plant his right foot, use a hesitation step, and then look off. If time permits, depending upon the type of pass, he may flag the ball. Then the quarterback should turn and step in the direction of the target and get set to throw. He should line up his left shoulder and lead foot with the receiver and deliver the ball quickly and accurately. His left arm should be extended ahead in the direction of the target for equilibrium. Assuming the passer is right-handed, he should follow-through with his passing arm and right shoulder.

7. This is an excellent early-season drill.

Middle Looking-Off Drill

The purpose of this drill is to provide the quarterback with practice in looking off. The drill coordinates those which have been discussed previously.

1. Place a center, quarterback, and just two receivers on offense.

2. Locate only one defender in the middle on defense. It is advantageous to place a

deep back on defense. The deep back will receive good practice in improving his interception distance.

3. The two receivers on offense line up approximately 7 yards from the center. They are not allowed to run all over the field, but must confine their routes to those the deep back has a chance to cover. However, they must not make things too easy for the deep back.

4. The deep back is instructed to play the quarterback's eyes 100 percent of the time.

5. Again, it is necessary to place a time limit on the passer to prevent bad habits from forming and to make the drill fair for the pass defender.

Split Vision Pass Drill

The purpose of this drill is to provide practice for the passer in spotting the receiver and looking off. Since there are three defenders versus two offensive receivers, the defense is favored. However, it is a drill that will test the passer, and should be used after he has mastered the other quarterback drills which have been discussed previously.

1. Station a center and a quarterback on offense with two offensive receivers.

2. Space the receivers a distance of 10 to 15 yards apart. They will execute the pass routes called by the quarterback in the huddle. A pass is called every time, providing the defense with the advantage.

3. As the quarterback retreats to pass, he looks straight downfield. This freezes the middle defender and keeps him out of the area where the pass is intended.

4. This is also a good drill for linebackers and one or two of the deep backs. Due to the distance separating them, quick reactions are necessary to break up the pass. If they can intercept the ball, they should. They should play aggressively and fight for the ball.

5. This is a fine early season or spring drill for sharpening the passer's timing in spotting the open receiver. It stimulates game conditions with a definite edge toward the defensive man. However, if the quarterback is going to connect with his ends, he must locate the uncovered receiver quickly.

6. We like to place a time limit on the quarterback so that he does not form bad habits.

Split Vision Drill (3-on-2)

The purpose of this drill is to develop split vision so that the quarterback can spot an open receiver quickly and unload the ball to him at once. It is a strong side passing situation.

1. Station two offensive ends, a center, and a quarterback on the offensive team.

2. Place three deep backs or linebackers on defense. Their job is to read the quarterback and play the ball.

3. As the quarterback retreats to pass, the defenders get depth to cover. The quarterback is looking off in the opposite direction as he goes back to throw.

4. Although the footwork and details of setting up to pass have been discussed in previous drills, they require constant attention.

5. Receivers are given a limited number of routes to use in getting open. The defense may gang up on one of them and leave the other wide-open, so that the quarterback is forced to hit that particular end. Defensive players are told that this drill is for the benefit of the quarterback and is used only for that purpose.

6. The coaching points of this drill are: 1. Proper footwork in going back to pass. 2. Position of the head and shoulders when going backward. 3. Looking in the off direction or directly ahead before throwing. Since the defenders will start to play his habits, the passer must not develop any telltale signs.

Split Vision Drill (2-on-1)

The purpose of this drill is to provide practice for the quarterback in looking off. It is similar to the other quarterback drills except that the offense has just one receiver.

1. Place a center, quarterback, and one offensive end on offense. The offensive end is limited in the movements he is allowed to make.

2. Station two deep backs on pass defense to read the quarterback and play the ball.

3. The quarterback receives the snap from the center and retreats to pass. He is looking straight ahead into center field as he goes backward. If he looks downfield, the defenders cannot read his eyes.

4. The essential coaching points of this drill are: 1) Always have the quarterback go back the same way. 2) Instruct him to look straight ahead into center field so that he will not tip off his intentions. 3) If time permits, the quarterback may flag the ball once in the off direction and then throw. This would depend upon the type of pass he is going to use. 4) Insist that he handle the ball as quickly as possible and release it to the target with fast arm and hand action.

Red-Dog Single Check-Off

The purpose of this drill is to provide the quarterback with necessary practice in throwing the check-off pass when encountering a red-dog.

1. Place a center, quarterback, and fullback on offense. Any offensive back will suffice; however, we prefer a fullback, and he must line up in the fullback position.

2. Station one linebacker on defense. This linebacker may vary his position and line up in any spot he desires.

3. Have the linebacker red-dog from his final spot. He may fake coming up and drop back to cover the pass.

4. Usually, he should come in from the middle and go either to the center's right or left.

5. The quarterback uses proper footwork in retreating to pass and looks straight ahead downfield.

6. The fullback must go in the direction indicated by the call of the quarterback, or he may block.

7. The coaching points for the quarterback to remember in this drill are: 1) When releasing the ball, look at the receiver. 2) He should break his wrist and lay the ball directly in the receiver's hands. 3) Since this is a most difficult catch, do not *rifle* the ball. 4) Throw the football directly into the receiver with a slight lead. If the ball is thrown with too much lead, the receiver could be shaken up. He must go for the ball and sometimes cannot see the defender, or the pass could be intercepted because the offensive man is usually closely covered.

Red-Dog Double Check-Off

The purpose of this drill is to provide the quarterback with essential practice in throwing a check-off pass with both a fullback and halfback in the backfield.

1. This drill should be used after the quarterback has mastered the single check-off drill.

2. Station a center, quarterback, and two backs on offense.

3. Locate one, two, or three linebackers on defense. They may vary their positions and assignments. One linebacker may red-dog and the other two should stay; two linebackers may dog and one may cover; or all three may rush the passer.

4. In this drill, the offensive backs are running a divide so that the quarterback is given practice in hitting either man, depending upon who red-dogs.

5. Coaching points for the quarterback in this drill are as follows: 1) If the quarterback is retreating, and the middle backer or the left backer dogs, he will usually unload the ball to the back on his right. 2) If the pass called in the huddle is a quick one, then the quarterback might go straight back rather than have his knees sideways, so he would be in position to see and hit either back. This would be advantageous if the right backer dogged, because he would want to hit the offensive back on his left side. 3) However, if the quarterback is retreating, and the right backer comes in, then the quarterback will turn up as he goes back and hit the offensive back on his left side. He must *sense* this man dogging, since he is coming in from the blind side. 4) Again, a key

coaching point to stress in this drill is the release of the ball so that the receiver can handle it without any difficulty. The passer must *ease* the ball into his teammate's hands.

Quick Pass Drill

The purpose of this drill is to serve as a warm-up and allow the passers to throw as many passes as possible in a limited period.

1. Many times a drill will serve its purpose, but is limited because it is too involved and does not provide enough repetition to be beneficial. However, here is a warm-up drill that allows the passer and receivers to throw and catch with little lost time. In addition, the passer and receivers are practicing frequently used maneuvers.

2. One major shortcoming in many passing and kicking drills is using an insufficient number of footballs. This point is particularly true in the case of the quick pass drill. Three to five balls are necessary, as well as one player or manager to feed the center.

3. Place a center, quarterback, and several receivers on offense. (The receivers may be all the tight ends.) No defensive players are employed.

4. The quarterback calls cadence, and the ball is usually snapped on a quick count.

5. All the receivers run the same pattern for the quick pass. If the drill is used as a warm-up, they are not allowed to line up wider than 7 yards.

Quick Pass Footwork Drill

The purpose of this drill is to develop the footwork and rhythm necessary in throwing a quick pass.

1. This drill is not designed to see how many passes can be thrown, but to perfect the footwork necessary in throwing a quick pass.

2. Station a center, quarterback, and several receivers on offense. The center should have at least two footballs so that valuable time will not be lost.

3. The quarterback receives the ball, pushes off his left foot with his right foot dropping back, and throws quick passes to the receivers.

Position Timing Drill

The purpose of this drill is to work on one particular maneuver of the passing game. We shall describe how the passer works on his footwork and timing for a 12-yard out.

1. Place a center, quarterback, and one receiver on offense. No defensive men are needed.

2. The receiver should assume the position he would be in if he were actually running an out or sideline pass. Since there is just one receiver and we do not want to tire

him, the position timing drill is used. This drill allows the quarterback to concentrate on any phase of the passing game and thus saves time.

3. With this type of drill, a coach can devote his attention to the quarterback. In turn, the quarterback can focus his attention and perfect his timing with the receiver, because he knows where the receiver will be stationed.

Opposite Drill

The object of this drill is to improve and emphasize a specific pass maneuver and provide practice in the essential skill of looking off.

1. Locate a center, a quarterback, and two receivers on offense. No defensive players are needed.

2. The quarterback is required to throw to either receiver. Both receivers are stationed 12 yards downfield. They are located in the final spot desired for a sideline pass.

3. The quarterback does not always know which receiver he is going to hit, but takes his cue from one of the ends. The end will usually have the quarterback throw to the man opposite the one he is looking at when he retreats. This procedure is used to avoid developing the habit of looking at the key receiver as the quarterback sets to throw.

4. In the early season, when sore arms are frequent, it is recommended that the quarterback go through the drill without releasing the ball.

Quarterback Production Drill With a Center

The purpose of this drill is to practice the essential fundamentals of ball-handling, pivoting, retreating to throw, and setting up to pass.

1. Place the three top quarterbacks on offense and provide a center for each. Make certain that the centers are experienced and not just fill-ins for this drill. Bad habits result from not using regular centers, and little learning is accomplished by anyone.

2. Each center must have a football. Since this is an early season drill, sometimes we use a weighted football, because it strengthens the fingers, hands, and wrists of the centers and the quarterbacks.

3. The quarterbacks do not release the football and throw in the early phases of this drill. We are concentrating on the fundamentals of setting up to throw. Later on, a receiver for each quarterback is added.

4. The quarterbacks begin by receiving the snap and alternate calling cadence. In this maneuver, we attempt to gain uniformity of voice.

5. A coach stations himself in front of, and slightly to the side of, the first group. From this position he has an excellent view of all six men and can detect any irregularity quite easily.

6. All quarterbacks go through the same maneuvers each time; however, only one quarterback calls cadence.

Quarterback Production Drill Without a Center

This is a pre-season drill that is used when the quarterbacks report before the rest of the squad. Generally, there are no centers available at this time; at the most, one center is on hand.

1. Locate three or more quarterbacks on offense. Each quarterback must have a football.

2. Align the quarterbacks 5 yards apart so that each has ample room to get depth and maneuver.

3. Since only the fundamentals of setting up to throw are stressed, receivers are not required. The quarterbacks do not release the football.

4. All quarterbacks execute the same play, with only one calling cadence.

5. Coaching points in this drill are as follows: The quarterbacks assume stance and only receive the snap. They receive the snap and push off. The quarterbacks receive the snap, push off, and retreat an exact number of steps (four). All quarterbacks receive the snap, push off, retreat four steps, and go through the complete motions of throwing the football.

6. With this step-by-step method, and a coach positioned in front of the lead unit, every detail can be examined.

7. Corrections should be made so that the three quarterbacks can benefit, because they are all within range of the coach's voice.

8. This is an excellent pre-season drill that will pay many dividends.

15 / **The Defensive Backfield**

COACHING THE LINEBACKERS

by Donald E. Fuoss

Don Fuoss
California State University, Sacramento

There is a difference of opinion among football coaches as to what and how much should be taught to linebackers. Arguments range all the way from, "Just turn them loose, do not bother them with details, and let them play football," to the other extreme, which is, "If the key (guard) moves his big toe, the linebacker reacts with a counter movement of twitching his big toe."

In response to these two extremes, many coaches do not have a detailed knowledge of good linebacker play with all of the coaching points. Second, teaching the keys and prescribed reactions are to aid and help the linebacker execute his position assignment, not to hinder him. Few linebackers are capable of finding the ball, attacking the ball-carrier, and making the tackle without adequate coaching. We are firm believers in teaching proper techniques so the linebacker knows who, when, where, why, and how to play his position. Rather than debate the issue further, however, perhaps we can best clarify our point by including the following dictionary definitions:

Key—"Something that gives an explanation or provides a solution; an arrangement of the salient characters of a group . . . designated to facilitate identification; of basic importance; fundamental."

Reaction—"Reciprocal or return or influence. The force which a body opposes to a force acting upon it. Activity aroused in an organism by a stimulus; a response."

Technique—"The method or the details of procedure essential to expertness of execution in any art, science, etc.—hence, manner of performance with reference to such expertness."

Following is a discussion of the keys, reactions, and techniques for the linebacker to help and aid him in doing his job effectively and efficiently.

The linebacker in a straight alignment, without employing defensive stunts, should

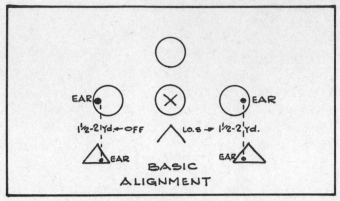

Diagram 15-1

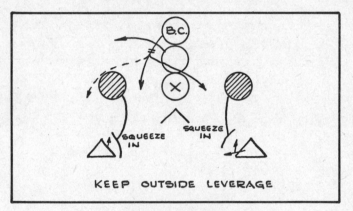

Diagram 15-2

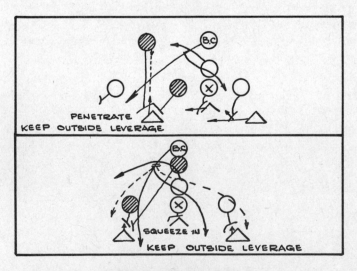

Diagrams 15-3 and 15-4

key the opposing guard on whom he takes his basic alignment (Diagram 15-1). As part of the forcing unit, the linebacker must be able to handle the running play to his area first. If the run does not hit in his area, then he must free himself and move to the football. He should stop inside plays and pursue the wide plays from inside-out. He must move to an angle which will put him in front of the ball-carrier at the earliest possible moment. If a pass shows, he must give underneath support to his secondary defenders. By keying the offensive guard initially, the linebacker is better able to read and identify backfield action and the offensive play. A linebacker must be drilled to watch his key and react properly in order to operate with maximum efficiency. If the linebacker merely watches only the backfield action, he can be pulled out of position by the deception of the offensive play. This neutralizes and destroys the linebacker's aggressiveness and effectiveness.

It should be kept in mind throughout, that while the linebacker is concentrating on his initial key, reacting as the key moves, he reads through the guard to the near back and the football. The initial guard key is merely a means of helping the linebacker find the football and get to it. Therefore, the linebacker should not permit himself to be locked up with his guard key unless backfield movement indicates the ball is right behind the attacking guard. The young linebacker, in particular, eliminates himself from pursuit when he reads only his basic guard key and becomes tied up with him when the ball is going away from his position.

Proper Reaction Techniques

1. When the guard key comes off to block the linebacker, he is either going to block him out or in.

A. As shown in Diagram 15-2, the guards are attempting to block from inside-out on the linebackers for an inside play up the middle, with the ball-carrier right behind the attacking key.

In this type of situation, as a rule, the guard key will step with the inside foot first in order to drive the linebacker(s) to the outside. The linebacker(s) should jab step forward, with the inside foot first, at the head of the blocker, maintaining the hitting position throughout. A common mistake is the failure of the linebacker to jab step forward into the attacking guard key when the blocker comes toward him.

When the football is behind the attacking guards, as shown in Diagrams 15-2 to 15-4, the linebacker(s) should deliver a blow to the blocker's chest with a forearm lift, the purpose of which is to raise the blocker and, if possible, destroy his balance in order to permit the linebacker to move to the football. If the linebacker can collapse the attacking guard and overpower him, he has done an excellent job in getting to the football. If he cannot shed the blocker, he should maintain an outside-in position (leverage) on the attacking guard and not be driven out. If he is physically capable of *stuffing the blocker in the hole*, he should do so. He should fight pressure and keep leverage on the blocker, squeezing his man and the ball-carrier to the inside, into the middle guard and the other linebacker. Should the ball-carrier attempt to pop to the outside (dotted lines in Diagrams 15-2 and 15-4) instead of coming inside his guards and running off the block of his center, the linebacker(s) will be in the hole in the original off-set position and should make the tackle. However, once the ball-carrier gets in the hole, as shown in Diagrams 15-2, 15-3, or 15-4, the linebacker(s) should release and come to the inside, filling the hole with the body, or drive the blocker into the hole, closing it.

The technique of delivering the blow from underneath the opponent is for the linebacker to jab step forward with his inside foot, dip his tail, get his shoulder up under the head of the blocker, and slam his forearm into the attacking guard's chest. The outside hand may be placed against the blocker's helmet, and by pushing with the outside hand and using a shoving action with the hitting arm, the linebacker can use leverage on the attacking guard to dispose of him in order to get to the ball-carrier.

Diagram 15-5 shows the offensive right guard taking an inside-out, cut-off position on the left linebacker. In this situation, the left linebacker does not want to become locked up with the attacking (right) guard, so he should slide off his block, using his hands after he reads his next key, which is the action of the ball and the backs going away from his position.

The reaction techniques for the right (off-side) linebacker (Diagram 15-3) are the same as those for the left linebacker (Diagram 15-5). However, should the ball-carrier come back to the inside instead of running off the lead block, the right linebacker plays it, keeping outside leverage (Diagrams 15-2 and 15-4).

The left (on-side) linebacker (Diagram 15-3) is confronted with a second blocker, the near back, along with the attacking guard. Other situations of the near back blocking the linebacker are shown in Diagrams 15-9 and 15-10. In this particular situation (Diagram 15-3), the left linebacker must keep outside leverage on the offensive right guard, jab stepping at his head and slamming with his inside forearm, as described previously and shown in Diagram 15-2. As he slams the guard and reads the near back coming toward the line of scrimmage, the critical point-of-attack must be directed at the left linebacker's position (Diagram 15-3). The linebacker must slam the guard and then step with his back (outside) foot and slam the near back. If the linebacker remembers nothing else except to try to get penetration slamming into the near back, he is likely to achieve a stand-off with the attacking blockers. While he might not be able to make the tackle, at least he will not be driven off the line if he gets penetration, and his body will be in the designated hole. If he fails to move into his blockers and catches on defense as the result of failing to react in the prescribed manner, it is likely he will be blown off the line of scrimmage and there will be a void in the defense. Under these circumstances, the ball-carrier cannot fail to make yardage.

The right (off-side) linebacker (Diagram 15-3) should use his hands to release from the block, and should also be filling the hole. It is somewhat difficult for the fullback to break back over the right linebacker's position. However, off an I backfield set, as shown in Diagram 15-4, the right linebacker must be careful not to overrun the ball and permit the ball-carrier to break back through his vacated area. He should squeeze the ball-carrier to the inside, as mentioned previously. The middle guard should also be moving laterally to the ball.

As shown in Diagram 15-4, the left linebacker must keep outside-in leverage on the attacking blockers, as shown in Diagrams 15-2 and 15-3.

B. As shown in Diagram 15-5, the offensive left guard is attempting an outside-in, cut-off block on the right linebacker. Since the critical point-of-attack is outside the defender's position, and the attacking key is trying to cut off the linebacker's pursuit, the guard is likely to step with his outside foot first.

When the linebacker was played with his inside eye on the outside eye of the offensive guard, we always instructed him to take a short, lateral (slide) step with his outside foot first in order to retain the outside-in, eye-to-eye relationship versus this situation. Since we are now lining up ear-to-ear with the offensive guard, the linebacker is off-set slightly wider in his outside-in position. However, we still teach the short, lateral slide step first with the outside foot and then the jab step forward, depending on the other keys. As shown in Diagram 15-5, with a diving action of the near back, the right linebacker must read his movement, and in this situation stay home, meeting force with force from the attacking guard. If the near back were to move laterally, as on the fullback option play (dotted lines), the right linebacker would slide off his blocker and pursue laterally. He should not stay locked up with his guard key if the point-of-attack is not directed at his position.

A common error is for the (right) linebacker to jab step forward with his inside foot first, as is proper (Diagrams 15-2 to 15-4) when the attacking guard is stepping for position or attempting to drive his head between the defender and the critical point-of-attack (Diagram 15-5) for the right linebacker. Therefore, as a coaching point, we instruct the on-side linebacker in situations A and B to step first with the same foot with which the attacking guard steps.

Maintaining proper alignment and not being caught out of position will always place the linebacker in a good position to deliver a blow to the attacking blocker. The purpose is to keep leverage on the blocker, destroy his block, control him, and at the same time do not permit the blocker to get to the linebacker's vulnerable area.

The reactions for the left (off-side) linebacker (Diagram 15-5) have been explained.

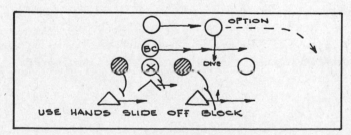

Diagram 15-5

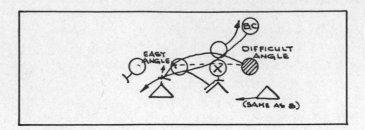

Diagram 15-6

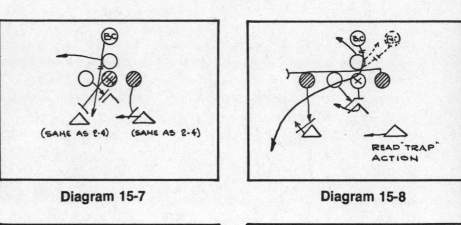

Diagram 15-7   **Diagram 15-8**

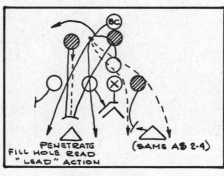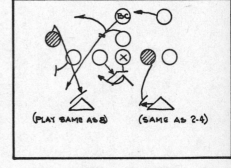

Diagram 15-9   **Diagram 15-10**

Since the critical point-of-attack is away from his position, as he picks up his next key and the action of the backfield, he should use his hands to slide off the guard's block in order to pursue the ball-carrier. He should not permit himself to be locked up inside with his attacking guard (Diagrams 15-2 to 15-4).

2. When the guard key blocks in on the middle guard, the linebacker is confronted with one of several situations which are as follows:

A. The trap or lead-through block of the off-side guard (Diagram 15-6) or the cross block of the center (Diagram 15-7).

B. The outside-in or down block of the on-side tackle (Diagram 15-8).

C. The lead or blast block of the back or backs (Diagrams 15-9 and 15-10).

In each instance, when the offensive guard blocks down on the middle guard, the on-side (left) linebacker (Diagrams 15-6 to 15-10) must discern quickly that the guard is blocking in or down, and is not stepping directly toward the linebacker, as shown in Diagrams 15-2 to 15-5, whether he steps with his inside or outside foot first. Second, the on-side linebacker should jab step forward with the inside foot first, playing the previously mentioned situations as a progressive sequence.

A. After the left linebacker's initial guard key blocks in on the middle guard (Diagrams 15-6 to 15-10), the defender picks up a secondary key from movement toward his position. Diagrams 15-6 and 15-7 show the left linebacker maintaining his outside-in position. He should play the attacking blocker, as described previously and shown in Diagram 15-2, fighting pressure, maintaining leverage, etc. By not crossing the line of scrimmage, it is difficult for the off-side (left) offensive guard (Diagram 15-6) and the center (Diagram 15-7) to trap the linebacker.

If the middle guard is doing a good job of hand shivering the offensive center, the latter should have difficulty getting free cleanly to block the linebacker (Diagram 15-7). Second, not too many teams trap or lead through on the linebacker (Diagram 15-6) with the off-side guard, unless the defender has a tendency to play too close in his initial alignment.

B. A more common and more dangerous situation is shown in Diagram 15-8, namely, the guard (right) key blocks in on the middle guard, and the tackle (right) blocks down on the on-side (left) linebacker.

As the on-side (left) linebacker takes a short jab step forward (inside foot) in his initial movement, reacting to the movement of his initial guard key, he should protect himself from the outside-in block of the tackle by bringing up his back (outside) foot and forearm, and by slamming the tackle if he blocks down on him. If this occurs, the linebacker should fight pressure through the tackle's head to keep from being wiped out to the inside. If the linebacker can get a stand-off with the tackle, and can make the play from that position, he may fill to the inside in tackling the ball-carrier. Otherwise, he should not go inside the tackle's block unless he is certain he can make the tackle in the hole.

If the tackle is blocking down on the linebacker, despite the fact the (left) tackle is supposed to keep the offensive (right) tackle off his (left) linebacker, the latter is protected and braced when he brings up his outside foot and flipper. However, the linebacker must release quickly from the tackle blocker by reversing his hands and using his outside hand for leverage on the blocker's helmet. If he stays locked up with the attacking tackle, the linebacker will not be able to fill the hole in the defensive line made by the trap block on the defensive tackle (Diagram 15-8).

C. The third progression is the situation faced by the linebacker, as shown in Diagrams 15-9 and 15-10. As indicated previously, even though the initial key is the offensive guard for the Oklahoma linebacker, the latter should always read through the guard to the near back (Diagram 15-9).

The linebacker's initial movement is a jab step forward with the inside (right) foot to play situation 2, (A), then he brings up the outside (left) foot to play situation 2, (B), and then steps up again with the inside (right) foot to play situation 3, (C), in this progression or sequence. As the linebacker reads the near back coming forward toward his position (Diagram 15-9), he must get penetration, and should end up with the inside foot forward, taking on the attacking (near back) blocker as he does the guard (Diagrams 15-2 to 15-4). He should keep outside leverage on the attacking blocker, or there will be a void in the defense.

The lead block of the halfback is more difficult to read (Diagram 15-10). However, when meeting a team that runs a lead play with a halfback in a close wing position, the defensive linebacker must be drilled to meet this situation just as he must be drilled to meet each of the other situations. Offensive tendencies usually dictate when a team is likely to run an isolation play with the close wing cracking back on the linebacker. Second, when the offensive guard blocks in and the tackle blocks out, situation 2, (C), if there is not a near back to lead through, then it must be the close wing cracking back (Diagram 15-10) or the off-guard trapping (Diagram 15-6), or the center (Diagram 15-7). As the linebacker reads progression (A) and the blocker does not come from the inside, he immediately brings up the outside foot, etc., for progression (B). Since there is no near back (Diagram 15-10 compared to Diagram 15-9), the on-side (left) linebacker is in a position to see the close wingback coming inside to block him. This is similar to the situation of the tackle blocking down on him (Diagram 15-8), and the linebacker should meet the blocker and fight pressure in the same manner described previously.

Once again, as we pointed out in Diagram 15-8, if the linebacker can shoot the gap and make the tackle before the blocker (close flanker in this case) can crack back on him, he should do so. Otherwise, if he meets the blocker in the hole, he should stack up the play at the line of scrimmage as long as he is not wiped off to the inside.

The reactions of the right (off-side) linebacker, as shown in Diagrams 15-7, 15-9, and 15-10, should be the same as those shown in Diagrams 15-2 to 15-4. The reactions for the off-side (right) linebacker when his initial guard key pulls, as shown in Diagrams 15-6 and 15-8, will be explained.

3. When the guard key blocks out on the tackle (Diagram 15-11), if the linebacker(s) will read this as the right on-side linebacker does in Diagram 15-5, namely, take a short side step laterally to the outside, going on the assumption the offensive guard is coming off to block him out, the defender will be placed close to the tackle who is coming behind the offensive guard. Then the linebacker should jab step forward with his inside foot into the tackle in order to keep outside-in leverage on the offensive tackle and the ball-carrier. The linebacker should squeeze the play into his middle guard, and stuff the tackle into the hole (Diagram 15-11).

4. When the guard key pulls to the on-side behind his tackle, as the offensive right guard does in Diagram 15-12, generally the (left) linebacker should go with his key to his

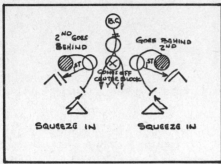

Diagram 15-11

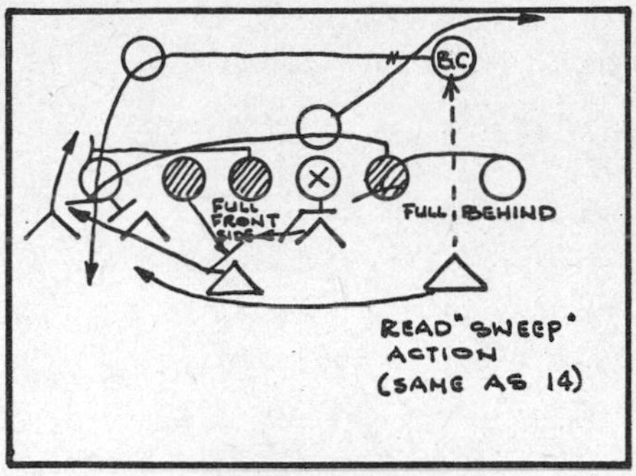

Diagram 15-12

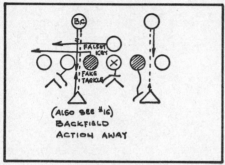

Diagram 15-13

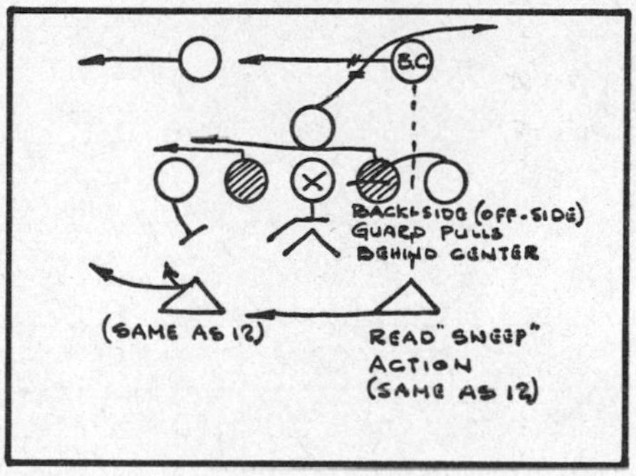

Diagram 15-14

side of the line of scrimmage. It is very likely the pulling lineman will lead the linebacker directly to the ball or reasonably close to the critical point-of-attack.

A. As shown in Diagram 15-12, the left linebacker should react as follows: as the offensive right guard opens and pulls to the front side, the (left) defender should also open step and turn in the same direction as his key, whip his inside (right) arm across the head of the offensive (right) tackle in the event the latter is blocking down on him, stay slightly behind the pulling guard, and play the ball-carrier from inside-out. The linebacker should not fire through the pulling guard's hole, unless a stunt has been called, because it might be a trap play. The play of the right (off-side) linebacker will be explained as the off-side guard pulls behind the center (Diagram 15-12).

B. Diagram 15-13 shows the false key or key breaker, where the offensive (right) guard pulls on-side and the quarterback hands off to the diving halfback, going on the assumption the left linebacker is going to run out of his initial position when his guard key pulls out.

While these plays look good on paper, they seldom break clean. As pointed out previously, any time a remaining back is in the near back position, the linebacker should key through his guard to the offensive back. Wherever the back starts forward toward the line of scrimmage (Diagrams 15-3, 15-9, 15-13, and 15-16), the defender must stay at home and be prepared to meet force with force until he is certain the critical point-of-attack is not in his immediate area. However, if a linebacker runs out of his initial position when his guard key pulls out, and ignores his other keys of the remaining back and the football, then a play as shown in Diagram 15-13 would be effective. Diagram 15-16 shows a false key play away from the right guard pulling behind his tackle.

.5. When the guard key pulls behind his center (Diagrams 15-14 to 15-17), by reading the near back the secondary key will indicate the type of play as follows:

A. As shown in Diagram 15-14, with the remaining (near) back coming across flat, read sweep action. The off-side (right) linebacker should pursue at a deeper angle, also shown in Diagram 15-12, and not permit himself to be tied up with his middle guard or left linebacker.

B. Diagram 15-15 shows the remaining back coming toward the line at a sharp angle. The right linebacker should read trap action, and fill as shown.

C. In Diagram 15-16, with the near back coming toward the line of scrimmage, the right linebacker is confronted with the same situation the left linebacker was confronted with in Diagram 15-13, namely, the false key. The right linebacker reads key or lead action, and should take on the near back from outside-in, just as though the offensive guard was attacking him, as shown in Diagram 15-2. The reaction of the left linebacker would be to pick up his secondary key, namely the football (Diagram 15-16), release from his pulling guard who is false-keying, and fill to the football, as shown in Diagram 15-16. Incidentally, the reactions of the left linebacker in Diagrams 15-14 and 15-15 have been discussed.

D. As shown in Diagram 15-17, with the backs going opposite the pulling guards, the linebacker(s) should read bootleg action and attempt to get back and pick up a crossing receiver coming through their zone.

6. When the guard key shows pocket or dropback pass (Diagram 15-18), the linebacker(s) should drop quickly to their respective hook zones, which are approximately 10 to 12 yards deep, opposite the offensive ends' normal positions. The reaction technique would be as follows: shout, *Pass,* shift attention quickly to the quarterback to read his dropback passing action, and drop-step, cross-over, and sprint back to the hook zone.

There is a difference of opinion among coaches as to the best technique for the linebacker to employ in getting back to his hook zone and covering the receiver on a dropback pass. One method is for the defender to watch the passer and continue to sprint back with cross-over steps until the passer pulls up. Then the defender should square off and continue to back up with short steps as he faces the passer, with his body under control, ready to react in any direction when the ball is thrown. Since the passer is not going to throw the football to the linebacker, the latter must move either to play the ball through the receiver or play the anticipated flight by reacting to the passer's first throwing motion. If the defender waits until the football leaves the passer's hands, he will not be able to get in front of the ball to intercept or to deflect it if the pass is thrown accurately.

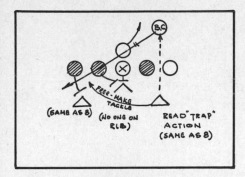

Diagram 15-15

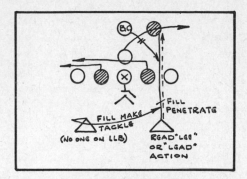

Diagram 15-16

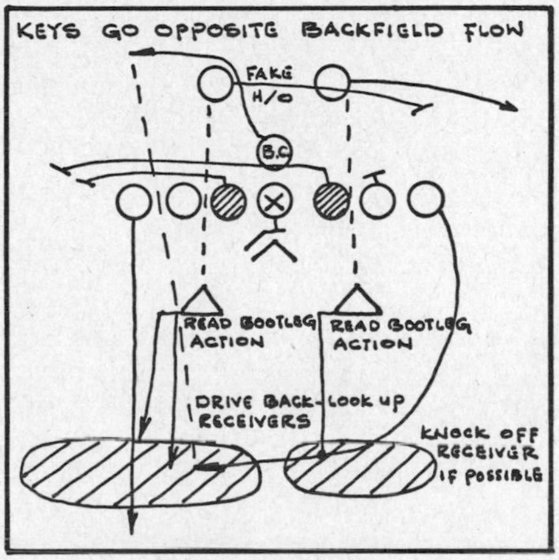

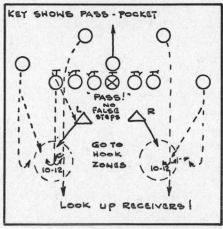

Diagram 15-17

Diagram 15-18

A second method is for the linebacker to turn away from the passer and look up the receiver immediately covering him closely. A third method is a combination of the two described previously. The defender should turn the sprint back toward his hook zone as quickly as possible, as soon as his initial key shows pass. Then he should square off and look up the intended receiver.

Regardless of the method employed, a linebacker should not false step forward when his initial key shows pass if the guard drop steps immediately. Second, when the linebacker takes his alignment, he should know immediately when the offensive set shows (Diagram 15-18), whether the tight end is to his side (left) or the split end is to his side (right). If it is the former, then the hook zone will be in the vicinity of the tight end's initial position approximately 10 to 12 yards off the line of scrimmage. If a split end is detached (right), then the linebacker (right) should work further to the outside as he drives back to his pass responsibility.

7. When the guard key shows sprint-out pass action (Diagram 15-19), the off-side (left) linebacker should play it just as if it were a drop-back pass, as shown in Diagram 15-18 and described previously, since the key shows backside pass action.

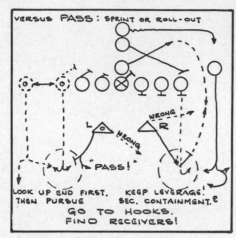

Diagram 15-19   **Diagram 15-20**

The on-side (right) linebacker should react by driving away from the line of scrimmage toward his hook zone, since the quarterback (passer) is sprinting away from the line of scrimmage, as shown in Diagram 15-19 by the number 1.

If the passer decides to run with the football, then the on-side (right) linebacker should come back toward the line of scrimmage because he has secondary containment, as shown by the number 2 in Diagram 15-19.

Basically, both linebackers play the sprint or roll-out pass the same as the pocket or drop-back pass in that both go to the hook zones first and look up the receivers.

8. When the guard key shows action pass (Diagram 15-20), the off-side (left) linebacker reads backside pass action and sprints to his hook zone, looking up a receiver, the same as shown in Diagrams 15-18 and 15-19.

The on-side (right) linebacker must play for the run first, because a good faking action will hold him in position, as shown in Diagram 15-20, by the number 1. If the fake is deceptive, the on-side (right) linebacker has no other choice but to tackle the offensive back whom he thinks has the ball. If the fake is poor, then the on-side linebacker should read the quarterback's actions the same as a sprint-out and the defender should go to his hook zone and look up the intended receiver, which is the same as shown in Diagram 15-19. The linebacker has secondary containment responsibility, marked number 2 in Diagram 15-20, in the event the passer decides to run with the football. The defender should keep leverage on the passer-runner.

These are basic zone coverage principles. The off-linebacker might be assigned man coverage on the remaining back to his side when the ball rolls away from his position. Or the linebackers might be assigned man coverage underneath as their basic responsibility.

SUPPORT FROM THE SECONDARY

by Steve Sogge and Tom Bielenberg

Steve Sogge
Formerly, University of Oregon

Tom Bielenberg
Welches Jr. High
Wemne, Oregon

Increased emphasis on the outside running game is placing a great deal more pressure on the defensive perimeter for run support. With the trend toward veer options, wishbone, run and shoot, and the sweep, the defensive backfield is required to accept more run responsibility. Many offenses are complementing their outside running attack with some sound play-action passes. This emphasis on the outside attack adds up to more pressure on the defensive secondary.

Our team defense is based on the premise of team pride and maximum pursuit to the football. We like to have our secondary support the run as aggressively as the linebackers and interior players. Conversely, our pass defense relies as heavily on the linebackers and interior players as it does on the secondary. When a mistake occurs on a running or passing play, the responsibility is placed on our total defense. By approaching defense using this team concept, we are able to build great pride and closeness into the entire defense. Thus, no player can ever point an accusing finger at a teammate without first pointing it at himself.

The team always lines up with four deep backs. Two basic coverages are used, although we have many other change-up coverages that are used in special situations. We do the best job possible to disguise the coverage to avoid telegraphing the particular coverage that is being used. This is done by always lining up the same, regardless of the coverage. Our alignment will vary, however, depending upon field position, down and distance, and the opponent. Diagram 15-21 shows our basic alignment.

Our communication begins when both the strong and the free safeties make a run and pass support call to the corner on their side of the formation. The terminology that we use is *sky* or *cloud*—sky being safety support, and cloud being corner support. If the call

271

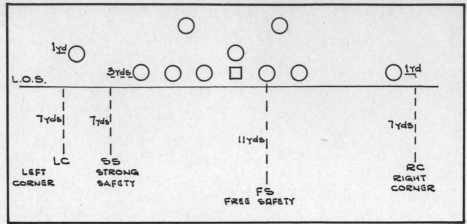

Diagram 15-21

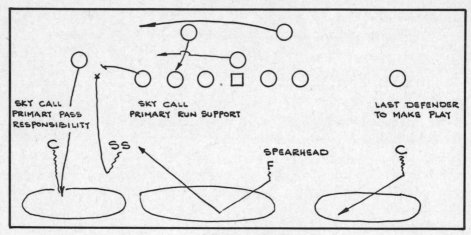

Diagram 15-22

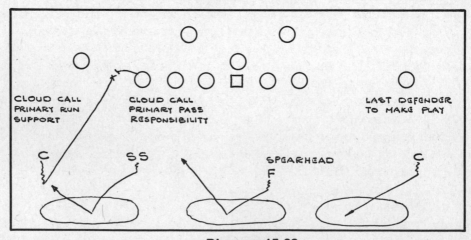

Diagram 15-23

is sky, the safety will be inclined to think run, prior to the snap, because he is the primary run support man. On a cloud call, the opposite is true. Now the cornerback becomes the primary support man. The call is made prior to every snap by the two safeties, and then echoed by the cornerback to their side. With run appearing to either side, both the safety and the cornerback know which player has primary run support and which one will play pass first.

The safeties make their sky and cloud calls based on differing criteria. The primary rule is the amount of split by the wide receiver to their side. In general, if the split is 7 yards or less, a cloud call is used. If it is over 7 yards, we go ahead with a sky call. Sky calls are made a large percentage of the time because the splits are over 7 yards, and due to the type of players we have as our safety men. Our safeties are tough individuals whereas the cornerbacks are the best athletes. Other criteria affecting the safety's call are: hash mark, down and distance, secondary coverage, prior support call, offensive techniques, game plan, and personnel.

The run-pass key which is used to determine whether the play is a run or pass is not restricted to one man or a single key. Our secondary reads run or pass by reading a combination of things such as backfield action, uncovered lineman, tight end or wide receivers coming off the line. Many times the overall play development based on opponent tendencies is the best key to determining the play.

As the running play develops, the away safety and cornerback disregard the run support call that was made previously to their side. The on-side safety and cornerback must now execute their sky or cloud call.

Diagram 15-22 shows the run support lanes versus a strong-side option. The strong safety must defeat the tight end's block. There are three techniques he may use. The on-side cornerback now has secondary run support and must be aware of the pass to the flanker or tight end. If the flanker runs deep, the cornerback mus un with him until he definitely recognizes run, and then he must explode toward the ball-carrier for secondary run support. It is his responsibility to cover play-action passes, pitch passes, and double passes. The receivers are his key.

The free safety gets depth and works strong-side, reading the play. As he moves strong, he reads the tight end and flanker for a possible pass. Once he definitely determines run, he moves up to an inside spear-head route, looking to eliminate the cut back. The backside cornerback gets depth while playing the split end man-for-man on any pass. He rotates through center field and is the last defensive man should the runner break into the open.

Diagram 15-23 shows a strong-side option versus a cloud call. Now the strong safety must get depth playing for any pass. The on-side cornerback must reduce the running lane and defeat the blocker. The backside safety and the cornerback are the same.

Emphasis, whether it is a sky or cloud call, is: 1) reduce the running lane, and 2) force the ball-carrier to cut back into the pursuit or take an unnatural path to the outside, stripped of his blockers (Diagrams 15-24 and 15-25).

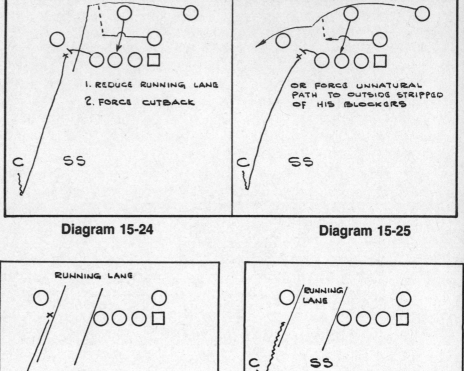

Diagram 15-24   **Diagram 15-25**

Diagram 15-26   **Diagram 15-27**

A ball-carrier must not be given a clean, natural path to the outside.

The secret of successful run support is to explode toward the line of scrimmage as soon as run is recognized. The more time it takes to get to the line of scrimmage, the less successful the defense will be. As an example, Diagram 15-26 shows fast, aggressive support whereas Diagram 15-27 shows slow, non-aggressive support. Notice the difference in the width and size of the running lane.

The proper type of aggressive support must be sold to the players, and they must have as much pride in supporting the run as they do in playing the pass.

Run support techniques will differ, depending on the type of play being run. Against the sweep, the primary run support man is instructed to explode to the line of scrimmage, reducing the running lane, and the chance of collision with the lead blocker. Our players are told always to keep the outside arm and leg away from the contact and throw the inside shoulder through the outside knee of the lead blocker, thus forming a pile and forcing the ball-carrier on an unnatural path.

Against the option where a tight end or lead back is being played, our basic method is to meet the tight end at the line of scrimmage, dipping the inside shoulder and driving through the tight end's outside shoulder. The important point to remember is that our two basic objectives also hold true on option plays: 1) reduce the running lane, and 2) force the ball-carrier to cut back into pursuit or take an unnatural path to the outside, stripped of his blockers. Our primary support man must not be washed out of the way.

We have other change-up techniques for playing off the blocker: 1) play the blocker with the hands, and 2) start up the field and dip underneath the blocker (Diagram 15-28). This technique can only be used when there is enough separation between the blocker and the ball-carrier.

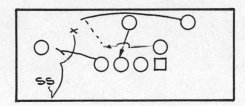

Diagram 15-28

On a sky call, many times cornerbacks are blocked by the flanker or split ends. This block is usually a stalk block and not a difficult one to defeat. Our cornerbacks are taught that there is no way a receiver can block them. The development of this attitude is important. The cornerbacks are given the opportunity to defeat the block by taking the outside or inside of the blocker. By this we mean that the cornerback may start a few steps to the inside, drawing the blocker's weight in, and then dip to the outside to beat the block. Having the freedom to go either inside or outside makes him difficult to block.

One coaching point that is important here is that the cornerback must read the relationship between himself and the ball-carrier. It is dangerous for the defensive back to take the inside route if the ball-carrier is close enough to beat him outside. Their primary rule is never to be washed inside and let the runner get outside when a sky call is being used. Generally, we teach getting their hands on the receiver and using their quickness to defeat him.

The cornerback's normal assignment is to take an outside path when the call is sky, and an inside path when the call is cloud (Diagrams 15-29 and 15-30).

Run support to the weak side of the formation is executed in the same manner. Crackback blocks are used, offensively, to a great degree. Without a tight end to block, the offense must crack back or use some sort of lead blocker. Our main coaching point for playing a crackback block is to defeat the block first. This means that all attention must be focused on the blocker and then move to the ball-carrier. Normally we will be in a sky call to the weak side so our cornerbacks are allowed to have the deep responsibility.

One of the axioms for success in the secondary is great communication on pass and run. Talking in all drills, scrimmages, and games is emphasized. Communication cannot

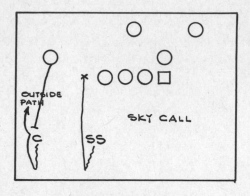

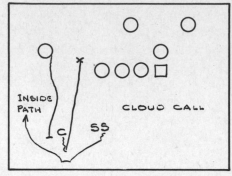

Diagram 15-29   **Diagram 15-30**

be overemphasized. It is a small aspect that will eventually contribute to success or failure in the secondary. We have found it necessary to emphasize communication at the very first practice and continue that emphasis throughout the entire season.

Important Coaching Points

1. Emphasize a team defense where 11 players are responsible for the run and 11 players are responsible for the pass.

2. Disguise coverages so that the quarterback is confused, as well as confusing the perimeter blockers.

3. Objectives of run support are: 1) reduce the running lane, and 2) force the ball-carrier to cut back into the pursuit or take an unnatural path to the outside, stripped of his blockers.

4. In order to be effective in run support, the play must be recognized quickly and the support executed aggressively. Effective run support cannot be passive.

5. This style of defense must be sold to the secondary.

6. When supporting the run, a player cannot be washed out of the way. He must be dedicated to holding his ground at all costs.

7. Always give 100 percent attention to defeating the blocker before attempting to make the tackle.

8. Communication can never be overemphasized. It is the most important element for success in the secondary.

Part V
COACHING THE LINEMEN

16 / The Offensive Line

OFFENSIVE LINE PLAY

by Hugh "Duffy" Daugherty

Hugh "Duffy" Daugherty
Formerly, Michigan State University

In offensive line play, everything starts with the stance. We give our players considerable leeway in the type of stance they may use. No two will use exactly the same stance. In other words, we permit them to use a square stance with their feet on the same plane, or to use a slight drag leg stance with one leg in back of the other.

We do, however, require them to follow certain fundamentals in arriving at an offensive stance. Their tails should be up with their backs on a plane so that they may move out in any direction. Linemen are asked to use a stance with the width approximately the same as their shoulders. They have little or no weight on their hand, and must be able to move equally well forward or to the left or right.

Next, we teach the linemen the method we want used in pulling. This is an important part of our line play, since each of our linemen will pull on various plays. In pulling, we always have the lineman step out with the foot in the direction he is going, using the step-out method of pulling rather than the cross-over method. We want our lineman to get his depth on the first step to enable him to clear the next offensive lineman. He pushes himself off his hand and shifts his entire weight on the foot he is stepping out with.

The course he will take will depend on the technique he is trying to execute, whether he is pulling to round the horn, or downfield blocking, or whether he is pulling to execute a trap block, or whether he is pulling for pass protection. We like our linemen to run low with a good, wide base so that they will always be in a blocking position and will be able to block any defensive man who unexpectedly crosses their path.

Lead Post Block

We use a shoulder block almost exclusively. In our offense, we do a great deal of

281

double-teaming or tandem blocking. Our most successful technique is what we call a lead post block. The post blocker has two functions: First, he should break the charge of the defensive man. Second, he should keep the seam closed between himself and his lead blocker. He does this by taking a short step toward his lead blocker with the foot nearest the lead blocker. He does not charge out at the defensive man.

The lead blocker steps or shoots, depending on the type of block used, over the shoulder of his post blocker, aiming where the defensive man will be, and not where he is before the play starts, attempting to hit the defensive man at the upper thighs or the waist with the full breadth of his shoulder. He immediately starts driving up through the defensive man's chest, bringing his outside leg up and around to prevent the defensive man from sliding into the path of the ball-carrier. In other words, we prefer to take the defensive man laterally rather than to take him straight back.

Inside-Out Block

Invariably when we are using a lead post block coming from one direction, we will have an inside-out blocker coming from the opposite direction. This is commonly referred to as a trap; however, in present-day football where the defensive linemen are not penetrating all of the time it becomes increasingly difficult to trap them. We, therefore, teach our linemen to execute an inside-out block by pulling and stepping with the foot in the direction they are going.

They get their depth on the first step, start right up into the hole on the next step, get inside position on the man and hit him at the upper thighs or the waist with a hard shoulder block, bring the forearm in as a hook for additional blocking surface, drive up through the defensive man's chest, and bring the outside leg around to prevent the man from sliding into the path of the ball-carrier. In other words, we are trying to block from the inside out. We are going to assume that he is not going to charge, as the waiting lineman is the tough one to take on a trap block of this nature.

Check Blocking at the Line

We use two types of check blocks, depending on the type of defensive play of the opposing lineman. If the defensive man is coming in strong consistently, we will use a high shoulder block, always stepping into the defensive man with the near foot, getting contact first and then getting position on the second step by placing the body between the defensive lineman and the path of the ball-carrier.

If the defensive lineman is hitting and sliding, we go out at him and hook his near knee, and crab block on all fours to try to pin him at the line of scrimmage and not let him slide to the play. We shoot the near arm and shoulder by the defensive lineman and hook his knee. The offensive lineman hooks the defensive lineman with his own leg and crab blocks on all fours.

Downfield Blocking

In downfield blocking, we try to give our men principles to follow. As they round the horn, we tell them either to block the first man to the inside or the first man to the outside. Modern football is a game of speed and movement, and a team is only as fast as its interference; therefore, we emphasize speed.

We also tell the players to follow the principle in the secondary that they never pass up one man to get to another. They will always block the first man who crosses their path. Regarding the type of block used, we like to have our players go into every downfield block with the intention of using their shoulder, and not go into a cross-body block or leave their feet until after contact has been established.

TRAPPING AND PULLING

by Ron Marciniak

Ron Marciniak
University of Miami

In our opinion, every young line coach should try to coach both offensive and defensive line play sometime during his career. If it is not possible to make the switch in an actual coaching assignment, then an effort should be made to study as much of the opposite type line play as possible. Football becomes more meaningful to the line coach when he has had the opportunity to work both with offensive and defensive line play. The change-over will also build his confidence and knowledge of the game. At times it is good to study defensive line play from an offensive point of view.

As a defensive line coach, in order to teach the techniques of destroying the offensive trap, we feel a coach must also know how the offensive coaches teach and train the trapper and the coaching points he uses.

Basically, the trap involves the trapper's fundamental techniques and the offensive influence of his teammate in the area of the defensive man who is to be trapped.

Trap blocking patterns (Diagrams 16-1 to 16-8) are broken down into the following basic patterns: 1. X block (Diagrams 16-1 to 16-3). 2. Quick trap (Diagrams 16-4 to 16-6). 3. Long trap (Diagrams 16-7 to 16-8).

The first important phase of trapping is the near split by the trapper of 2 feet without giving the play away. He should not lean or point before the snap count. The teammate alongside the pulling trapper must move quickly and clear the area where the trap blocker will take his first step.

The next important phase of trapping is the course the trapper takes initially. That first short step of the near foot must be into the line of scrimmage on about a 45° angle. He should pivot on the ball of the other foot and then step off that same foot. His near arm and elbow should be lifted against the rib cage of his body as he steps with the near foot on that first step. His body should be low, head up, and eyes on the spot of contact. He should place his chest over his near leg as the first short step is taken.

284

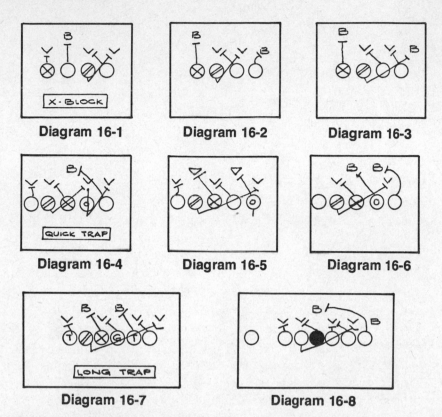

Diagram 16-1   Diagram 16-2   Diagram 16-3

Diagram 16-4   Diagram 16-5   Diagram 16-6

Diagram 16-7   Diagram 16-8

It is essential that the trapper approach the defender from inside-out. If he is parallel to the line of scrimmage, he is increasing his chances of being defeated. When pulling, the trapper's first step should be directed into the line of scrimmage. On the second and third steps, he should gain ground into the line of scrimmage, achieving a proper inside-out approach on the defensive man. Trap the defensive man by using a drive block through the man's inside hip, making contact with the outside shoulder and forearm. As contact is made, drive up through the man. Position is more important than movement. The trapper should get into the hole between the defensive man and his ball-carrier.

Basically, there are three types of influence blocks: 1. Pass influence. 2. Pull away. 3. Fire out.

The offensive man over the area of the defensive man to be trapped should split out the opponent. Split to a point where the defensive lineman will still remain head-up and become removed from the defensive man next to him.

An influence blocker must experiment with his split as the game progresses. He should keep in mind that oversplitting will tip off the trap play. Undersplitting will cause the trap play to be less successful.

The type of influence block used should complement other blocking patterns in the offensive scheme. Strong and correct influence techniques are essential to the success of the trap play. The coach should emphasize the same fundamentals for the influence block as he does in his regular basic blocking techniques.

Quick Trap Blocking Rules

On-Side

On-Side End—Blocks the safety and the deep man on his side.

On-Side Tackle—Takes the most dangerous linebacker from inside out. If there is no linebacker, then he should block No. 2.

Center—Block the backside.

Off-Side

Off-Guard—Pull and trap the first man past the center on the line of scrimmage.

Off-Tackle—Block No. 2.

Off-End—Takes the deep man on his side.

Trap Techniques

The trapping game must be developed with fundamental techniques and drills. These trapping drills must be progressive, and should be taught versus dummies. After the basic fundamentals have been learned, then five men and contact should be used. Following this individual, fundamental stage, progress into team pattern work.

The three fundamental trapping drills we favor are: 1. Bag approach drill. 2. Bag reaction drill. 3. Bag follow-through drill.

In all drills, it is important that the two adjacent men in the pattern work side-by-side. This procedure will teach proper timing in stepping and moving. The center should work alongside the guard in a quick trap drill (Diagram 16-9).

Diagram 16-10 shows the bag approach drill. After the trapper takes his first step, the coach will call the numbered bag to be trapped. The coach calls out position 1, 2, or 3 to stimulate penetration of the defensive lineman.

For the drill shown in Diagram 16-11, use air bags or hand dummies. The bag holders face the coach with their backs toward the trapper. Prior to starting the cadence, the coach signals 1, 2, or 3 to the bag holders. On the starting count, the designated defensive bag holder spins into the trapper low and strong. This drill causes the trapper to react to the type of defensive penetration developed on the snap of the ball.

For the drill shown in Diagram 16-12, lay the bags flat on the ground with the bottom facing the trapper. Repeat the same procedure explained in the approach drill. The low level of the base of the bags will demand proper techniques of contact and leg drive. Emphasize head-up, proper shoulder contact, leg drive, and follow-through.

We believe these fundamental techniques of trapping are sound and workable. The drills will develop a sound trapping game. They must be sold to the players, taught properly, and worked on diligently. Pride in the trapping game will develop and success will result. The properly executed trap pattern is one of the most exciting and explosive plays in offensive football.

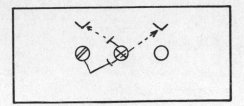

Diagram 16-9

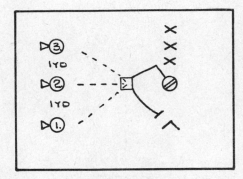

Diagram 16-10

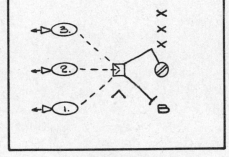

Diagram 16-11

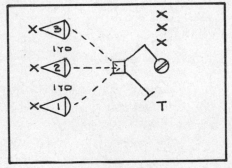

Diagram 16-12

Pulling to Trap—Guards and Tackles. The important phase of trapping is the trapper's course. It is essential that he approach the defender from inside out. If he is parallel to the line of scrimmage, he is increasing his chances of being defeated. When pulling, his first step should be directed into the line of scrimmage. On the second and third steps, he should gain ground into the line of scrimmage, achieving a proper, inside-out approach on the defensive man. Trap the defensive man by using a drive block through the man's inside hip, making contact with the outside shoulder and forearm. As contact is made, drive up through the man. Position is more important than movement. The trapper should get into the hole between the defensive man and his ball-carrier.

Pulling to Lead. The trapper's first step should be a parallel one. As he continues down the line of scrimmage, he should stay as close as possible to the tails of his offensive linemen. Turn up into the first daylight and block the first color to show.

Pull on Flip—Tackle. On the first step, get as much depth as possible and continue to get depth on the second and third steps, aiming at the outside knee of the defensive halfback. Drive through the outside and roll.

Pull to Protect—Guards on Action Passes. When pulling, the first two steps should be parallel to the line of scrimmage. On the third step, get depth, aiming at the outside knee of the defensive man, usually the end. If he hangs on the line of scrimmage, attack his outside leg immediately with a cut-off block. If he crashes inside, cut him immediately with a cut-off block and pin him inside. If he boxes deep, the trapper should drive his face for the outside leg of the man and reverse him quickly, whipping his hips into the inside to tie up the man's inside leg.

Inside-Out Long Trap. Materials: Dummies and men. Objective: Correct technique of the trap block after running a distance. Method: The men should line up to the side of the dummy and, on the snap count, execute correct pulling technique with inside-out position, lift, and follow-through.

Chute Drill. Materials: Men, dummies, and chutes. Objective: Spring through the chute after pulling and running in a good, low hitting position. Method: Emphasize body position, hitting technique, follow-through, and proper base.

Sweep Drill No. 1. Materials: Men, chalk line, and dummies. Objective: Pulling to the 1 or 9 hole, executing correct technique. Method: Three men line up adjacent to each other and, on the snap count, pull through to the designated 1 or 9 hole by going to the horn, planting, pivoting, and sealing to the inside on a dummy.

Sweep Drill No. 2. Materials: Men, chalk line, and dummies. Objective: Pulling to the 1 or 9 hole, executing correct technique. Method: The players line up adjacent to the cut-off men on the line of scrimmage and pull laterally either to the right or left. They clear the cut-off man in working for the horn to seal to the inside, again on a dummy.

Check Drill. Materials: Men. Objective: To keep normal stance and not telegraph the pull either to the right or the left. Method: The players line up on the chalk line in a four-point stance. Then the coach calls the direction straight, pass right or left, using correct pulling techniques. The coach checks the blocks back on the dummy. Thus he is able to give the direction to the player at the last moment. Check for any changes in a player's stance after the direction is given.

THE INSIDE TRAP

by Frank Kush and Don Baker

Frank Kush
Arizona State University

Don Baker
Arizona State University

The guiding principle of our offensive game is, ''How much time does it take to perfect, and how much will it contribute to the offense?'' Practice time that is spent without any return on game day is wasted effort. We do not like to spend more than an hour and a half per day on the practice field during the season. As a result, the team cannot afford to be working on things that are not going to be used. Our short, inside trap game has produced the best results for the time spent than has any other phase of the offense.

Our trapping game is started in the spring by teaching the fundamentals in the individual technique period of practice. The guards learn to pull and post, the centers to scramble, post, and lead, while the backs work on their individual routes. In the combination period, which lasts about 20 minutes, the team gets together. During this time, the centers, guards, quarterbacks, and fullbacks are working on the inside game. At the same time, the tackles, ends, wingbacks, and halfbacks are working on the outside game. The quarterbacks are rotated between each drill.

The rule for the inside trap is: Trap the first man past the center, on or off the line of scrimmage. We start by having the players go against the big bags in a 5-4 defense (Diagram 16-13).

The first technique practice consists of the double-team and trap. Emphasis is placed on the pulling guard being split at least a yard. To impress upon him the necessity of quickness, the fullback is lined up no deeper than 3 yards from the ball. He is instructed to beat the guard through the hole. During the combination period, quickness to the hole is emphasized, rather than concentration on technique. We want the blocker and the ball-carrier at the point of attack almost at the same time. The fullbacks are not looking for daylight—they are flying up to the line, trying to break through the seam.

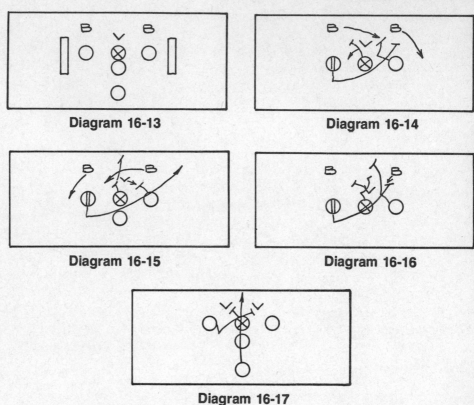

Diagram 16-13   Diagram 16-14

Diagram 16-15   Diagram 16-16

Diagram 16-17

The faster the offense can get to the line of scrimmage, the less time the defense is given to react.

After working against the big bags, then the players work against the air bags. Diagrams 16-14 and 16-15 show the *doodad*, which is used against reading and stunting teams. If a team can be caught stunting, sometimes we have two extra blockers downfield.

Against a reading team, the *doodad* would work similar to a lead block. Against a stunting team, it would be an area block (Diagram 16-16).

Against a reading team, the center starts a lead block and then works into a reverse body block. The guard starts for the middle guard and then turns off for the linebacker.

Against an even defense the same rules prevail, except the on-side guard now sets up and influences. Our off-side tackle is responsible for the nearest linebacker to the hole. Again, the *doodad* is used if the opposing team has a history of stunting.

As the players' techniques improve, we go from dummies to live work. However, a certain amount of time is spent every day on the execution of the *doodad*.

During the fall, about 15 minutes of each practice session are spent on the *doodad*. At this time, emphasis is placed on quickness through the use of a different method. Two defensive players are lined up off-side and are instructed to crash straight ahead

(Diagram 16-17). This really forces the center and guards to hustle in order to get to their blocks.

From gap work, the team progresses to working against the defenses we feel will be encountered in the coming game. Every day the players go against stunts, gaps, and every imaginable defensive combination. We usually have three sets of guards with whom to work, so it is necessary to hustle. That is exactly what we want—quickness to the hole and simplicity once the players reach there.

Of course, it helps to have fast players on the team. The depth of the fullback is regulated according to his ability to get to the hole. The faster he can start, the deeper he will be lined up. Even with the emphasis on quickness, the fullback never lines up deeper than 4 yards from the ball. As can be seen, the guards and center have to fly in order to get out ahead of the play.

The players have confidence in our trapping game. They feel they can execute against any defense and hope to be able to take advantage of any adjustments that must be made to stop them. In our opinion, the advantage is on our side, because the opponents only have a week to get ready to stop something that we have been working on all spring and every day of fall practice.

Simplicity and repetition are emphasized until the players master execution. It is not how much the team knows, but what the players can do that wins games.

OFFENSIVE LINE TECHNIQUE AND DRILLS

by Herb Deromedi

Herb Deromedi
Central Michigan University

When studying game films, coaches should check to see whether or not their linemen were able to block bigger opponents successfully. Often blocking assignments release men downfield with little or no results. Defensive pursuit can also be a factor in destroying the consistency that is required for ball control. If any of these situations presented a problem to offensive success, may we suggest that the merits of the blocking techniques, and the manner in which they are used, be examined.

Defensive alignment requires certain techniques in order to block the one-on-one, double-team, the linebacker, and downfield. The major portion of coaching emphasis is placed on proper execution of the one-on-one and the linebacker block. In teaching these techniques, either live or dummy drills are used with the blocking chute every day that the team is on the practice field. The chute is similar in design to the types that are being used in a number of football programs at the present time. Constructed of wood, it is divided into five segments, each of which is 4 feet high, 4 feet wide, and 5 feet deep (Diagram 16-18).

The one-on-one, or what is referred to as the crotch block, is the essence of the technique used by the offensive linemen. This block is used when a defensive lineman who is in a three- or four-point stance is on any part of an offensive lineman. It is a technique which must be practiced and perfected just as are the techniques of the kicker, punter, or passing specialist. By using this block, the following can be accomplished: 1) Provide an easier method for an offensive lineman to keep the defender occupied. 2) Cut down on the pursuit of a defensive lineman. 3) Enable a play to be successful without requiring the defender to be defeated physically.

When coaching the crotch block, the major teaching points are as follows:

1. Get off on the snap of the ball.

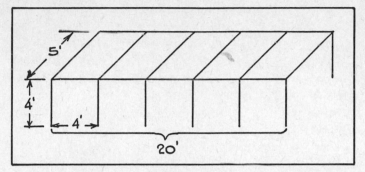

Diagram 16-18

2. Step with the near foot. This step should be short and under control.

3. The shoulder should be driven toward the crotch of the defensive man. If the defender is in the gap, then the offensive lineman should drive his shoulder into the defensive man's far hip. Maintain contact, square up, and drive downfield.

4. Keep the eyes open.

5. Keep the neck bulled and the head up.

6. Keep the hips lower than the shoulders.

7. Drive off the balls of the feet and keep the toes, heels, and knees in a straight line.

8. Use short, choppy steps. Work to keep the feet under at all times. Do not extend.

9. If the offensive man falls to the ground, he should recover quickly on all fours and scramble block the opponent.

10. Sustain the block until the whistle blows.

The linebacker block differs from the crotch block in the point of aim for contact. In teaching this block, the following points are emphasized:

1. Get off on the snap count.

2. Make contact as quickly as possible, stepping with the near foot.

3. Keep the body under control. Do not lunge or overextend.

4. The offensive man should maintain good hitting position as he moves to make contact.

5. Be aware of the flow of the play so the movement of the linebacker can be anticipated.

6. He should look into the defender's numbers and perform a shoulder block.

7. If the linebacker reacts to the flow of the play, the offensive man should run with him as he moves to the point of attack. By placing his shoulder on the far number of the opponent, blocking the defender past the hole will often result.

8. Sustain the block until the whistle.

When coaching both blocks, a major portion of the emphasis is placed on sustaining the block. If an offensive man does not sustain his block, it usually means that one or several of the other teaching points must be examined. Often he fails to keep his head up and his feet under him, causing him to overextend.

In our opinion, an offensive running play requires five seconds of time from the snap of the ball until the tackle is made. The offensive lineman is instructed to occupy the defensive man until the official's whistle blows the play dead. How many times have coaches seen a defender get hit with a good solid block only to recover and make the tackle after a short gain? If the blocker had maintained contact for one or two more counts, the play would have been more successful. The block must be sustained, and it is easier to do so by using the crotch and linebacker blocking techniques.

A second factor that has contributed to the success of our ball control philosophy has been the blocking design that releases only the backside tackle to block downfield. Six linemen can be used at the point of attack. Therefore, by requiring the backside tackle to block first at the line and then downfield for an off-tackle play to the opposite side, the possibility of the run to daylight for the ball-carrier is increased. His block becomes just as important as the block of the on-side tackle, and even more important. He cannot afford to let up, because in the back of his mind he feels that the play is being run to the opposite side. Diagrams 16-19 and 16-20 show the blocking design for the off-tackle play and the ball-carrier's adjustment to the defender's movement after the snap of the ball. We believe this adjustment would be less likely if the backside tackle was released to block downfield.

As mentioned previously, the team is drilled either live or dummy using the blocking chute. Furthermore, the fundamental blocking techniques of the crotch and linebacker blocks are taught in the following drills.

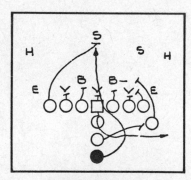

Diagram 16-19

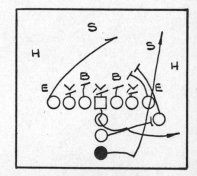

Diagram 16-20

Board Charging Drill

Purpose—to teach the proper stance and explosive get-off under control.

Procedure— a. The boards should be approximately 10 feet long and 1 foot wide. They should be placed directly in the middle of each chute, on the ground. b. The offensive linemen should assume their stance with the hand placed on the ground, just in front of the edge of the board. Each stance should be checked before the snap count is called. c. On the snap count, the linemen fire out, straddling the board on all fours as they charge the length of it.

Board Blocking Drill

Purpose—to teach good hitting technique, sustain the block, and not drop to the knees.

Procedure— a. A blocking shield is held at the front of the board so that the lower edge is almost touching the board. The holder should exert three-quarters resistance. b. The blocker must drive the dummy straight back to the end of the board and then turn it one way or the other. c. During the early season, the dummy may be eliminated and the drill conducted live.

Linebacker Sustain Drill

Purpose—to teach delivering a blow and maintaining contact with a linebacker.

Procedure— a. To be used primarily against dummy shields. b. The blocker lines up inside the chute, straddling the board. The holder of the dummy assumes a linebacker position just outside the chute. c. On the snap count, the blocker fires out and executes a linebacker block, placing his shoulder on the defender's numbers upon contact. d. This block should be sustained for a minimum of five seconds.

The boards and chute are also used to drill our players to trap block.

CENTER TECHNIQUE AND DRILLS

by Rich Welborn

Rich Welborn
Niles High School
Niles, Michigan

The stance of the center should be slightly wider than that of the other offensive linemen. He should have an even stance, one from which he can move in any direction. His feet should be slightly staggered, toe to instep. If the center is right-handed, his right foot should be placed behind. The ball should be placed in front of the center's nose. It is our recommendation that the center sit back on his haunches.

We want the ball placed flat on the ground, laces up, with the center's right thumb across the front of the laces (right-handed center). His left hand should be nearer the rear of the ball, flush against the surface, and should guide the ball to the quarterback's hands.

The center should keep his arms stiff on the snap, and bring the ball up in a quarter turn. A quarter turn takes place with the natural movement of bringing the wrist to the crotch. The ball should pop into the quarterback's hand. By turning it a quarter of a turn, the quarterback receives a large portion of the ball. The ball, if it is turned properly, should hit the quarterback with the laces right at his finger tips.

As the center drives the ball back and up, the weight of his body starts forward. As contact is made with the quarterback's hands, the center takes his first step forward. Reversing the exchange is one approach we might suggest in obtaining the correct touch in transferring the football. We feel the quarterback can show the center the exact, desired placement of the ball. Also, the reverse exchange of the ball defines the exact placement of the hands so the center knows where to place the ball.

If a fumble occurs in the exchange of the ball between the center and the quarterback, the center is held responsible. We feel every opportunity to prevent fumbling must prevail between the two players involved. Practicing the reverse exchange has been beneficial in our program.

When the ball is being snapped to a punter or a holder, we recommend that the laces be flat on the ground. No adjustment of the ball is necessary for a right- or left-handed center.

His elbows should be down and in, with his arms completely relaxed from the shoulders to the wrists.

His right hand should be placed under the forward point of the ball, and his finger tips should be placed on the laces. The center's right hand is the power in snapping the ball back to the punter or the holder. His right wrist should turn downward to produce a good spiral and a quick pass to the kicker or the holder. The center's right hand should be placed on the ball as if he is throwing a forward pass.

The center's left hand should be placed so that his first finger is close to the tip of the ball. It is our contention that the thumb should be placed across the seam of the football. We like to emphasize that the center's left hand serves only as a guide to the flight and direction of the ball.

A center must concentrate on the follow-through of his hands and his arms which are between his legs. Emphasis should be placed on the speed and direction of the ball to the receiver. We feel the center must execute a manageable snap, so our entire kicking game will not consume over a total time of two seconds. Not over a total of two seconds should elapse from the time the ball leaves the center's hands until it is kicked.

It is our philosophy that more games are lost due to some poor phase of the kicking game than in any other phase of football. Thus, we feel that some aspect of the kicking game must be included in every practice plan. However, centering the ball for 15 minutes in our pre-practice is emphasized, and some type of centering (point after or punting) is used for ten minutes in our regular practice. In our opinion, it is important enough to include in every practice for no less than 25 minutes.

Another coaching point we would like to emphasize is the importance of not allowing the center's motion to be restricted. In all drills and practices, a defensive man should shock the center with his hands or hold a dummy over him. Obviously, this provides an opportunity for the center to learn the necessary habit of blocking after he has snapped the ball. When selecting a player for the center position, he must be able to block as well as center the ball.

We feel the center must cover every situation he will encounter in a game in a single practice. Time must be provided for the center-quarterback exchange, center-punter exchange, and the center-holder exchange.

Drill No. 1—Warm-Up

Purpose: This drill is used to provide the center with a stretching exercise for warm-up.

We have the center stretch his legs as wide as possible. This stretching limbers hamstrings and quadriceps when he alternates twisting his torso.

Drill No. 2—Extended Arm Drill

Purpose: We use this drill to mirror the mechanics the center will encounter when he is snapping the ball to the punter.

Two centers are placed 11 yards apart and one is instructed to extend his arms above his head. The other center snaps the ball with both hands to his counterpart. Then they reverse the procedure. We start all centers with this drill to show them what they will be doing from their stance.

Drill No. 3—Head-Up Drill

Purpose: This drill is used to teach the center to snap his head up after firing the ball to the holder or punter.

A player with a dummy is placed in front of the center and he observes whether or not the center has snapped his head up before the ball reaches the receiver.

Drill No. 4—Accuracy Drill

Purpose: We use this drill to teach the snapper to center the ball to the appropriate spot for the punter or holder.

Two centers are placed 11 yards apart and they exchange snaps for accuracy. We like to have the center place the ball on the inside of his thigh, at belt-buckle level of the kicking leg of the punter. The center is instructed to fire the ball to the hands of the holder for extra points. For the balance of the practice, the centers will have the opportunity to engage in exchanging the ball with quarterbacks, punters, and extra point holders.

When working on our punting game, the ball is always snapped from the 1-yard line to the punter, who is standing 2 feet away from the baseline. Pressure is placed on the center for accuracy and to make the punter comfortable under the goal posts. A bad snap in the end zone could be disastrous. Thus, our kicking unit practices in this pressure spot every day once the season starts.

17 / The Defensive Line

DEFENSIVE LINE TECHNIQUE

by Sid Gillman

Sid Gillman
Formerly, Chicago Bears

Defensive football has developed tremendously over the past several years. The change has occurred, not only in theory, but also in the conception of individual techniques. For instance, it was common practice, not too many years ago, to utilize one defensive pattern. Each defensive player was equipped with an assortment of individual stunts which he applied at his own discretion and without regard for the stunts executed by any other member of the defensive front. In other words, the only change of pace that aided the defensive player in attaining his objective was strictly of an individual nature.

Most present-day coaches, in an effort to obtain greater and more effective change of pace, resort to several group patterns. These group patterns unite the entire defensive front, and each individual involved is a part of a specified design. Their individual stunts carry restrictions, depending upon the dictation of the pattern. When several such patterns are utilized, the defensive player need not be equipped with individual stunts.

We believe in, and adhere to, the use of variation by the group rather than by the individual, and, as a consequence, use very simple principles of defensive line play. Before going into a discussion of these principles, we feel it may be of interest to the reader to mention the nature of the group pattern variations.

Variation in Spacing. Many football teams find it extremely difficult to cope with last-second shifting of the entire defensive front from odd to even spacing. They rely on calls from offensive linemen that dictate a combination of blocks. An effective stunt is to call two defenses, the first of which is a stem or a camouflage, with a quick shift to the second defense. Timing the movement so that it is made in unison, after the offensive call, is important.

Gaps or Shaded Locations. Some offenses are geared for the on-the-nose locations of defensive linemen, whether or not there is odd or even spacing. Gapped and

301

off-the-shoulder locations are effective at times because of the difficulty in the definition of such alignment. A cleverly designed system of defense that includes movement from a stem to odd or even locations, or to offset locations, can be puzzling and very troublesome.

Variation in the Intensity of the Charge. Variation in the intensity of the charge is a method of change of pace that has great merit. An offensive lineman is granted an edge if his defensive opponent applies movement repeatedly at the same tempo. Varying the degree of speed by applying a complete sell-out movement at one time, then an extremely soft movement at another time, makes for problems in the execution of offensive line techniques.

Variation in the Distance Off the Ball. Variation in the distance off the ball provides the defensive line another excellent change of pace. Any coach of an offensive team will appreciate the problems involved in attempting to attack an enemy who is varying his distance from the line of scrimmage. Attacking this type of defensive man requires a short sprint technique which involves a series of fast, short strides in an effort to close quickly the distance between the offensive man and his opponent. Once contact is made, the offensive man will be doing well to match the reactions of the defensive man, in the hope of keeping him entertained long enough to permit the ball-carrier to run through whatever daylight is provided him.

Loops and Angles. Loops and angles provide an excellent change of pace. These angles are very effective when they are executed from man-to-man, gap-to-gap, and in combinations, with the linebackers collaborating occasionally by crashing to support these line stunts. The offensive team is forced to restrict its attack to a specific type of offense that will lend itself best to angles, and the limitations are many.

Because of the character of the variation of the patterns that are used, the techniques that we teach are very simple in nature. We have discarded the old chestnuts such as double coordination, limp-leg, dip-split, and all those highly coordinated movements that we planned and practiced. Upon examining our movies, we found these techniques were seldom effective under the pressure of game conditions. Our primary objective is to attack a man in an effort to create a stalemate, with subsequent reaction to offensive pressure. The explanation of the defensive line techniques employed by our linemen is set forth in the following eight principles:

Stance

The stance of our linemen is of great importance. Speed of movement is essential in one of the several directions that the pattern may dictate. Stance provides a springboard from which the linemen derive their explosive movement. We use the four-point stance. It is our belief that better balance and control of the body are obtained when two hands are in contact with the ground. The feet, which provide force for movement, are well under the body so that it can be thrust forward with speed, accuracy, and power. A heel-and-toe stagger is maintained, with the feet placed parallel to each other. The knees are bent and under the body, since it is the extension or straightening of the legs which provides the force for uncoil. In our defensive stance, the linemen hold their hips high and backs flat, with their shoulders squared to the ground. A player maintains a slight, upward tilt of his head, but it is not carried so high as to stiffen or tense the neck and back muscles. Distribution of the weight should be concentrated on the forward or springboard foot.

Vigorous Contact

The second principle indicates that with the snap of the ball, the defensive player must attack his opponent and attempt to destroy his offensive charge, thereby creating a stalemate until such time that the action of the offensive backs has taken place and the ball is given true direction. At that time, all of the defensive linemen pursue the ball-carrier along definitely designated routes. Our defensive candidates are taught four methods of defensive attack.

Hand Lift. When the pattern of defense calls for an extremely soft movement, the hand lift is used. We like this charge because it facilitates quicker disengagement from the blocker, thus faster play reaction and pursuit will follow. The heels of the hands are driven upward into the blocker's shoulders. At contact, the arms of the defensive men are extended fully and locked at the elbows. The upward blow is necessary, since its purpose is to straighten out the blocker and destroy the impact of his offensive charge. As the heels of the hands are thrust into the opponent's shoulders, the rear foot moves forward simultaneously and plants on a line with the forward foot.

This is an important coaching point, since it will enable a defensive player to shuffle right or left, depending upon the pressure of the blocker or the movement of the ball. The legs must be free and moving, because regardless of the power or strength of the block, the defensive man cannot be defeated badly if his feet are under him and free for movement. It is extremely difficult to secure execution of the hand lift. Our movies show that when our men are encountering good, tough blockers, they are forced to resort to the use of the forearm rather than the hands. Effort must be made, in the execution of the hand lift, to maintain the opponent directly in front of the defensive man and keep him under control until such time that the ball is given true direction.

Forearm Lift. The forearm lift is essentially the same as the hand lift. The forearm lift provides a greater area of impact on the offensive target. Contact is more vigorous and intense, and as a consequence, it is more useful in attacking a strong blocker. Designating the numbers on the jersey of the blocker as the target, the defensive player strikes upward with the forearm, and at the same instant contact is established, the rear foot advances and plants on a line with the forward foot. Toe and toe alignment is necessary so that lateral movement may be attained in either direction. This is essential for good play reaction.

The opposite hand is delivered to the shoulder as it is in a hand lift. As contact is made, the head must come up in an effort to locate the true direction of the ball. To neutralize the offensive charge, the defensive player applies upward pressure with the forearm and raises his opponent as he raises himself. The defensive player must be warned that in any charge involving the hands, the impact must be struck from underneath on up. The defensive man should never play off the back of a blocker, since this will allow the blocker to gain contact with the body. Again, as in the hand lift, the defensive player must control his opponent.

The opponent is controlled in this manner until the ball is given true direction, at which time the defensive player disengages himself and enters into play reaction and pursuit.

Shoulder Charge. We feel it is necessary to retain the old-fashioned shoulder charge as a defensive maneuver. During the course of a game, tactical situations will arise which necessitate the use of a power charge. The target for the shoulder charge is slightly below the level of the blocker's shoulder. The defensive player uses the forward foot as a springboard, and as contact is made, the rear foot is advanced well ahead of the forward foot. In the power charge, the torso must travel parallel to the ground. The head should be up, since the defensive player must see the ball, and secondary reaction must be accomplished. Due to the sell-out nature of this charge, working against pressure becomes more difficult, hence reaction to the play and entry into pursuit are delayed.

Since these two items make any defense workable, they must be drilled on constantly. The shoulder charge may be controlled against trapping attacks by rocking on the knee of the forward foot and grounding the hands simultaneously. For execution of the controlled blast, we drill for sharp, crisp shoulder contact. The hands are grounded and are not to be used until after shoulder contact is made. The charge may be of a sell-out nature, with the player instructed to go all the way, depending upon the depth of penetration desired.

Angle Charge. Our defensive pattern involves occasional angles. It is a very effective maneuver when used in conjunction with regular group patterns.

The defensive player takes a lead step in the direction of the angle. The object of this step is to gain ground rapidly across the face of the blocker on the right. Contact is made with the left forearm on the far number of the blocker's jersey, and is accomplished as the cross-over step is being completed. The defensive player must square away as contact is made, in order to facilitate the location of the ball. The angle may also be of a sell-out nature or it may be controlled.

Get to the Assigned Spot

To indicate the degree of depth of the penetration and the direction of charge, certain spots are designated. The spot definitely indicates a point to which the charge is to be made and serves to make our defensive coaching more objective. One spot may be established at the point where the blocker's hand contacts the ground, or under the right or left shoulder of the blocker's original stance. Another spot may prevail immediately behind the hips of the blocker, his right foot, left foot, or either gap. We are careful to remind the defensive player that his defense does not begin until he completes his movement to this spot.

Protect Your Territory

Each player must appreciate his territorial responsibility and also the degree to which he fits into the pattern. He must understand the area he must maintain, and that his secondary reaction and pursuit must not take place until the ball has taken direction over another position. A lineman who is placed on the nose of an offensive man is responsible for an area the width of which includes up to the far shoulder of the next offensive lineman on either side of him. If he is positioned in the gap, the same rule applies (Diagram 17-1). He must control and maintain that area and he must not be moved laterally to either side. If forced to retreat, the lineman's retreat must be over the territory that he came from.

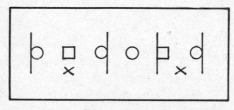

Diagram 17-1

React to Pressure

The ability to react to pressure is of great importance. Most of our practice time is spent drilling the candidates on working against pressure and attempting to disengage themselves quickly from that pressure for pursuit of the ball-carrier. The whip-out is a most effective method when it is used to escape an offensive block.

As the defensive player feels the pressure of an angle block, he drives off the left foot and simultaneously throws his left arm and shoulder around and behind in the direction of the pressure. The throw of the head also adds momentum and thrust to the whip-around. Under the most adverse conditions, a drop step with the foot to the side of pressure should be taken first in order to gain clearance before attempting the whip-out.

Locate the Ball

The primary objective of a defensive maneuver is to engage a blocker with the purpose of creating a stalemate. When the ball is given true direction to a certain area, the defensive player must go after it with all the speed that he can muster. In the execution of any defensive charge, the head must be up so that the defensive player is able to locate the true direction of the ball. Once the ball is located, the fifth principle is in effect.

Line Pursuit

Line pursuit is to the defense what downfield blocking is to the offense. Each defender must have an approximate course of pursuit to the ball-carrier. With proper execution of these pursuit courses, the individuals in the defense form a net, and thereby eliminate long runs, since the ball-carrier's area of maneuverability becomes restricted. He is forced to run the gauntlet with each and every defender in position to make the play.

In order to obtain and maintain field balance, the angle of pursuit is dependent on the following circumstances: 1. The amount of time a defensive man delays before entering into pursuit. 2. The progress made by the ball-carrier. 3. The distance to the defender's goal line.

The coaching points for proper pursuit are as follows: 1. A player should never follow his team's color. 2. The longer a player delays before entering into pursuit, the deeper will be the course. 3. The deeper the penetration, the greater the angle of pursuit. 4. The ball-carrier should always be kept in the line of vision.

Gang Tackling

This phase of defense is essential to the total defensive picture. Mob tackling makes certain that when a good ball-carrier is hit, he stops right there. Great ball-carriers are extremely difficult to bring down by one or two tacklers, but must be met by a number—two or three tacklers setting him up while three or four more complete the job. It is our feeling that 70 per cent of tackling is desire and 30 per cent involves technique.

The following are the coaching points we stress: 1. When a tackler hits a ball-carrier, he is to stop there. 2. A ball-carrier should be approached with balance, wide base, and short stride. 3. The tackler should keep his head up and his eyes open. He should focus his eyes on the opponent's hips. That is the target. 4. The tackler should get in close enough to the ball-carrier to step on his toes. 5. The tackler's knees should be bent and his body squared away. 6. The arms should be wrapped around the opponent's legs, and the tackler should drive with his shoulders. 7. Good leg drive and follow-through are essential for a tackler. 8. A tackler should hit and lift with one movement. 9. Never push a man out of bounds, drive him out. 10. The tackler should always finish on top of the ball-carrier. 11. Hold on until the whistle is blown.

DEFENSIVE END PLAY

by Joe Szombathy

Joe Szombathy
Formerly, Syracuse University

We have always felt that defensive end play has been an important and complicated position to play and master. It has become progressively more difficult, and now requires a totally dedicated and talented player to give the top performance needed to win.

Through the years, we have seen defensive ends blocked by every one of the eleven offensive players, including the quarterback. The great variety of modern offensive formations and sets has made this possible. It places extreme pressure on the defensive end. He must face every type of block and play that is possible. Double-teams, finesse blocks, crack-backs, power traps, and others all must be met. Varied plays such as the sweeps, flips, sprint-outs, powers, reverses, bootlegs, and the most difficult to defend, the option play, all must be handled differently. Often we hear players say that the defensive end's position is hard to play. We agree. If someone wants a challenge, he will find it there. It is complicated but enjoyable and satisfying to the player who faces and meets the challenge.

From our basic 5-3-3 defense, the defensive ends line up about one yard outside a tight offensive end. Basically, they use a three-point stance and face into the backfield at about a 45° angle (Diagram 17-2). They key through the offensive end into the nearest back. On the snap of the ball, we want them to move rapidly into the backfield to a point behind the offensive end, setting up in a football position with the inside foot slightly ahead. Two or three steps should be necessary to reach the point. As they move to the point, they should be concentrating on their key. This key man will tell them their next move. If he is blocked immediately, the defensive end should meet the blocker with his forearm and hands, fight head pressure, get rid of the blocker, locate the football, pursue, and tackle. On any type of pass play, he becomes an all-out pass rusher, keeping leverage on the passer from an outside position. If his key flows away from him, he

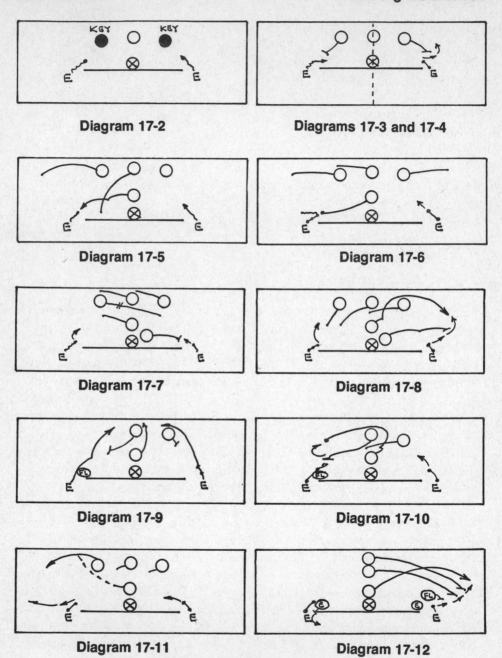

Diagram 17-2

Diagrams 17-3 and 17-4

Diagram 17-5

Diagram 17-6

Diagram 17-7

Diagram 17-8

Diagram 17-9

Diagram 17-10

Diagram 17-11

Diagram 17-12

should check for reverses, bootlegs, or scissors first; if the ball has gone away from him, then he should pursue at the level of the ball through the offensive backfield.

Our coaching points are: stress a good, balanced three-point stance; proper line-up; aggressive movement across the line of scrimmage; concentrate on and read the keys properly; react to the blocker and the ball; pursue or pass rush properly; and tackle sharply.

The defensive end's responsibilities are: close down and stop the off-tackle play (Diagram 17-3); contain and turn in the power sweeps (Diagram 17-4); force the quarterback with the ball on the belly (ride) option (Diagram 17-5); play the quarterback with the ball on the quarterback (down the line) option play (Diagram 17-6); close down with the shoulder and forearm on the nose of a lineman who is trapping (Diagram 17-7); keep the ball inside on any delayed play such as a reverse quarterback bootleg, etc. (Diagram 17-8); rush the pocket pass from an outside-in position (Diagram 17-9); contain and keep leverage on all play- or run-action (Diagram 17-10). Basically, the players are instructed to keep the ball inside if possible and turn it into our pursuit. Secondly, at least, they should keep the ball in front by staying squared off (toe and nose toward the goal line), and by giving ground grudgingly, not letting the ball cross the line of scrimmage (Diagrams 17-11 and 17-12).

The five basic techniques of defensive end play that we teach are:

1. *Normal*—Cross the line of scrimmage quickly to the point. Concentrate and react on the key. Play the depth of the ball—contain it. Be aggressive. Always cover the last man out of the backfield if a pass develops.

2. *Control*—Cross the line quickly at a 90° angle. Be cautious. Clear the area. Key and look for the ball. If a pass shows, cover the first man out. If it is not a pass, play normal.

3. *Anchor*—Line up on the outside eye of the tight end or slotback and unload through him. Be tougher off-tackle initially, and then play normal.

4. *Cat*—Line up on the inside eye of the wide receiver. Unload on him. If a pass shows, cover anyone in the wide flat zone. He should force the ball if it comes to him.

5. *Stunt*—A special maneuver such as crashing, looping, etc.

In order to remain as constant as possible in the teaching of our theories of defensive end play, only minor changes are made when the defenses are shifted. The adjustments really only stress lining up a little tighter or wider according to the basic defense called. As an example, in the wide six defense, the line-up is about 2 to 2½ yards outside the opponent's offensive end.

Initially, the terminology and techniques of defensive end play must be taught and learned. Then the defensive end must face and recognize all the various types of sets and plays. He must become familiar with them and learn how to handle them. This is accomplished mainly through repetitious teaching.

Our defensive ends are given a great deal of responsibility. They must defend a large area—from the off-tackle hole to the sideline. They are asked to defeat, not only one blocker, but many times three or four on one play. We expect them to be strong pass rushers, and sometimes pass defenders. However, the most difficult job a defensive end has is to play the option properly. This is the most complex of his tasks because there are many types of option plays which he must face. Many are concealed by double fakes and deceptive ball-handling. In others, the manner in which the defensive end plays dictates what option the player with the ball will use. There are pass-run options, two-way quarterback options, three-way football ride options, halfback options, and quarterback sprint-out options. These all place considerable pressure on the defensive end.

In normal defensive end play, when confronted with an option play, the ends must read the key properly, play through any immediate blocker, and then play the player with the ball. The simplest coaching point to stress is to have the defensive end stay and play at the depth of the ball in the backfield, trying to buy time and keep the ball inside.

Theoretically, if a quarterback is trying to option off the defensive end, the longer the defensive end can prevent the quarterback from making his decision, the more time the defensive players will have to react and pursue to the ball. Therefore, the defensive ends are taught to stretch or string out the quarterback by using waiting tactics. They are instructed to play about 1 to 1½ yards away, but on the same plane with their feet parallel and toes toward the goal line. They should stretch their arms and use their hands to reach in at the ball, trying to distract the quarterback or deflect the ball. If the quarterback keeps, the defensive ends should turn into him for the tackle. If he pitches, the ends should turn quickly to the outside, taking a good pursuit angle to meet the ball-carrier at the crossroads. If the quarterback comes to the ends and stops, they should stop; if he moves, they also move, keeping relative distance to him. The defensive ends must be alive, on their toes, and ready to move decisively with great second effort to the ball-carrier when he makes his decision.

The first four drills are called our daily basic four, and as the name implies, we work on them every day. The objective is to work on hitting, reaction, quickness, movement, balance, and the use of the hands.

Blast. The blocker should line up nose-on the defensive end. Both players should be in an upright football position. On a signal, the defensive end should pump his feet in place. Then using alternate sides, he should unload with his forearm and shoulder four times into the blocker. Again alternating his feet, the defensive end should extend his arms and deliver four quick hand shivers on the blocker's shoulders. After the fourth hand shiver, the defensive end should grab one shoulder or arm, pull, and turn the blocker. Then he should explode past and aggressively rush the passer. He should raise his arms to deflect a pass thrown by the coach, who has been standing behind the offensive end.

Inside Reaction (Shoulder). The blocker should line up at a slight angle to the defensive end. Then he should drive out with a shoulder block on a signal as the defensive end steps toward him. The defensive end should strike a blow with his forearm and shoulder, and fight the head pressure of the blocker, trying to close down but staying squared off.

Outside Reaction (Hands). The blocker should line up at a slight angle to the defensive end. On a signal, the blocker should drive out low and hard at the defensive end's legs. He should try to hook or cut the defensive end and use a crab block on all fours. The defensive end should react to the low block and use his hands to fight off the blocker. The defensive end should try to keep his feet spread and free and give ground to the outside, trying to contain. Stress use of the hands and a shuffling out movement along the line of scrimmage.

One-on-One Tackling. The blocker should be nose-on the defensive end, and both players should assume three-point stances. The defensive end should deliver a blow, neutralize the blocker, locate the ball-carrier, and pursue to make a solid shoulder tackle, driving the ball-carrier 3 or 4 yards toward the goal line. We try to vary our tackling drills slightly from day to day. Some days quick pitch-outs are used, and other days the quarterback option and then the pitch, etc. Stress quickness, hit, and a crisp tackle.

In addition to the daily basic four, we have a number of other drills which are used in pre-season practice and also throughout the season.

Single Tackling Sled. Two hits—left and right shoulder. Stress hit, lift, both arms around, and a four- to five-step drive. Forearm lift—drive into the cushion low, hit the inside forearm, and lift up through. Then with the free hand deliver a strong blow on the side of the cushion, trying to turn it over. Explode around the sled and raise the hands on a pass rush.

Defensive Reaction Machine. The coach operates the machine, moving the lever in all directions. A defensive end assumes a squared-off football stance and pumps his feet in place. He reacts to the helmet and pressure by stepping with his near foot and delivering a hard hand shiver. Make the drill short, but stress quickness and reaction. This drill can also be started from a three-point stance, and hitting with the forearm can be emphasized.

Two-Man Sled. Two defensive ends assume a three-point stance. On the coach's signal, they explode out, delivering a low forearm blow, and should hit. They should recover immediately into their stance. After the fourth hit, they should roll out quickly to the side, get up, charge ahead, and deliver two forearm hits into the blocker. Stress quickness and forearm hit.

Stance, Starts, Point, Steps (Diagram 17-13). A defensive end assumes a good three-point stance. On the coach's command, he explodes quickly to his point, taking two or three steps and setting up in a low, squared-off position. Then he cross steps out along the line of scrimmage, moving his hands and feet quickly. Slide steps can also be used.

Key Drill (Diagram 17-14). A defensive end crosses to the point and keys the blocker. He reacts to an inside or outside block. Against a straight-on block, he should hit the blocker nose-on. Then he should give ground backwards, and stay squared off. He should explode toward the ball-carrier and make the tackle.

Ballet Scissors Drill (Diagram 17-15). Line up three or four blockers and a ball-carrier 4 to 5 yards apart. The defensive end should face the blocker on the line of scrimmage. The blocker tries to hook the defensive end, who fights out. Then the next

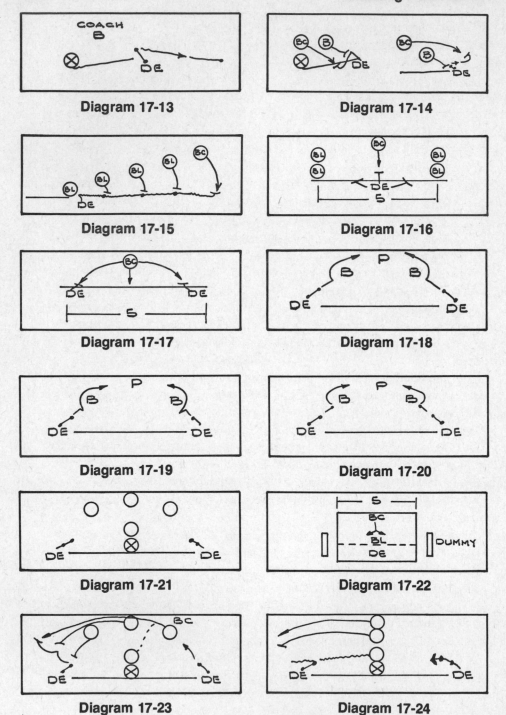

Diagram 17-13

Diagram 17-14

Diagram 17-15

Diagram 17-16

Diagram 17-17

Diagram 17-18

Diagram 17-19

Diagram 17-20

Diagram 17-21

Diagram 17-22

Diagram 17-23

Diagram 17-24

blocker approaches and the defensive end fights him, etc. A defensive end must fight head pressure, keep his legs free, stay squared-off, hit down and out with his hands, and make a crisp tackle.

Angle—Shed—Tackle (Diagram 17-16). A defensive end pumps his feet in place. On command, a blocker attacks the defensive end. The defensive end unloads on the blocker under his shoulder, lifts up through, and sheds him. He recovers and squares off. Then the next blocker attacks. Alternate four hits from left to right.

Tackling Drill (Diagram 17-17). Two defensive ends line up 5 yards apart. Both pump their feet in place and stay in a low football position. The ball-carrier tries to run through or inside the defensive ends. As the ball-carrier approaches, a defensive end moves in front of the ball-carrier, squares off, makes a shoulder tackle, and stops the ball-carrier's progress.

In addition, we use a variety of warm-up drills such as the backward run, carioca, cross step, quarter eagle, etc.

For our pass rush we use the following drills, always trying to keep outside containment and leverage.

Unload (Diagram 17-18). The defensive end drives hard into the blocker, unloads with his forearm, dips his shoulder up through the blocker's chest and follows through using his hands. Then using quickness and second effort, the defensive end drives hard toward the passer.

Head and Shoulder Fake (Diagram 17-19). The defensive end drives hard toward the blocker and makes a good fake to the inside. He changes direction quickly, trying to evade the blocker. To come in on the passer from behind, the defensive end uses speed.

Hand Grab (Diagram 17-20). The defensive end drives toward the blocker, extends his arms, and tries to grab the blocker's arm or shoulder. Then he pulls, pushes, or turns the blocker to the side and explodes past him to rush the passer. Raising the hands early, tackling high, and keeping leverage should be emphasized.

Apron Drill (Diagram 17-21). Two defensive ends don full body aprons and line up in their respective positions facing the offense. A complete offensive backfield will run a variety of plays against the defensive ends. Emphasize running the best offensive plays. Make the defensive ends work hard since their movement is restricted. Outside linebackers or cornerbacks can be added in this drill.

One Versus One Hand-Off Drill (Diagram 17-22). Place a defensive end and a blocker on a 5-yard square. The blocker takes the defensive end in any direction. The ball-carrier veers off the block. The defensive end attacks the blocker, fights pressure, sheds, and tackles the ball-carrier, trying to drive him back.

Contain Drill (Diagram 17-23). The defensive ends take normal line-up positions. Then they cross the line to the point. They fight for depth to contain and turn the play to the inside. Then they shed the blockers and make the tackle. If the ball-carrier cuts back, the defensive end folds to the inside to make the tackle.

Quarterback Option Drill (Diagram 17-24). The defensive ends cross to the point. They play at the depth of the ball. Their feet should be kept parallel with their noses, and their toes should be toward the goal line. Use delaying tactics and buy time. Shuttle out as the quarterback moves. If he turns up the field and keeps, tackle him. If he pitches, turn out and use good pursuit to tackle him at the crossroads.

BASIC DEFENSIVE LINE DRILLS

by Pat James

Pat James
University of Oklahoma

We teach our linemen to hit an explosive blow, trying to develop that snap, like a punter, batter, or fighter. The team must strike with authority.

One of our drills is a two-on-one setup, where two men line up side by side on their hands and knees, shoulder to shoulder, making a good, high, solid target for the defense to hit (Diagram 17-25).

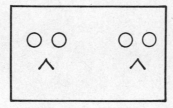

Diagram 17-25

We work on the defensive lineman's stance as he explodes into his target. He should drive his shoulder low and quick, and as contact is made, whip his tail down. His legs should be extended straight as the blow is completed. He should neither draw back, nor raise up. The first move should be forward. After he has the feel of really popping, then he hits the same blow, bringing his feet up under him, moving them hard and fast and holding in a position ready to react to blocks and the ball-carrier. Sometimes when defensive linemen start to bring their feet up they will not really explode but start to raise up, and then when they do explode, they cannot gain control of themselves to react.

Spinning out of a block is a continuation of the exploding drill. It is a technique of getting out of a block, and makes a defensive lineman pressure conscious. Our players use the technique during a game. We do not know how often they use it, but we do know that many times it is not executed as it was taught. However, our players are encouraged to use little maneuvers of their own that are not taught. Our teams have made some great plays by spinning out.

In spinning out, we want the defensive lineman to explode on the blocker, bring his feet up under him, and then spin right or left (Diagram 17-26). As he starts his spin and drives off his other foot, he should push with his arms and hands, keep his eyes on the action as long as possible, and at the last instant, whip his head around. His quickness and the speed with which the play is hitting the hole will determine where the defensive lineman will try to spin. If he is late in the spin, he will have to spin deeper. The most common mistake is that he will step to the inside with the foot that he is collapsing, and will spin in the blocks rather than out of them. The defensive lineman will not strike a blow, and is forced too deep on his spin.

When teaching defensive linemen to read blockers, we continue with the two-on-one setup, with live blocking. Place the defensive man in the gap about 1 yard off the line, and the coach behind him (Diagram 17-27). The coach gives the offensive men the charge signal and the block to be used, which amounts to a cross-block or short trap action. The defensive man explodes on the man who is blocking him and fights through his head or spins out. We start the defensive man off the line so that he will have more time to recognize the block, which gives him confidence. The quicker he recognizes the block, the better blow he will strike and the closer he can play on the line of scrimmage. The mistake made by defensive linemen is to step forward on movement and not parallel into the blocker.

To get penetration, we teach the defensive linemen to drive hard and low, and at the last second, turn their shoulders and body, and scramble through and to the ball. This works effectively when the defensive man has been reading or when an offensive man is tipping off. This technique has forced the offense to fumble. The defense must keep the offensive blocker guessing. We also allow the defensive men to jump over to get penetration if we feel they have the ability.

Diagram 17-26

Diagram 17-27

We also have the defensive men fake penetration. This is effective if the offense has been hurt with the previous technique. The defensive man lines up the same way he did on the penetration defense. Then on the snap he jumps back on all fours and most of the time the offensive man will miss contact on his block. This maneuver is good when looping out of a gap.

On the goal line and short yardage charge, we want the defensive linemen to line up in a low stance, watch the ball, and aim for a point 1 yard deep in the backfield. They should drive their shoulders at the shoe tops of the offensive man. As they achieve penetration, they should grab everything and fight back up. The charge should be slightly in with a good, strong, wide base. As a change-up, it is good to let the man go over the top occasionally.

Playing one man is good for preventing blockers from getting to the defensive linebackers. It also places the defensive man in good position if the offensive man is blocking on him. If the man the defensive man is playing does not come on him, or he receives the two-on-one block, we want him to throw his weight and hip back into the blocker and spin out.

As shown in Diagram 17-28, four men line up on offense and a defensive man lines up head-on on one of the inside men. The coach stands behind the defensive man and gives the signal for either a wedge, two-on-one, trap, or pass block, and the defensive man must react to the type of block that is being used. Start the defensive man off the ball about a yard.

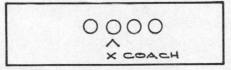

Diagram 17-28

When he is playing against the wedge, the defensive man must drop to all fours and hit the wedge on the rise with penetration. If the wedge straightens him up, he should shove and jump back away from the blockers, go to the ground, and drive back under the wedge.

Against the two-on-one, first we want the post man whipped, and the defensive man should finish on the shoulder that the turn man is coming from. If the turn man drives straight at him, the defensive man will normally recognize the double-team quicker, and then he should fight through or spin out. If the turn man is going for, or stepping for, position, then the defensive man usually finishes up splitting the crack.

When playing against the trap, we want the defensive man to drive low under the trapper, almost straight back down the line of scrimmage. If the trapper has position and it is too late, we want the defensive man to fall back at about a 40° angle into the hole.

The defensive man's play versus a drop-back pass or setting lineman should be as follows: When an offensive lineman sets, he should look to the inside and stay in a head-on position until he recognizes the play. If it turns out to be draw, the defensive man should slow down and make the ball-carrier show.

The 7-on-3 and the 11-on-3 drills (Diagrams 17-29 and 17-30) are good for working more than one defensive man at a time and reading with the backs faking away from the blocking scheme.

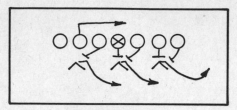

Diagram 17-29

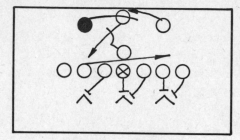

Diagram 17-30